ENDORS

In Dr. Naim Collins' book, *Power Prophecy,* you will be ignited to begin using the gift of prophecy for supernatural signs, miracles, and wonders. Prophecy is a key that opens the dimensions of the supernatural, and Dr. Collins gives biblical basis in the Old and New Testaments, which help you learn the Word to unlock these realms. I know and agree with him on the power of prophecy to invade the earth and change environments. This book is more like a manual, which covers so many topics of the supernatural where prophecy is the key that opens the door. You will become armed with power when you dive into *Power Prophecy.*

Dr. Candice Smithyman
Host, *Glory Road* TV show and *Your Path to Destiny* on the It's Supernatural Network
Author, *Releasing Heaven: Creating Supernatural Environments through Heavenly Encounters* and *Angels of Fire: The Ministry of Angels in the End Time Revival*
www.candicesmithyman.com

Naim Collins has a proven prophetic track record. Throughout the years he has gleaned revelation from the unseen realm, captured it in his spirit, and then released prophetic words that have brought forth mighty demonstrations of God's power on earth. He is a true prophet, one who can be trusted. And now, through the pages of this book, you are being given an invitation to sit under the counsel of prophetic instruction to learn the ways of the Spirit and grow in your own spiritual capacity.

As a hungry seeker, I am always looking for Spirit-filled books that can help enlarge my knowledge of God's Word and provide greater insight into the glory realm. In your hands, you hold such a book. In my own life and ministry, I've been well acquainted with the realm of miracles, prophecy, and angels, so I was delighted to read the fresh revelation the Spirit has given to Naim on these subjects, and I know you will find them fascinating as well.

This book is a tool for navigating the world of *Power Prophecy* and learning how to release it into your own personal spheres of influence. Read, revelate, and then allow God to speak these truths through you!

JOSHUA MILLS
Cofounder of International Glory
Bestselling author, *Seeing Angels* and *Power Portals*
www.joshuamills.com

Naim Collins aims to be culturally relevant without watering down the potency of the raw, authentic message of the Gospel of the Kingdom of the Lord Jesus Christ. You are holding a stick of dynamite in your hands! But what are you going to do with it? If you just hold it, you will absolutely blow up! But if you give the power of the prophetic away, you will see multiplication take place! Take it from Naim and me, you can be used in Christ to transform lives!

JAMES W. GOLL
Founder of God Encounters Ministries
GOLL Ideation LLC

The anointing of the prophet is more than prophesying; in the function of the prophet is a tangible release of the power of God expressed through miracles, signs, and wonders.

I want to recommend an incredible, well-written book on this matter by Naim Collins. His newest release, *Power Prophecy,* unveils key revelation on the nature of the prophet, including diverse types of gifting available through prophecy, angelic partnership, prophetic deliverance, and much more. You'll be glad you dove into this great read.

CHARLIE SHAMP
Destiny Encounters International
Vice President, Renaissance Coalition
Author, *Angels* and *Transfigured*

There is a new but old dimension of power being released in the prophetic. God is releasing a pioneering company who are preparing the way for a generation who will prophesy and move in signs, wonders, and miracles. Naim Collins is one of these pioneers who is helping lead the charge for this generation to move in *Power Prophecy*. In Naim's book *Power Prophecy* be prepared to be provoked for a new expression of the prophecy. You will receive an impartation not just hearing the voice of God to prophesy but to become a worker of miracles with signs and wonders following you. Come to the banqueting table and feast upon the revelation and faith in the pages of this book!

STEVEN SPRINGER
Cofounder Global Presence Ministries
GPS School of the Prophetic
International Speaker, Author

One prophetic word from God can shift a person into their purpose and God-given destiny. In this book, *Power Prophecy,* Naim Collins unpacks revelatory content on the potency of Spirit-led prophecy and why it is so needed for today. Collins unlocks the miraculous as he challenges readers to grow in prophetic understanding. The powerful words that fill these pages will stir you, ignite you, and activate the spirit of prophecy within you. I highly recommend this book.

JOSHUA GILES
Pastor and Founder, Kingdom Embassy Worship Center
Founder, Joshua Giles Ministries
Author of *Prophetic Forecast*
www.JoshuaGiles.com

POWER PROPHECY

DESTINY IMAGE BOOKS BY NAIM COLLINS

Realms of the Prophetic:
Keys to Unlock and Declare the Secrets of God

POWER PROPHECY

Release Miracles Through the Power of Prophecy

NAIM COLLINS

DESTINY IMAGE® PUBLISHERS, INC.

P.O. Box 310, Shippensburg, PA 17257-0310

"Promoting Inspired Lives."

This book and all other Destiny Image and Destiny Image Fiction books are available at Christian bookstores and distributors worldwide.

For more information on foreign distributors, call 717-532-3040.

Reach us on the Internet: www.destinyimage.com.

ISBN 13 TP: 978-0-7684-6034-6
ISBN 13 eBook: 978-0-7684-6035-3
ISBN 13 HC: 978-0-7684-6037-7
ISBN 13 LP: 978-0-7684-6036-0

For Worldwide Distribution, Printed in the U.S.A.

1 2 3 4 5 6 7 8 / 26 25 24 23 22

CONTENTS

FOREWORD

BY

Dr. Hakeem Collins

What you hold in your hand is not just a book written on the subject of prophecy but a living epistle written by God's true modern-day prophet, Dr. Naim Collins. *Power Prophecy's* author has more than 25 years of experience in the prophetic, supernatural, and healing workings of the Holy Spirit. The reason I can attest to what is written is because I am his twin brother who has traveled the nations with him releasing the power of prophecy in the lives of God's people. We are nationally and internationally known as the "Twin Prophets." Basically, twin brothers who are also called as prophets of God in our generation.

This literary work, in my opinion, is a continuum of Dr. Naim Collins' last book, *Realms of the Prophetic.* He now takes readers on the biblical practicum of how to operate in the creative force of the spoken word of the Lord. Words that bring total healing, miracles, and signs and wonders through speech. Words do matter, and everything in our reality is the product of what has been vocalized by sound and vibration.

Power Prophecy goes beyond the surface and the obvious where Dr. Naim thoroughly explains and outlines chronologically, Scripture by Scripture, the nature of the supernatural that every believer has access to through the prophetic. The title of this book alone is self-explanatory to what you will glean. The takeaways held in these anointed pages will assist every believer on their journey of releasing the supernatural in the natural, moving in the realm of miracles, activating the prophetic that unleashes signs and wonders, and partnering with the Holy Spirit to unlock creative miracles, healing, and breakthroughs.

Power Prophecy, I believe, is a prophetic manual for every believer ready to discover the ancient truths that the prophets of old experienced and encountered in their day. Unlike them, today's believers can discover their prophetic DNA to host the supernatural everywhere they go to advance the glory of God on earth.

Dr. Naim Collins brilliantly composed a reference cheat sheet for all believers to understand the biblical history and relationship between prophecy and miracles—then and now! I have personally witnessed countless miracles, testimonies, and stories contained in this book that you will read, which will ignite your faith to go beyond the surface to the supernatural.

This book assists you in breaking every spiritual faith blockage or hindrance by speaking life into dead situations. The author provides a balance and consistent evidence of ordinary people performing extraordinary things by the power of prophecy. Supernatural ministry and prophetic declaration are gifts available to every believer, including you! It's time to cast aside doubt and fear, and begin to prophetically release God's miraculous glory into the world around you.

Are you or someone you know in dire need of a breakthrough miracle? Do you want to operate in the supernatural and power of prophecy to see many healed, delivered, and transformed? If so, this book has been written with you in mind! We must understand that the supernatural is the element and ingredients of Heaven. It is essentially our God-given gift to release Heaven on earth, here and now!

The enemy's desire is to kill, steal, and destroy—but Jesus comes with good news that we may have life and live it more abundantly.

Power Prophecy by Dr. Naim Collins gives you, the reader, the prophetic advantage to change, shift, and create atmospheres, climates, and environments that are conducive for miraculous manifestations in the life of believers. This book will help you to become not just a reader of God's Word but a doer also.

Dr. Collins shares the heart of God lodged in the content of this book of what I believe is Psalm 29:2-4 (NIV): *"Ascribe to the LORD the glory due his name; worship the LORD in the splendor of his holiness. The voice of the LORD is over the waters; the God of glory thunders, the LORD is thunders over the mighty waters. The voice of the LORD is powerful; the voice of the LORD is majestic."* You will find your voice and sound after reading this power-packed book.

The voice of the Lord can be thundered through you for His glory to be revealed. Psalm 18:13 (ESV), says *"The LORD also thundered in the heavens, and the Most High uttered his voice, hailstones and coals of fire."* There are key elements contained in *Power Prophecy* of the prophetic that create a supernatural environment in which miracles become normal or made simple. But many contemporary believers today do not realize the vital connection between these gifts of the Holy Spirit. In *Power Prophecy*, Dr. Naim Collins uses Old and New Testament examples, stories, and comprehensive references, as well as firsthand experiences, to show that the prophetic and miracles go hand in hand—and the supernatural is for today just as the prophetic is too.

I am tremendously honored to read and recommend this life-changing and eye-opening revelatory book for every student and disciple of the supernatural and prophetic. After reading it in its entirety, you will come away with the fundamental biblical principles and power to become supernaturally prophetic!

Dr. Hakeem Collins
Author of *Unseen Warfare, The Power of Aligning Your Words to God's Will, 101 Prophetic Ways God's Speaks*

FOREWORD

BY

DR. CINDY JACOBS

You are about to read a very important book. The author, Dr. Naim Collins, has done the whole Body of Christ a service in writing it. While there are excellent books on the gift of prophecy, this one takes our knowledge of how to both function and manifest the full scope of its name, *Power Prophecy.*

There are many excellent prophets today who are walking in the supernatural elements lined out here, however, in general, I believe that many, both with the potential and gifting to expand their gift, who will be challenged to have faith to release this gift on a greater level.

As I read the following pages, I loved how deeply Collins had researched his points. He did an excellent and thorough job.

I have been prophesying on various levels for over sixty years as of this writing. While I was always aware that what I had was gifted by God, through those years, I have had seasons in which God challenged me to stretch myself more in the use of the gift.

One of those seasons occurred when I realized that I had believed something that I now believe is an error in theology concerning the office of the prophet; by that, I mean that the New Testament gift was a lesser one than the Old Testament. I had somehow been limited as a prophet not to challenge myself to walk in the full manifestations of what God wanted to express through me. What a change I experienced when I corrected my thinking! I began to understand the role of prophets in miracles concerning nature, such as storms, miracles of physical healings, and the scope and sphere of authority concerning declarations.

As I read this book, I saw that Naim Collins had no such problem! He teaches truth that took me many years to discover.

I love the section where he expands on the nine gifts of the Holy Spirit. Sadly, there isn't a lot of teaching on the various gifts and how to operate in them today.

Even if you don't see yourself as a prophet or think that you will flow in prophecy on a regular basis, this book is for you. We are all responsible to learn how to cooperate with the gifts of the Holy Spirit. It is critical to ask God for wisdom and discernment. Bottom line, we who are in Christ and empowered by the Holy Spirit must learn how to manifest His power to the generations.

This is not just a book; it is a manual that you will want to study carefully and apply in your everyday walk with God. It will change your life!

Dr. Cindy Jacobs
Generals International
Dallas, Texas

INTRODUCTION

There is a resurgence of an anointing being released through the ministry of the prophet and those carrying prophetic grace to unlock signs, wonders, and miracles. As we explore the different dimensions of the prophetic, there lies ancient powers, started ages ago in the prophets, that are needed more now than in any time and in the future. Threaded through the pages of history and the Old and New Testament Scriptures, there is a correlation and connection between prophecy and miracles.

The prophetic ministry today in many circles, streams, and churches is not regarded as a ministry of signs, wonders, and miracles; rather, it is only relegated to divine communication of preaching, praying, and prophesying through inspired utterance, *"Thus saith the Lord."* Prophets were in fact vitally important in demonstrating the powerful gifts of prophecy and the Holy Spirit that were a catalyst for displaying the supernatural through the power of prophecy.

Throughout the ages, God has always uniquely blended and combined the prophetic with signs, wonders, and miraculous powers to equip His people for supernatural ministry to ultimately change the worlds for Jesus. The church in the New Testament—within different, circles, streams, denominations, and organizations—have not fully embraced the role, ministry function of the prophet, even in our modern epoch and schools of thought. Prophets are not just communicative ministers but supernatural ministers of power. Signs, wonders, and miracles will serve as an astounding witness to the mouth of God through His prophets in every generation according to Hebrews 2:4 (NKJV):

> *God also bearing witness both with signs and wonders, and various miracles, and gifts of the Holy Spirit....*

Power Prophecy introduces you to discovering your prophetic genes that are inherently imparted and imputed by the Holy Spirit to function and operate as supernatural beings. Through this prophetic nature and DNA, we have the capacity and faculty to call and speak things into being. The mysteries of the prophetic and the various understandings of the supernatural have been hidden for ages in the ancient prophets, until now.

The anointing of the prophet is more than prophesying; the anointing is discerning, disarming, dismantling, disengaging, and defeating demonic forces and powers. There is an army of prophetic forces that will manifest the power of God unapologetically. God, through the ancient prophets, has provided us with terminology and etymology that is genetically developed in the prophetic believer. *Power Prophecy* provides readers insights on how to discover and embrace their supernatural DNA to wrought miracles.

As you explore each chapter, you will receive an impartation of revelation that will break the limitation of prophecy to just vocalization of the mind, will and intent of God, and release the dimension of miraculous power through the prophetic. God's prophets are agents of the impossible who understand that they were born to manifest unseen power. You will discover the power behind defeating the odds, accomplishing, and creating opportunities for the impossible to happen. Each chapter in *Power Prophecy* helps you learn how to partner with both angels and the Spirit of God to exhibit unusual miracles with the finger of God. Prophetic believers are able to not only speak the word of the Lord but to touch many people with power and anointing to minister the unexplainable.

Power Prophecy gives a prophetic perspective where the prophetic is more than hearing the voice of God—it is uncapping and untapping the power of prophecy. It is the power that releases the residential anointing of healing and deliverance that lies within the ministry of the prophetic. The power of deliverance starts and ends with the prophets.

My goal is to show how you can operate in revelatory deliverance through the power of the prophetic. Prophets walk in revelatory and demonstrative power. This book introduces you to the anointing and power of prophecy that will activate and acclimate the miracle-working power.

The prophetic is one of God's choice and most powerful vehicles to manifesting signs, wonders, and miracles in and through His sons and daughters. To be prophetic is to be supernatural. This book teaches you from both Old and New Testament Scriptures and firsthand experiences of key elements in the prophetic that will help create an atmosphere, climate, and environment for miracles. You will see how the ancient prophetic and the modern prophetic are working together to unlock an unprecedented prophetic anointing of power prophecy.

Unfortunately, there are a number of false beliefs around the subject of the supernatural where people have created fear, doubt, and unbelief in trying to comprehend the unexplainable in the ministry of miracles.

This book is an interactive guide to unlocking the supernatural miracles of prophecy. The primary purpose is to teach the dynamic power of prophetic demonstration. The ministry of signs, wonders, and miracles collates with the prophetic and the manifestation gifts of the Holy Spirit. Diversities of miracles will be demonstrated through the ministry of the prophetic in the believers. Miracles is one of the revelatory powers of the prophetic that cannot be ignored, remised, or overlooked. My goal in this book is for all to understand the supernatural as it relates to the prophetic.

Power Prophecy unlocks the anointing and power to not only see miracles but to speak miracles. One of the most powerful secrets and realities that has been invested in every believer in Christ Jesus is to access different dimensions of power through prophetic communication. Let this book charge and empower you to release the miracle-working power. Your mouth prophetically is the conduit on earth touched by Heaven to release miracles through *Power Prophecy.*

PART I

THE POWER OF PROPHECY

1

MIGHTY PROPHETS

And He said to them, "What sort of things?" And they said to Him, "Those about Jesus the Nazarene, who proved to be a prophet mighty in deed and word in the sight of God and all the people."
—LUKE 24:19 NASB

And Moses was learned in all the wisdom of the Egyptians, and was mighty in words and in deeds.
—ACTS 7:22 NKJV

God is revealing the next wave of the prophetic people who will carry signs, wonders, and creative miracles like that of Moses, Elijah, and Jesus. The *super prophets* whom I call *"mighty prophets"* are among us and they have the understanding of dealing with the supernatural, the prophetic, and are the ministers of signs and wonders, knowing that miracles go hand in hand. Throughout the ages God has always uniquely blended and combined the prophetic with signs, wonders, and miraculous powers to equip His people for supernatural ministry to ultimately change the world for Jesus.

The prophets, historically through the pages of the Old Testament, pointed prophetically to the greatest revelation of all times in the Person of Jesus Christ. No one who has ever had history or a supernatural resume with God has done anything apart from the revelation of the Christ Jesus. No one in history has performed the type of miracles that our Lord Jesus Christ performed. He is the epitome of a Miracle Prophet. Miracles is an aspect of prophetic revelation demonstrated. It is a method that God uses in the prophetic or the prophet to either reveal something, or to point to something in the case of a sign. The Elijahs among us as mighty prophets will carry the powers of Heaven.

No man or woman, with any history with God, carrying prophetic revelation has ever had a genuine encounter Jesus Christ who was not to some degree also endued miraculously to make Jesus known to others in both word and deed. The prophetic and the miraculous are inseparable. David declared revelation knowledge in the God of miracles according to Psalm 77:14 (AMP):

> You are the [awesome] God who works [powerful] wonders; You have demonstrated Your power among the people.

In the ancient Scriptures, there are examples of extraordinary prophets whom God has placed special anointings upon, which separated them in their class of prophetic operations. These type of prophets have recreated a restored paradigm to the school of the prophetic today, that if prophets in the Old Testament were able to communicate the mind of God with demonstrations of the supernatural, then today's prophets and prophetic people can now work mighty miracles too.

We are seeing a resurgence of these types of prophets with special, unique, rare, and unusual mantles and grace upon their lives to meet the demand of their age and ages to come. These phenom prophets and prophetic believers are going to be known as *mighty prophets*.

A MIGHTY PROPHET DEFINED

A *mighty prophet* is simply a chosen spokesman or spokeswoman who speaks on the behalf of God who operates in powerful miracles as a revelatory expounder or teacher in divine communication and in the Scriptures. This prophet has a unique grace to manifest mighty acts of God. The word *mighty* in the Greek is the word *dynatos* according to Strong's Concordance, which means "to be able, powerful, mighty and strong." It is the ability and power to do something or a person's capability. This word *mighty* speaks relatively to one's capacity. Therefore, a mighty prophet has the ability, capability, and capacity to do something powerful or supernatural. It's interesting to note that *dynatos* is also defined as a "might man" or "powerful man."

This is the same as calling someone a "powerful man or woman" of God because of his or her supernatural abilities or communicative capacity to minister the word of God effectively. Jesus was regarded as a prophet because of His ability and power in both word and deed (Luke 24:19). Moses as a prophet in the Old Testament was recognized as being *mighty* according to Acts 7:22 *"in his words and deeds."*

Consider the ministry of Apollos who was with Paul, whereas he was recognized by his competency, skills in speech and oracle ability in ministering, and powerful communication in the Scriptures:

> *Now a certain Jew named Apollos, born at Alexandria, an eloquent man and mighty in the Scriptures, came to Ephesus* (Acts 18:24 NKJV).

When you look at the ministry of Paul and the ministry of Apollos, you will see that both were distinctively regarded—Paul being powerful in signs, wonders, and special miracles and Apollos being powerful in word and an eloquent communicator of the

Scriptures. Paul speaks of us as believers as being *mighty* in God in the area and arenas of spiritual warfare of those possessing spiritual power when he wrote, *"For the weapons of our warfare are not carnal but mighty in God for pulling down strongholds..."* (2 Corinthians 10:4 NKJV).

Prophets are men and women of the supernatural and extraordinary in divine communication. It is important to understand that one of the dimensions of the prophetic office is a ministry of signs and wonders. Prophets according to the Old and New Testaments were not just revealers and expounders of the Word of God, they were also demonstrators of the Word.

Prophets manifested the power of God. They walked in the very power of the prophetic. This is what we would consider as power prophecy exhibited in both word and mighty miracles. Prophets walk powerfully in both demonstrative power and communicative prophecy. Miracles are in the mouth of the prophets and the prophetic. You can speak a miracle into existence.

Historically, prophets walked in the power that they talked. "Walk the talk" is a saying we use to describe someone who walks in and lives what they talk. One of the most powerful revelations of a prophet is his or her ability to walk mightily in both word and deed in the sight or eyes of God and all the people. Mighty prophets are simply "power prophets" who essentially do mighty miracles through the word of the Lord. It is the communicative power of the prophet to release miracles in their prophetic ministry. Power prophecy is the aspect and dimension of the supernatural that is displayed in their preaching, teaching, praying, and of course prophesying and speaking forth the word of God. It is ministering the word of God with miraculous power. They are known and earmarked for doing all kinds of notable miracles.

THE PROPHET REVEALED

Jesus was revealed and recognized as a reputable Prophet of God by the people due to the manifestation of the miraculous deeds and words done among them. Prophets are revealed by both their works and their words. Prophets were the first in the Scriptures to walk in healings, miracles, signs and wonder (Genesis 20:7,17-18). This is not a foreign phenomenon to the ministry of the ancient prophets.

Unfortunately today, prophets are not quite regarded as ministers of the supernatural but primarily as ministers of prophecy. We need thorough foundational understanding and functional revelation of the full scope of the prophets' ministry in order to properly benefit from Christ's prophetic ministers in His church today and beyond.

Moses and Jesus were both revealed and recognized as prophets by the people who encountered their supernatural ministries from the biblical accounts in the Old and New Testaments following Old Testament revelation of the spokesman and New Testament revelation of the prophet:

Old Testament Revelation of the Spokesperson

> *The LORD your God will raise up for you a prophet like me* [Moses] *from among you, from your fellow Israelites. You must listen to him* (Deuteronomy 18:15 NIV).

New Testament Revelation of the Prophet

God prophesied through Moses that He would raise up a prophet like him who later manifested in the Person of Jesus Christ who was revealed and recognized by the masses as a Prophet: *"The multitudes said, 'This is Jesus, the prophet from Nazareth of Galilee'"* (Matthew 21:11 NKJV).

Jesus is seen as a Prophet by a woman personally: *"Sir, I perceive that You are a prophet"* (John 4:19 NKJV).

Prophets are recognized both individually and corporately. There is anointing upon a prophet to minister miracles to those personally and corporately. On the road to Emmaus, two disciples were having a conversation about all the things that had just happened in Jerusalem concerning Jesus's death, burial, and eventual resurrection. Jesus appeared to them and walked with them as they were talking of Him, but these two disciples' eyes were restrained so they were unable to recognize Him.

It is important to keep in mind that Jesus appeared to them *after* His resurrection and is walking and talking with them in His resurrected form and body. He was walking in what many regard as His glorified body. The two were heartbroken about everything that had happened to Jesus.

Jesus asked the two the nature of their conversation and the reason for their sad countenance. One of them, named Cleopas, answered Him, essentially questioning if Jesus was a stranger in Jerusalem and did not know what had happened to the Prophet recently.

Jesus responded to him saying, "What things?" So the two disciples said to Him, *"The things concerning Jesus of Nazareth, who was a Prophet mighty in deed and word before God and all the people, and how the chief priests and our rulers delivered Him to be condemned to death, and crucified Him"* (Luke 24:19-20 NKJV).

I love the translation and rendition of Luke 24:19 in the New Living Translation to best describe the type of prophet Jesus was recognized as by the people:

> *"What things?" Jesus asked. "The things that happened to Jesus, the man of Nazareth," they said. "He was a prophet*

who did powerful miracles, and he was a mighty teacher in the eyes of God and all the people"

PROPHETIC REPUTATION

Jesus was used mightily in powerful miracles and was reputable as a power teacher in the eyes of the people. His teaching was marked with power. Moreover, His teaching was glaring with direct revelation, power, authority, and miracles following. The prophets today are known as and will continue to be known for their dynamic revelatory teaching and preaching of the word that will be reinforced and confirmed with accompanying signs and fulfillment of prophecy. Jesus's reputation as a Prophet was characterized by word and demonstration. Teachers can typically demonstrate what they teach.

Power prophecy is the epitome of both working the word of God and mighty deeds being communicated and demonstrated among the people. A prophet's reputation precedes them. Their ministry can make them famous or infamous among the people.

And immediately His [Jesus] *fame spread throughout all the region around Galilee* (Mark 1:28 NKJV).

The type of miracles that Jesus performed among the people, I should say, must become the model, prototype, and example for all prophets and prophetic believers today. The revelation of Jesus being a mighty Prophet was not just in His talk but also in His walk. He walked in the revelation of what He both taught and preached. Prophets must become one with their revelation and become practitioners of what they preach and teach.

The basis of this understanding for all believers to grasp in their prophetic practicum is founded in the following statement of Jesus Christ in Mark 16:17-18:

And these signs shall follow those who believe: In My name they will cast out demons; they will speak with new tongues; they will take up serpents; and if they drink anything deadly, it will by no means hurt them; they will lay hands on the sick, and they will recover.

Jesus even tells His students in John 14:12 (ESV) saying, *"Truly, truly, I say to you whoever believes in me will also do the works that I do; and greater works than these will he do, because I am going to the Father."* Jesus was referring to miraculous works. Prophets were discipled in the different facets of prophetic powers. Similarly we should become understudies of the supernatural. We must become students of the prophetic that is validated with authentic signs, wonders, and miraculous healings. Miracles not only set the prophets apart—miracles validated their ministry and their words.

Prophets will do special miracles by the power of God in their prophetic ministry. It will be commonplace to see literally uncommon miracles released by the mouth of the prophet. Prophets will walk in a realm of the supernatural where they will do notable miracles and remarkable signs that serve as evidence, verifiable, and undeniable proof to all the people they are sent to minister and serve (Acts 4:16 NIV).

Documented miracles will further substantiate their ministerial prophetic office. Special miracles were done by the hands of the apostles in the New Testament—and equally, special miracles will be done by the mouth of the prophets of the New Testament. Prophets carry revelatory power to manifest mighty signs, wonders, and extraordinary miracles through their prophesying, preaching, and praying.

REVELATORY TEACHING POWER

Miracles is one of the revelatory powers of the prophetic. Prophets have a unique way of ministering revelation. Teaching is no different as prophets are innately powerful in miracles and dynamic in teaching. Prophets teach, preach, and prophesy with attesting signs following their ministry of the word. They teach with power and authority that is unequivocally different from traditional or orthodox teachings. There is a measure of authority with which prophets teach.

Prophets teaching will develop a seek and insatiable hunger in people to come to learn more about Jesus. The greatest revelation of prophets is to reveal Jesus Christ in both word and deed.

Jesus's dimension of teaching was so highlighted with miraculous signs that His ministry got the attention of a Pharisee by the name of Nicodemus who visited Him at night to comprehend Jesus's teaching, to learn how to access the supernatural, and essentially how things were possible *(dynatos)* that he witnessed in Jesus's ministry. Nicodemus saw revelatory power on Jesus through His teaching and the miracles that followed thereafter.

> *There was a man of the Pharisees named Nicodemus, a ruler of the Jews. This man came to Jesus by night and said to Him, "Rabbi, we know that You are a teacher come from God; for no one can do these signs that You do unless God is with him"* (John 3:1-2 NKJV).

Nicodemus knew Jesus was sent by God because of His teaching and His ability to do miraculous signs. Demonstration of miracles is an indicator that God is with a man or woman of God. Prophets teach with wisdom and mighty works of miraculous power. This measure of power in the prophetic will cause people to question or consider the source of these capabilities:

> *He* [Jesus] *came to His hometown and began teaching them in their synagogue, with the result that they were astonished, and said, "Where did this man acquire this*

wisdom and these miraculous powers?" (Matthew 13:54 NASB)

Prophets have the capacity by the authority of Jesus to minister in the realm of teaching that will be fresh, new, unprecedented, unorthodox, and unfamiliar to others, and it will be marked with the power to bring deliverance:

> *And they were all amazed, so that they questioned among themselves, saying, "What is this? A new teaching with authority! He commands even the unclean spirits, and they obey Him* (Mark 1:27 NASB).
>
> *And He went down to Capernaum, a city of Galilee; and He was teaching them on the Sabbath, and they were amazed at His teaching, because His message was delivered with authority. In the synagogue there was a man possessed by the spirit of an unclean demon, and he cried out with a loud voice* (Luke 4:31-33 NASB).

Prophets typically speak words or communicate in a way that many have not heard spoken before:

> *When they heard these words, some of the people said, "This really is the Prophet." Others said, "This is the Christ." But some said, "Is the Christ to come from Galilee?"...The officers answered, "No one ever spoke like this man!"* (John 7:40-41,46 ESV).

Prophets will minister itinerantly to great crowds while teaching and preaching the gospel and administering healing of all types of afflictions, diseases, and sicknesses: *"And he went throughout all Galilee, teaching in their synagogues and proclaiming the gospel of the kingdom and healing every disease and every affliction among the people"* (Matthew 4:23 ESV).

Prophets do not teach by their own authority—they speak just as they were taught by revelation by the Holy Spirit: *"So Jesus said to them, 'When you have lifted up the Son of Man, then you will know that I am he, and that I do nothing on my own authority, but speak just as the Father taught me'"* (John 8:28).

I often teach that everything a prophet does is prophetic. Therefore, whether a prophet calls a person out in a meeting and ministers to them in personal prophecy or not, every word spoken under the canopy of their prophetic office and authority is subject to change the life and trajectory of anyone who dares to believe what is being released. Their power is in the preached or taught word of God, which is a surer word of prophecy (2 Peter 1:19).

I have literally seen in my prophetic ministry manifestations of healing and deliverance as I taught prophetically. One of the keys to unlock the supernatural is to teach on the supernatural. For example, when my brother, Dr. Hakeem Collins, and I, who are widely recognized as "The Twin Prophets," would teach and preach the word of God regarding the Kingdom of God, we would see powerful manifestations of the Kingdom in miracles, healings of the sick, and casting out of demons, similarly as Jesus commissioned His disciples to practice what He preached and taught them according to Matthew 10:6-8.

Jesus was a practitioner of miracles, signs, wonders, healings, and deliverance. It was common to see diversities of miracles as an attesting witness of what He taught by the Spirit. As a teacher, Jesus provided many infallible proofs, and this is what prophets, teachers, and leaders today must demonstrate in their ministry (Acts 1:1-3). In other words, in His ministry, Jesus did both—He provided proof and He also taught Scripture.

When one hears a prophet minister the word of God, he or she ministers with such revelatory knowledge that you know that it came from above (Heaven). Prophets operate in revelatory power. Their teaching carries the same weight to manifest the power of God. As the prophet ministers and teaches the word, demons can come out of people as we see in the example of Philip in Acts 8:4-8.

Prophets historically were known for being sent by God by the miracles upon their lives and their word of prophecies not failing. Prophets of God carried such a formidable reputation among the people they ministered to that God was with them because of the miraculous powers upon them and God allowing none of their words to fail—all came to pass. Cindy Jacobs who is a global and reputable major prophet of our time has written in her book, *The Voice of God* which was the very first book I read on the prophetic that helped me fully embrace my call to the prophetic ministry. She recently after having a valuable phone conversation with her during the writing of this book corrected and tweaked a standard of thinking that many not all have been taught that the Old Testament prophets had a reputation that they were always 100 percent accurate in prophecy. Unfortunately, this erroneous thinking and paradigm created a standard in the prophetic community that for years that New Testament prophets or prophets today are lesser prophets incomparable to our ancient prophetic predecessors in prophesying and that prophets today have to be 100 percent acaccurate, or they are not true spokesman and spokeswoman of God.

This have created much confusion, criticism and conflict among prophetic voices operating in a greater measure and advanced levels of prophecy to our fully potential than the biblical prophets. Many may not still agree with this school of thought but I agree wholeheartedly now that unlocked the power of prophecy in me with humility but without reservation.

She writes in her book, *The Voice of God* on page eighty-eight where she addresses this issue and teaching that all Old Testament prophets were consistently 100 percent accurate, or that they were false if they were not and inference developed a sense that devalued the New Testament prophets and prophecy of being of a lesser caliber. She adjusted and corrected my perspective on this matter as a Mama prophet.

She writes: "The Old Testament prophets, however, were human—they made mistakes, but the were not always stoned for doing so. If Old Testament prophets who gave inaccurate words were stoned, why wasn't Nathan stoned when he prophesied inaccurately to David? Why wasn't Micaiah stoned when he lied before giving God's true word (see 1 Kings 22:15)? I love what she further says in principle regarding New Testament prophets and prophets today that, "God seems to always save the new wine, or the best, for the last, Wouldn't it be the same with prophecy?"[1]

Samuel was one of the prophets in Israel who carried such a track record in the word of prophecy. Accuracy was one of the qualifiers of genuine prophets of God but not the only qualification (Deuteronomy 18:22). Samuel had developed a notable and honorable reputation in all of Israel as a confirmed and credible prophet whose words did not fall to the ground according to First Samuel 3:19-20 (NKJV):

> *So Samuel grew, and the LORD was with him and let none of his words fall to the ground. And all Israel from Dan to Beersheba knew that Samuel had been established as a prophet of the Lord.*

First Samuel 3:19 in the New Living Translation puts it this way: *"As Samuel grew up, the LORD was with him, and everything Samuel said proved to be reliable."*

First Samuel 9:6 shows Saul's servants revealing and speaking of the prophetic reputation of Samuel with regard to receiving directions and guidance in locating his father's lost donkeys:

And he said to him, "Look now, there is in this city a man of God, and he is an honorable man; all that he says surely comes to pass. So let us go there; perhaps he can show us the way that we should go."

Prophetic Rarity

Now the boy Samuel ministered to the LORD before Eli. And the word of the Lord was rare in those days; there was no widespread revelation (1 Samuel 3:1 NKJV).

Samuel had such a rarity in the prophetic that his reputation went from as far north as Dan to as far south as Beersheba, confirming and establishing him as a prophet of God (1 Samuel 3:19-20). He carried a rare word during a time when prophetic operation and revelation was limited and not widespread. Because there was a shortage of prophets and prophecy, it was precious in the era of Samuel the prophet.

Prophets today will carry rare prophetic anointing and grace in communicating the word of the Lord in seasons of prophetic limitation or famines of hearing the word of God (Amos 8:11-13). Samuel's fame, notoriety, credibility, recognition, and respect as God's prophetic voice were honored beyond his geographical location.

Samuel's prophetic acuity and navigational ability was unmatched, which set him apart in his day. Samuel's ability to prophetically locate the time, duration, and place of Saul's father's lost donkeys was unheard of and warranted such reputation (1 Samuel

9:20). Reputation speaks relative to the prophet's character, notoriety, honor, influence, name, prominence, and standing.

A prophet's reputation must precede him or her. Prophecy is the prophet's most primitive power in the supernatural to reveal the past, present, and future. God is restoring the relevance and the prominence of the prophets as a supernatural agency of miraculous power and not just for their communicative power. Mighty deeds were integrated within the very essence of the prophetic that has always been the standard by which the timeless prophets lived by, and what they were essentially known for. Miracles were integrated into the ancient prophetic ministry.

Power and prophecy were the reputation and recognition of the ancient prophets. Prophets and prophetic believers today will be famous for not just prophecy but also the power of God working in and through their ministry—or notorious for inaccurate prophecy and the lack of the character and power of God working in and through their ministry.

Prophetic Powers

Prophets were the pioneers in ministering with miraculous prophetic power. The prophetic ministry is the forerunner of the apostolic ministry. Therefore, the prophets were the first to walk in power ministry. In other words, before the New Testament apostles' ministry of signs, wonders, and miracles according to Second Corinthians 12:12, there was first the Old Testament prophets' ministry of signs, wonders, and miracles according to Second Chronicles 20:20 and Genesis 20:7,17-18.

Abraham was the first in Scripture to be recognized as a prophet by God and that honorable mention was to reveal the foundational function of prophets to the ministry of intercession and healing (see Genesis 20:1-18). You will see in the ministry of the apostolic a merging of miracles and the prophetic working hand-in-glove together. In fact, the prophetic is the fuse behind the apostolic.

The apostle Paul in his apostolic ministry taught and ministered with prophetic powers according to his definition of it in First Corinthians 13:2 (AMPC):

> *And if I have prophetic powers (the gift of interpreting the divine will and purpose), and understand all the secret truths and mysteries and possess all knowledge, and if I have [sufficient] faith so that I can remove mountains, but have not love (God's love in me) I am nothing (a useless nobody).*

Paul defined *prophetic powers* as having the gift of interpreting the divine will and purpose, and understanding all the secret truths and mysteries and possessing all knowledge. This was most certainly a key element of his apostolic ministry. You cannot be genuinely apostolic without being prophetic. He further explains that *prophecy* is also regarded as part or fragment of the integration of his teaching according to First Corinthans 13:9 (AMPC) saying, *"For our knowledge is fragmentary (incomplete and imperfect), and our prophecy (our teaching) is fragmentary (incomplete and imperfect)."*

Paul essentially functioned as a prophetic apostle in both mighty deeds and prophetic powers in his teaching. The prophetic powers in the gift of prophecy gave him the ability to explain the mysteries of the Scriptures by the Spirit. Miracles have always been and will always be also one of the marks of the prophetic ministry. The notable power of the prophetic is in the mouth of the prophets. Prophets release healing, deliverance, and miraculous signs through the power of prophecy. The powers of hell recognized the validity of the powers of Heaven that is bestowed upon God's servants the prophets. That is one of the reasons why prophets and prophetic people endured an enormous amount of warfare due to the power that is invested in them as vocal instruments and spokesmen of God. The devil works tirelessly to shut the mouths of the prophets in order to keep God's creative, revelatory, and miracle-working power from being released.

One of the ways that the devil tries to weaken, diminish, or soften the weight of the prophetic officers of God is to mimic, mock, and/ or muzzle the prophets. This was clearly and distinctively what separated Moses as a *mighty prophet* from the magicians of Pharoah who could not copy, duplicate, or recreate his prophetic powers in signs, wonders, and divine judgments. Moses as a prophet was empowered by the Lord to perform before Pharoah the king of Egypt all the miracles and wonders that God had given him power to do. He was to show or display them to Pharoah:

> *And the Lord said to Moses, "When you go back to Egypt, see that you do before Pharaoh all the miracles that I have put in your power. But I will harden his heart, so that he will not let the people go"* (Exodus 4:21 ESV).

It was not just the miracles that Jesus performed, but the way He ministered in word was just as powerful. There was an extraordinary dimension in the prophetic ministry of the Word that Jesus walked in that was unexplainable. He would preach, teach, and prophesy the Word with signs, wonders and mighty deeds. His prophetic ministry redefined and refined the prophetic ministry in the New Testament as *"Power Prophecy,"* which is releasing miracles through the power of prophecy.

The following are just a few examples of Jesus's supernatural Kingdom ministry that serve as a model for prophets and prophetic ministers.

- The people recognized that Jesus was sent from God by the miracles He performed. People will identify, testify, and verify a prophet of God today in the church, the marketplace, and the world globally by the same standard of impossible signs that he or she will do among them. Prophets will be able to do uncommon, unheard, unseen, and unexplainable miracles that will directly challenge people's opinions, doubts, and unbeliefs (see Luke 5:12-26).

  Then some of the Pharisees said, This Man [Jesus] is not from God, because He does not observe the Sabbath. But others said, How can a man who is a sinner (a bad man) do such signs and miracles? So there was a difference of opinion among them. Accordingly they said to the blind man again, What do you say about Him, seeing that He opened your eyes? And he said, He is [He must be] a prophet!... Since the beginning of time it has never been heard that anyone opened the eyes of a man born blind. If this Man were not from God, He would not be able to do anything like this (John 9:16-17, 32-33 AMPC).

- Jesus was anointed with the Holy Spirit and with power. The anointing of power by the Holy Spirit upon the prophets today will be key to ministering in miracles, healing, deliverance, and salvation. Prophets and prophetic believers will function in an anointing of miracles. People will know that Jesus's Spirit is working not only with His prophets but in His prophets working by the Spirit: *"how God anointed Jesus of Nazareth with the Holy Spirit and with power, who went about doing good and healing all who were oppressed by the devil, for God was with Him"* (Acts 10:38 NKJV).

▪ New Testament prophets and ministers of prophecy will be commissioned by Jesus Christ through the power of the Holy Spirit to demonstrate the Kingdom of God according to Matthew 10:6-8 ESV: *"But go rather to the lost sheep of the house of Israel. And proclaim as you go, saying, 'The kingdom of heaven is at hand.' Heal the sick, raise the dead, cleanse lepers, cast out demons. You received without paying; give without pay."*

Equipped With Mighty Works

Miracles, signs, and wonders are parts of incredible supernatural equipment. The word *miracle* in the Scriptures is used interchangeably as *"mighty works, signs and wonders."* Miracles are simply supernatural works not stemmed from natural or external causes. It is imperative to comprehend that a *"mighty work"* aims our focus to the points of the Bible that have supernatural acts of God. The word *wonders* directs our attention to the impression made by miracles. The word *sign* is used more frequently for miracles in the Gospel of John. More than likely this use of the word *sign* is meant to point or direct our attention to God or reveals a specific message. In fact, miracles validate the truthfulness of the one sent and equipped by God.

The miraculous works provide more credibility of the supernatural minister and the message that is in his or her mouth. God will confirm the word of His prophets as truth with testifying signs to authenticate God's message and messenger. We can see an example of this validation in John 10:25 (NKJV) where Jesus says, *"I have told, and you do not believe. The works that I do in My Father's name, they bear witness of Me."*

Miracles are an important and purposeful act of God to deliver people from danger (Exodus 14:21-31) and to demonstrate that the God of the Bible is the one true God (Exodus 7:2-5; 2 Kings 18:16-38). A miracle is a supernatural exception or override to the laws of nature. A miracle is an event in which God temporarily makes an exception to His rule and to the way things usually happen. A miracle is a supernatural phenomenon or mystery that is done by God Himself or through His ministers of power. According to the Merriam-Webster Dictionary, a miracle is an extraordinary event manifesting divine intervention in human affairs, as in the healing described in the Gospels and even in the Old Testament prophets.

GOD GIVES MOSES MIRACULOUS POWER

And Moses was learned in all the wisdom of the Egyptians, and was mighty in words and in deeds (Acts 7:22).

In the book of Exodus, God clearly states to Moses that the purpose of the miracles is to show to the Israelites that Moses is truly sent by God. Mighty works, signs, and wonders may have many distinct names and point to many distinct instances; however, they all have one unifying theme and that is to prove that the people who perform them are gifted with the power from God and are sent by God to serve His purposes. God gave Moses, as His divine communicator, miraculous signs as proof to the Israelites and Pharoah that he was sent by Him. The miraculous powers invested in Moses were to support and reinforce him as God's chosen spokesman and prophet.

Moses, in the Old Testament, was clearly a mighty prophet similar to Jesus Christ in the New Testament. Moses was an understudy in all the wisdom of the Egyptians, and was mighty in words and in deeds. Moses and Aaron were given a staff and rod as symbols of their power and authorization as official prophets. God gives Moses two confirming and convincing signs (miracles) during his initial calling as a prophet. God was sending His prophet with power. Whenever God sends someone to do anything for Him, He will send him or her with power and authority.

THE PROPHET'S VOICE

God will supernaturally support not only His prophets but their voice. God chooses and confirms His prophets that He will give them a voice that people will listen to. There is an authority in the prophetic voice where God will provide them with convincing miraculous signs as reinforcement to the words of the prophets. If they do not believe, listen, and obey the prophet, then the miracle serves as a witness for them to believe. God will reveal and make Himself known to His prophets by way of direct revelation, audible or inner voice, visions, dreams, appearances, and some special experience or encounter, and even miracles (see Numbers 12:6; 1 Samuel 3 and Hebrews 1:1).

We can see in the following Scriptures that Moses needed assurance from God as a prophetic voice with respect to being a spokesman on His behalf to the people if they had questions about God appearing to him in Exodus 4:1:

> *Then Moses answered, "But behold, they will not believe me or listen to my voice, for they will say, 'The Lord did not appear to you.'"*

The miracles or signs done by a prophet is for people to believe the message. A miraculous sign is given to reveal a message. It is to confirm the message or a specific revelation. God said in Exodus 4 that if the people did not believe or obey the message of the first sign (miracle) that they may believe the message of the latter miracle sign. There is a message in the sign or miracle given to the prophet. Even in the miracle (sign) done by a prophet there is a message being communicated. Prophets are messengers of the supernatural and even their miracles, signs and wonders serve as divine messages; this truth is revealed in Exodus 4:6-8 (NIV):

> *Then the Lord said, "Put your hand inside your cloak." So Moses put his hand into his cloak, and when he took it out, the skin was leprous—it had become as white as snow.*
> *"Now put it back into your cloak," he said. So Moses put his hand back into his cloak, and when he took it out, it was restored, like the rest of his flesh. Then the Lord said, "If they do not believe you or pay attention to the first sign, they may believe the second."*

The miracle is connected to the mouth, voice, and message of the prophet as a sign. Moses was given two signs (miracles) as a prophetic voice for the people to believe he was sent by God as a prophet. The final miracle would be of the water turning into blood as a wonder on earth to point to their authority to execute judgment due to unbelief, blatant disobedience, or refusal to obey God's official spokesmen and the signs in Exodus 4:9 (NIV):

> *But if they do not believe these two signs or listen to you, take some water from the Nile and pour it on the dry ground. The water you take from the river will become blood on the ground.*

God trains and equips His prophets with the tools and the supernatural resources needed to complete His works. A prophet's voice can be used as a tool, instrument, or a weapon. Moses and Aaron were to represent the correlation of the prophetic and miracles as they are sent on assignment to lead God's people. God teaches His prophets what to speak.

In the following Scripture passage, God reassures Moses. Though he felt inadequate to be a solidified spokesman and prophetic voice on God's behalf, God provided Moses with all the undeniable and irrevocable power tools he needed as a mighty prophet of God. According to Exodus 4:10-17 (NIV):

> *Moses said to the LORD, "Pardon your servant, Lord. I have never been eloquent, neither in the past nor since you have spoken to your servant. I am slow of speech and tongue." The LORD said to him, "Who gave human beings their mouths? Who makes them deaf or mute? Who gives them sight or makes them blind? Is it not I, the Lord? Now go; I will help you speak and will teach you what to say." But Moses said, "Pardon your servant, Lord. Please send someone else." Then the LORD's anger burned against Moses and he said, "What about your brother, Aaron the Levite? I know he can speak well. He is already on his way to meet you, and he will be glad to see you. You shall speak to him and put words in his mouth; I will help both of you speak and will teach you what to do. He will speak [spokesman] to the people for you, and it will be as if he were your mouth and as if you were God to him. But take this staff [rod] in your hand so you can perform the signs [miracles] with it."*

Moses was equipped with tools. His and Aaron's staff, rod, and mantle (cloak) as God's sent ones (apostolic) and spokesmen (prophetic) were essentially symbolic to represent the audacious nature and demonstrative power of their prophetic ministry.

THE PROPHET'S ROD AND STAFF

Aaron's rod refers to any walking stick—part of a prophet's equipment. The Bible reveals how along with Moses's rod, Aaron's rod was endowed with miraculous power during the time when the plagues of Egypt were released prior to the Exodus. There are two occasions where the Bible tells of the rod's power. In the culture of the Israelites, the rod was a natural symbol of authority, as the tool used by the shepherd or leader to correct and guide his flock (Psalm 23:4). Rods were sometimes used as weapons of defense or offense and, as mentioned, as walking sticks (Genesis 32:10).

The staff or walking stick shows the power and authority that prophets walk in and walk with. As a mighty prophet, this would be equivalent to what a superhero would have in his or her utility belt and/or their special weapon against their enemies. Prophets carry a spiritual staff as a leader and a rod of authority. The rod and staff serve dualistically in the power and authority of prophets. They walk in authority with the staff as leader; but they execute power, alignment, or correction with the rod. This is the pure power and authority of the prophets revealed in Exodus 4:2-5 (NIV):

> *Then the LORD said to him, "What is that in your hand?" "A staff," he replied. The LORD said, "Throw it on the ground." Moses threw it on the ground and it became a snake, and he ran from it. Then the LORD said to him, "Reach out your hand and take it by the tail." So Moses reached out and took hold of the snake and it turned back into a staff in his hand. "This," said the Lord, "is so that they may believe that the LORD, the God of their*

fathers—the God of Abraham, the God of Isaac and the God of Jacob—has appeared to you."

Consider the following biblical accounts of the prophetic and supernatural power and authority invested in the prophet's *rod* and *staff*:

- Moses's Rod—Performing miracles (Exodus 4:1-5); he lifted his rod and the Red Sea parted miraculously (Exodus 14:16); while in the wilderness he struck a rock with the rod to produce a spring of water (Exodus 17:5-7). He thereafter raised his hands with his staff in warfare and obtained victory with the help of Aaron and Hur (Exodus 17:11).

- Aaron's Rod—Swallowing the magicians snakes (Exodus 7:8-10); performing miracles (Exodus 7:19). Summons miraculous plagues of frogs (Exodus 8:5-6). His rod budded at three different developmental stages prophetically to verify and authorize the prophet's anointing, authority as God's appointed leadership (see Numbers 16–17).

- David's Rod and Staff as Shepherd—(Psalm 23:4) David was a shepherd boy in his youth and he described his use of the rod to King Saul saying, *"Your servant used to keep his father's sheep, and when a lion or a bear came and took a lamb out of the flock, I went out after it and struck it, and delivered the lamb from its mouth; and when it arose against me, I caught it by its beard, and struck and killed it"* (1 Samuel 17:34-35 NKJV).

- Elisha's Staff—Elisha understood the supernatural power and miracle-working properties in his prophet's staff or rod when he sent it with his servant Gehazi to heal and raise the widow woman's son from the dead (2 Kings 4:29).

- The Lord's Rod and Staff—The Lord disciplines the ones He loves and chastises every son whom He receives (Hebrews 12:6). The rod is also an instrument of correction, alignment, and discipline (Psalm 94:12 and Proverbs 3:12).

The account of Elisha sending his staff with his servant was just like Elisha sending himself to be laid on the child. It was believed that there were supernatural properties in the walking staff of the prophet to release healing and miracles. The walking staff or rod described the prophet *walking* in the supernatural.

THE PROPHET'S MANTLE

It is like the New Testament account of Paul sending cloths and handkerchiefs from his body for others to be healed and delivered (Acts 19:12). There are miraculous properties and powers also in the prophet's *mantle*. As a prophet I have given my own ministerial garments, robes, watches, and personal belongings to those who were sick, and even to my spiritual mentees and sons in ministry, and there have been literal manifestation of the healings as result of the anointing of the office upon my life.

In the early tenure of my ministry, I had a spiritual mentee whom I had given my ministerial garment (cassock) to minister in, and it was said by his grandmother (a prophetess) that he had ministered, preached, and prophesied in the same prophetic grace that I walked in as result of the garment due to the transference of my anointing that was saturated in it. There is a prophetic anointing and transference of power in clothing because of the prophet. This happened in the ministry of Jesus—when anyone touched His garment, they were healed by virtue of His clothes or mantle (see Mark 5:30; Luke 6:19; Luke 8:46). It is important to note and understand that healing power and anointing was not in the garment, mantle or cloak in itself that heals. It is the Holy Spirit's power and anointing working through the office of the prophet and in his or her article of clothing that heals. We do not seek healing from a prophet's clothes, possessions or personal belongings but from God working through the prophet in any way He sees fits.

The mentee's prophetess grandmother went on to say that she had seen my prophetic spirit and power—the spirit of the prophet—upon him and asked if I could take back the garment because it was heavy for him to walk in at such a young age at the time. I have witnessed my twin brother, Dr. Hakeem Collins who is also a prophet, give our grandmother his prayer shawl and instruct her by the leading of the Holy Spirit to sleep with it for seven days after she had received a cancer diagnosis. After following the prophet's orders, she was miraculously healed to date. The prophet's rod and staff were the prophet's equipment. The power and authority were not just in the prophet's rod and staff, miraculous power was also in the prophet's mantle.

The prophet's mantle is another piece of equipment and tool of the prophet. The cloak (mantle) of Moses represented the mantle of miraculous power to demonstrate and administer healing as a prophet in Exodus 4:6-8 (ESV):

> *Again, the LORD said to him* [Moses], *"Put your hand inside your cloak* [mantle]*." And he put his hand inside his cloak, and when he took it out, behold, his hand was leprous like snow. Then God said, "Put your hand back inside*

your cloak." So he put his hand back inside his cloak, and when he took it out, behold, it was restored like the rest of his flesh. "If they will not believe you," God said, "or listen to the first sign, they may believe the latter sign."

Moses and Aaron were given signs, wonders, and the miraculous to accompany their prophetic voices (Exodus 11:10). These endowments of power were for the people to know and believe that they were commissioned by God—providing overwhelming proof of their mission. There was miraculous power in the mantle of Elijah that was eventually transferred and transmitted to Elisha.

As we have previously seen the power of the prophet's staff, we cannot ignore the mantle of the prophet. Elijah and Elisha both struck the Jordan river during their time of transition and transference of the spirit and power of the prophetic office. Elijah struck the water and it, in God-like fashion, opened up for them to walk on dry ground (2 Kings 2:8). Elisha, after receiving and taking up the mantle of Elijah, activated the power of the mantle by striking the same water to cross back over as evidence that he is now the newly anointed prophet carrying the spirit of Elijah (2 Kings 2:14).

AUTHENTICALLY PROPHETIC

The supernatural phenomenon of miracles, mighty deeds, acts, signs, and wonders add authenticity to the prophetic voice as one sent as God's official spokesperson. Miracles in the ministry of the prophet can be revelatory or signifying. Prophets, in fact, function in the revelatory and signifying aspects of their office. When the prophet is operating, it is sometimes difficult to distinguish the revelatory or signify the miracles. All in all, the mighty deeds and words done by the prophet of God is simply to reveal the true and living God and proves God is stamping His approval on His messenger communicating His message as truth. God's prophetic voices are stamped with miracles, signs, and wonders.

Prophets do not need people's approval or validation because they have God's seal of approval and He watches over His word to perform it (Jeremiah 1:12). Acts 2:22 in the New Living Translation teaches us that Jesus was approved of God by miracles, signs, and wonders:

> *People of Israel, listen! God publicly endorsed Jesus the Nazarene by doing powerful miracles, wonders, and signs through him, as you well know.*

Jesus was accredited by God as one fully equipped, credentialed, and qualified by Heaven's endorsement with miraculous exploitation in His earthly ministry. He was schooled in the supernatural and was a qualified teacher (rabbi) in spiritual things. Jesus was sent with conferred power to work miracles. In other words, God signs off on His miracle workers. God puts His signature on His people to distinguish them from and against counterfeit and false signs and wonders.

Moses was stamped with glory to signify that the presence of God was with him. Moses was a glory carrier who walked with tangible glory that all of Israel was able to see visibly. There was no secret to his ministry, that he was God's prophet. Another example of being authentically prophetic was when Moses asked for the glory and presence of the Lord to go with him and the children of Israel under his prophetic leadership. Moses understood that only the presence and glory of God could distinctively set him and God's people apart from other nations, according to Exodus 33:15-17.

Moses had a grace of God's presence on his life that people were able to easily recognize and know that he walked with God and that God was with him. There was something different about Moses than anyone else. Prophets and prophetic people carry something uniquely different that distinguishes them from the world, and the world takes notice. Prophets having phenomenal prophetic abilities were regarded in ancient Israel as distinct, mighty men or heroes displaying miraculous and prophetic powers and as possessing inner experiences, impressions, and visions that can be regarded as divine interventions or as manifestations of divine or supernatural powers.

MIRACLES OF AUTHENTICATION

Miracles of authentication—miraculous occurrences or happenings—can serve as the following in the ministry of the prophet:

- Authorization—as credentials and credibility of the prophet's spiritual authority in the form of leadership in Exodus 4, in which Moses convinces the Israelites of the authenticity of his mission by miraculous performances.

- Verification of Prophecy—as verified prophecy in Deuteronomy 18, where it is written that a prophet is disqualified if the sign that he has predicted does not come to pass. Prophets' prophetic words are sure and come to pass as the verification of prophecy.

- Demonstration—as the demonstration of the divine and superior power of God over counterfeit, demonic, false gods, or prophets in Exodus 7, which recounts Aaron's staff swallowing up the staffs of the Egyptian magicians, thus demonstrating the superiority of the God of the Israelites, Elijah on Mount Carmel against the prophets of baal. Prophets are powerful instruments in the spirit against opposing forces. They are not just oracles of truth but also demonstrators of truth.

- Sanctification and Consecration—as proof of the sanctity of a holy person, a holy site, or a holy object, Moses called from a place and where he was standing was holy ground (Exodus 3:5); or God appearing to prophets miraculously in different places or sites (Genesis 22 and Joshua 5:15).

- Manifestation and Exhibition—more generally as evidence of the truth. We can see this example in the Gospel of Mark where Jesus Christ working with the preaching of the word of the apostles as accompanying and attesting sign (Mark 16:19-20), which the true essence of power prophecy where there is accompanying and attesting signs exhibiting the preaching, preaching, and prophesying of the word of God.

There are four main purposes of miracles in Scripture:

1. To strengthen the faith of believers.

2. To produce faith in unbelievers.

3. To confirm that a particular message/messenger was from God.

4. To display God's divine power.

DEFINING MIGHTY DEEDS AND WORKS

Jesus was revealed and His ministry defined as being a *mighty prophet*—marked by *mighty deeds*. The phrase "mighty deeds" means miracles or powerful works. Jesus describes the works He did in His ministry as testifying on His behalf when He said, *"...The works I do in my Father's name testify about me"* (John 10:25 NIV). Miracles testify on the behalf of the prophet, minister, and believer. The Greek word *ergon* literally means "works." This is a description from the standpoint of what is normal and natural to God. As such, they are called "works" or "deeds." The word denotes work of God, Christ, believers, unbelievers, and/or the devil.

In the New Testament, this word *works* is used 169 times. It is used by Jesus to describe His distinctive works; those works that no one else has done. Several times in John (5:36; 7:21; 10:25,38), Jesus spoke of His miraculous works in an effort to spur people to believe in Him saying:

> *If I do not do the works of My Father, do not believe Me; but if I do, though you do not believe Me, believe the works, that you may know and believe that the Father is in Me, and I in Him* (John 10:37-38 NKJV).

We are called to *believe* the works—the miracles. These are works that no mere human can do. These works point to divine or miraculous power. It is important as believers to believe in miracles. Miracles were part of the ministry of the prophets, and it became a tool to draw people to believe in the God of miracles. We as disciples of Jesus Christ through the power of the Spirit are to continue in the works of producing miracles. Jesus essentially was saying in John 10:37-38 setting a New Testament precedence, *"If I do not do the works or miracles of God, do not believe Me."* This should be the desire of the prophets to press in for more of God's power flowing through them.

Prophets will be called upon in their generation to release miracles, signs, and mighty wonders through the power of prophecy. We will see prophets emerge prophesying physical and divine healings. People with all kinds of diseases will be healed by the word of the Lord spoken by the auspices of the prophetic. There will be instantaneous healings occurring before people's eyes as we speak healing into existence. This will happen through the believers who are bold, courageous, and fearless.

Mighty prophets will perform remarkable feats that will baffle the minds of the naysayers.

According to Strong's Concordance, the word *deed* is *ergon,* which is the original Greek for the English word *works,* which is translated as "deed, doing, labor, or toil." When used in the sense of a deed or act, the idea of working is stressed.

Jesus labored in working miracles. The supernatural was part of His works as a prophet. Miracles take laboring, toiling, and working to manifest results. The key to unlocking miracles prophetically is simply laboring in prayer as did Elijah in order to open and close the heavens when he prophesied that there would be no rain for a span of three and a half years (see 1 Kings 18:41-45 and James 5:13-18). The power behind the prophetic is continual fervent prayer and intercession that produces the miraculous.

We see also this principle demonstrated first with Abraham being a prophet who prayed for King Abimelech and his entire household, consequently being healed from barrenness (see Genesis 20:7, 17-18 NKJV). Jesus was doing the work or business of His Father. Miracles were part of what Jesus used to complete the work. The word *ergon* is also defined as business and/or employment, in which anyone is occupied.

WORKING MIRACLES

The root word and etymology of the word *miracles* comes primary from the word *ergo,* which simply means "to work." *Ergon* speaks of working as an act or deed. It simply means to "work miracles" as part of one's job, task, assignment, and occupation. Miracles was an undertaking of the prophets. Miracles, mighty deeds and acts of God were byproducts of servants of God—the power of God through the energy of the Holy Spirit flowing in the prophets as they ministered in word. The people asked for a miraculous sign to be done so they would see and believe Jesus. At times, miracles served as confirming signs for people to believe the message of the prophet or messenger of God:

> *They answered, "Show us a miraculous sign* [work] *if you want us to believe in you. What can you do?"* (John 6:30 NLT)

According to the Merriam-Webster Dictionary the word *deed* is something that is done. It is an illustrious act or action. It is a feat or exploit. Deed also means an action that is performed intentionally or consciously. Jesus was very intentional when He performed a miracle of healing or deliverance. Prophets are intentional in working a miracle. No miracle in the Bible was done accidentally or haphazardly. In the Old Testament, the very acts of the prophets to perform miracles were signs of their authenticity and them working as servants on behalf of God. Prophets are in essence miracle workers. Mighty or power prophets specifically function with divine power, while false prophets operate with demonic or human power.

There must be a radically and unwavering obedience to the prophetic word of the Lord. Mighty prophets are those who are hearers and doers of what God reveals to them to speak and demonstrate without reservation. This act of extreme obedience produces unusual miracles.

NOTE

1   Cindy Jacobs, *The Voice of God* (Bloomington, MN.: Chosen Books, 1995, 2016), p. 88

2

PROPHETIC HEALING

He sent His word and healed them, and
delivered them from their destructions.
—PSALM 107:20 NKJV

The centurion answered and said, "Lord, I am not
worthy that You should come under my roof. But
only speak a word, and my servant will be healed."
—MATTHEW 8:8 NKJV

There is power in the release of the word of healing. In the Old and New Testaments there are biblical examples of various types of healings that have happened through a prophetic release or a prophetic word. It is important to understand that there is power in the prophetic. The simplest definition of prophecy is to speak forth or to utter by inspiration the word of God. Power prophecy is to speak forth the word of God that produces God-type results. The power of prophecy through prophetic healings is to speak forth the word of God that produces tangible healing.

The anointing of a prophet is activated when he or she opens their mouth to release the word of God. Healing is one of the manifestations in the mouth of the prophets. Many are one prophetic release away from their healing, miracle, deliverance, and breakthrough.

Whether you have been ordained or gifted to be a prophet or prophetic voice, you have the power to employ the word of healing and watch it work for you in the name of Jesus Christ. One of the most powerful manifestation of the prophets, prophecy, and the prophetic is *healing*.

This chapter reveals the residential anointing of healing that lies within the ministry of the prophetic. We will discover the power of healing that has always been in the anointing and grace of the prophets of old and how it is accessible for the prophets and prophetic believers today. All believers have been commissioned by Jesus Christ to minister in prophetic healing (Matthew 10:1,7-8). The first mention, biblical account and demonstration of healing was done by a prophet. Healing and the prophetic have an ancient history recorded for us to see.

The first act of healing in relation to a prophet through prayer and intercession is that of Abraham whom God Himself first called a prophet in Genesis 20:6-7 (NIV):

> *Then God said to him* [Abimelech] *in the dream, "Yes, I know that you did this with a clear conscience, and so I have kept you from sinning against me. That is why I did not let you touch her* [Sarah, Abraham's wife]. *Now return the man's wife, for he* [Abraham] *is a prophet, and he will pray* [intercede] *for you and you will live. But if you do not return her, you may be sure that you and all who belong to you will die."*

For the purpose of this chapter, any form of healing demonstrated by a prophet through the laying on of hands, prophetic intercession, or any word or prophecy spoken through the different realms of the prophetic will be described as *prophetic healing*. Abimelech's restoration was predicated primarily on the intercession of Abraham.

Prophetic intercession can release healing and restoration to an individual, people, nations, and kingdoms. Life is created or incubated in the mouth of the prophet. Prophecy spoken over someone can impart life and it can give birth and create extraordinary things in those who may have been physically and spiritually barren.

There is power in the prophetic to open spiritual and physical wombs. This can be best described as *prophetic intercession.* Prophetic intercession creates wombs for the supernatural to happen. It is praying until something happens or is birthed.

We can view this as two sides of the same coin where we see healing and even deliverance working interchangeably. Abimelech and his entire kingdom and household were healed by the prayer of the prophet to produce children. It can also be viewed as prophetic deliverance, and we will discuss this further in the next chapter as possibly a divine reversal from the curse of God shutting up all of the wombs of the women causing barrenness. No matter which way you slice it, healing and deliverance came through the prayer and intercession of a prophet. Healing was only in Abraham as the designated mouthpiece of God.

Curses can be broken or physical conditions can be reversed through prophetic intercession. Prophetic healing is in the mouth of the prophetic. Divine reversal of curses or judgments are broken by the mouth of the prophetic. Healing from barrenness was as result of the intercession of the prophet.

OPENING SPIRITUAL WOMBS

Abraham, as God's prophet, prayed for Abimelech and he was healed. When a prophet intercedes or prays for or on behalf of God for a person's healing and restoration of health, it happens as a result according to Genesis 20:17-18 (NKJV):

So Abraham prayed to God; and God healed Abimelech,
his wife, and his female servants. Then they bore children;
for the LORD had closed up all the wombs of the house of
Abimelech because of Sarah, Abraham's wife.

It is important to note that God did not heal Abimelech and his entire kingdom from barrenness until Abraham the prophet of God prayed to God on his behalf to be healed. It would not have mattered if the king found another prophet, soothsayer, magician, or wiseman to pray for him, the healing was in the mouth of the prophet that God ordained to speak and pray on His behalf.

Abraham was the prophet from whom this healing from barrenness would come. Prophets do not just *speak* on God's behalf, they *pray and intercede* on His behalf. There are answers in the mouth of the prophet. There are answers to medical conditions in the release of the prophetic. Prophets in ancient Israel carried medical breakthrough in their prophetic release. We will see more and more modern prophetic voices prophesy by revelation regarding emerging medical and scientific breakthroughs in times of an epidemics, pandemics, and urgent global crises.

WHAT IS PROPHETIC HEALING?

I define the term "prophetic healing" as any form of healing, recovery, and restoration of health through inspired and activated utterance in faith of the word of prophecy, preaching, or praying. In other words, it is better understood of any prophecy, word-inspired utterance, and release of the word of God both written or spoken in faith that results in someone's physical healing. This healing is directly and consequently associated to the mouth of the prophet through praying, preaching, and prophesying. The faith behind the release of the word spoken literally empowers that word to produce the results you are praying, hoping, and believing to manifest in the person you sent it to. *Prophetic healing* essentially can be released through prayer, intercession, laying on of hands, and prophecy that is spoken out of the mouth of any believer in Christ Jesus. Simply, it is someone being healed as result of a prophetic word spoken, an inspired utterance, and/or infallible Scriptures imparted by faith.

The following is a powerful example of the word being sent. He sent and the word healed as a result through intercessory prayer, and the Lord answering the prayer of the people according to Psalm 107:19-20 (NIV):

> *Then they cried out to the LORD in their trouble, and he saved them from their distress. He sent forth his word and healed them; he rescued them from the grave. Let them give thanks to the LORD for his unfailing love and his wonderful deeds for mankind.*

When reading different Scripture translations of Psalm 107:19-20 and the word usage, you will get a better understanding of the potency of the word of God sent out of the mouth of a person prophetically to deliver them out of their serious conditions.

HEALING THROUGH PROPHETIC INTERCESSION

Prophetic intercession is another way that healing can be released through a prophet. Praying to God on behalf of someone for healing is one the most common practices of the prophets in the Old Testament. Prophets were practitioners of prayer and intercession. Elijah the prophet is a great example for us regarding the power of prophetic intercession. Elijah's intercession unlocked the power of miracles through his mouth in prayer. We can see the incredible power of prayer in the prophetic anointing.

Power prophecy is developed in the example of Elijah praying first and prophesying out of that intercession to Ahab and Jezebel that the heavens will be opened and closed at His command. God has always released His power of healing through prophets and prophetic intercessors. Prayer is the source of supernatural power of the prophets. There is absolutely no power in prophecy without prayer and intercession.

The following is an example of *prophetic healing* where Elijah the prophet shut the door of his chamber and intercedes over the boy who had recently died from an unknown sickness in First Kings 17:17, 21-22,24 (AMP):

> *It happened after these things, that the son of the woman, the mistress of the house, became sick; and his illness was so severe that there was no breath left in him. ...Then he stretched himself out upon the child three times, and called to the LORD and said, "O LORD my God, please let this child's life return to him." The LORD heard the voice of Elijah, and the life of the child returned to him and he revived. ...Then the woman said to Elijah, "Now I know that you are a man of God and that the word of the LORD in your mouth is truth."*

Elijah's intercession created an opportunity for a healing miracle to manifest by his relentless prayer and intercession three times—continually—for the child. He shut the door and went into immediate intercession to God on behalf of the widow woman and her son. He cried out to God and called life back into the child's body; and the Scripture says above that, *"The Lord heard the voice of Elijah."* Prophets have a voice in prayer that God hears and responds to with answers.

Prayer is the key that gives you access into untapped and unlimited powers. The ancient prophets understood this phenomenon of power prophecy. There is an ancient secret behind praying in private and intimately with God that rewards and produces answers openly (Matthew 6:6).

Prayer was and is the key and power behind a prophet's divine communication. Prayer and prophecy are the channel of communication by which supernatural power flows in and out of the prophet's ministry. Jesus healed in the same manner by shutting out the noise and putting the people out the door, and thereafter raising a child from the dead (see Mark 5:40-42).

Look at the same results of miraculous healing demonstrated in Elisha when he followed the same prayer and intercessory model established in him by Elijah, his predecessor, in Second Kings 4:32-35 (AMP):

> *When Elisha came into the house, the child was dead and lying on his bed. So he went in, shut the door behind the two of them, and prayed to the LORD. Then he went up and lay on the child and put his mouth on his mouth, his eyes on his eyes, and his hands on his hands. And as he stretched himself out on him and held him, the boy's skin became warm. Then he returned and walked in the house once back and forth, and went up [again] and stretched himself out on him; and the boy sneezed seven times and he opened his eyes.*

KEY TO PROPHETIC HEALINGS

You can see the power of prophecy demonstrated in the ministry of Elijah praying and prophesying through the prophetic release that shut up the heavens (drought) and the release of rain at his word or command in First Kings 17:1 (NKJV): *"And Elijah the Tishbite, of the inhabitants of Gilead, said to Ahab, 'As the LORD God of Israel lives, before whom I stand, there shall not be dew nor rain these years, except at my word.'"* This power of prophecy to be able to prophesy drought and then the release of rain at his word all happened because of constant, avid, and penetrative prayer and intercession to God. This is the master key that opens the heavens for healing, deliverance, miracles, signs and wonders, and salvation.

In First Kings 18:41-46 as you read that passage of Scripture, you learn about Elijah's position and posture in prayer where through his continual intercession—in what many would describe as a birthing position—produced miraculous results. Prophets' spiritual position through prayer and intercession becomes the womb and cradle for healing, deliverance, and miracles to happen.

Elijah heard the sound of abundance of rain in prayer that gave him the prophetic forecast and release to prophesy essentially that heavy rain is coming (1 Kings 18:41). He had the prophetic insight of what was being released by revelation in prayer to God.

Our position in prayer is critical to what we are able to release from Heaven and what we can produce on earth. We can see that Elijah's position with his face between his knees was a prophetic act representing that Heaven was pregnant and what he was carrying in his spiritual womb, the waters (rain) were about to break forth on the earth. Prayer brings breakthroughs of supernatural release. His prophetic intercession was key to him prophesying the rain is coming. Rain was in the mouth of the prophet.

Elijah prophesied to Ahab and Jezebel there would be no dew or rain except at his word. Elijah waited in prayer for the sound of his prophetic release. He saw as a prophetic sign, a cloud in the sky the size of a man's hand. The hand was symbolic of a release coming. Hands spiritually represent power. Therefore, this manifestation and sign of the cloud was a prophetic release through the power of prophecy and intercession. Prayer is a position of humility, reliance, and absolute submission on God to answer our earnest petition, cry, and intercession.

In the book of James, the author of the text makes an interrelation and connection with healing through active, fervent prayer and intercession by using Elijah the prophet as a prayer model for us to demonstrate the power of prayer that produces. This prayer from the prophet touched Heaven to produce on earth. The powerful key of prayer and intercession that manifests the supernatural, specifically *healing,* is revealed in the following Scripture passage regarding Elijah:

> *Therefore, confess your sins to one another [your false steps, your offenses], and pray for one another, that you may be healed and restored. The heartfelt and persistent prayer of a righteous man (believer) can accomplish much [when put into action and made effective by God—it is dynamic and can have tremendous power]. Elijah was a man with a nature like ours [with the same physical, mental, and spiritual limitations and shortcomings], and he prayed intensely for it not to rain, and it did not rain on the earth for three years and six months. Then he prayed again, and the sky gave rain and the land produced its crops [as usual]* (James 5:16-18 AMP).

Healing was an active function of the prophetic ministry in the Old Testament. As we embrace fully a lifestyle of prayer and understand the art of praying prophetically from the heart, mind, and intentions of God, we will see the exploitations of God. Prophetic intercession is not praying from our prayer request or a prayer list given by people, though there is nothing wrong with it; it is praying earnestly from what is downloaded by revelation of God's will.

Prophetic intercession is simply praying as the Holy Spirit leads or inspires. It is not to say that we cannot pray for someone on our own or by a person's request; but when we learn to pray according to God's will, supernatural things will be done on earth as it is in Heaven (Matthew 6:9-13 and Luke 11:2-4).

PROPHETICALLY CHARGED FAITH

Prayer is the lifestyle of the prophets and the prophetic. Prayer is the foundation of everything that the prophets do. I have discovered in my prophetic ministry that praying for many hours in the Spirit has afforded me divine access into the mysteries, secret and hidden things, revelations, realms and dimensions in the supernatural that I would not have otherwise. Praying in tongues (in the Spirit) gives you spiritual endurance and strength to eventually manifest the power of God through praying, preaching, and prophesying.

The secret to developing and accessing power is praying in the Spirit. This is a crucial part of spiritual maintenance that charges up the faith of the believer to produce the power needed to accomplish the works of God. The source of unfathomed power is in prayer—but how we can plug in or connect into that power is praying in the Spirit.

Every believer's faith has to be charged up in order to produce the highest level of output needed in the moment. The strategy is to build yourself up in your apex of faith, which is to pray continually in the Holy Spirit. The higher the faith input in prayer, the more powerful the output of manifestations. Simply put, our input in prayer determines the type of output of the supernatural. Prophets are men and women of revelation; therefore, their private prayer manifests public power. In other words, what we do in secret, God will reward us openly (see Matthew 6:6-7). Secret prayers produce revelatory power.

Jude 1:20 reveals how to charge your faith in prayer: *"But you, beloved, building yourselves up on your most holy faith, praying in the Holy Spirit."* The word *building* in Jude 1:20 also literally is translated "to supercharge."

Therefore, when we practice praying in the Holy Spirit or in our heavenly, spiritual, secret, or stealth tongues (languages), not only do we build up our most holy faith, simultaneously we are literally supercharging our faith. This form of praying is practically praying to God who empowers our faith to do the unfathomable. Through prayer, Jeremiah the prophet could gain access to great, mighty, and hidden things that he had yet to fathom or understand what was accessible to him according to the following verse when God said, *"Call to Me, and I will answer you, and show you great and mighty things, which you do not know"* (Jeremiah 33:3 NKJV).

This Scripture teaches us that great and mighty things that are beyond our comprehension are manifested and revealed through engaging God in prayer. Prayer gave Jeremiah access and revelation into the unexplainable and incomprehensible. Praying in the Spirit increases exponentially our capacity to comprehend, encounter, and demonstrate different facets of God in the supernatural. It becomes our direct line of communication as prophets and prophetic people.

Legally, prayer is the only way to align and connect our "natural" to the "supernatural." In other words, prayer is communicating supernaturally. Whether a person believes it or not, prayer is a spiritual practice and discipline of the believer. Those who manifest the supernatural have developed a mastery and discipline in prayer and intercession. The prophets had a mastery of discipline as they spent an enormous amount of hours in prayer to God.

HEALING INTERCESSORS

God is raising up *healing intercessors* who will pray according to revelation of the measure of healing needed. This is an aspect of prophetic healing. Prophets by default are intercessors. Examples of Moses's intercession of healing in the following two accounts are in the book of Numbers. Let's examine closely both accounts in Numbers 12 and 21, and you will see God's judgment on an individual and judgment on an entire people being divinely reversed because of the prophetic intercession of the prophet.

1. Miriam and Aaron, siblings of Moses, criticized and spoke against Moses because of the Ethiopian woman he had married, and they went on to say, *"Has the LORD indeed spoken only through Moses? Has He not spoken through us also?"* This statement in Numbers 12:2 (NKJV) challenged the prophetic legitimacy and authority of Moses as the mouthpiece of the Lord (Numbers 12:1-3). God made it absolutely clear that though He speaks to both Miriam and Aaron as prophets, the status and leadership position of Moses is uniquely different and above in rank even the prophets (Numbers 12:4-8).

God did not speak to Moses like he did to the prophets, He spoke to him face to face as someone talks with a friend (Numbers 12:8). Consequently, Miriam was stricken with leprosy and subsequently healed (Numbers 12:9-15) as result of the intercession of Moses crying out on her behalf to God, *"So Moses cried to the LORD, 'Please, God, heal her!'"* (Numbers 12:13 NIV).

2. The Lord through Moses's intercession removed from the people the fiery serpent (snakes) who had bitten the people and they died as a result of speaking against God and His prophet. Moses by

revelation was directed to make a fiery serpent and set it on a pole, which is similar to the symbol of the snake on a pole on today's ambulances, EMS vehicles, and hospitals to represent healing. Through the direction of the prophet, if those who were bitten by the deadly snake looked at the bronze serpent, they would live. Obeying the prophetic directive—or I would say prophetic prescription—meant manifest healing. This is *prophetic healing!*

> *So the Lord sent fiery serpents among the people, and they bit the people; and many of the people of Israel died. Therefore the people came to Moses, and said, "We have sinned, for we have spoken against the Lord and against you; pray to the Lord that He take away the serpents from us." So Moses prayed for the people. Then the Lord said to Moses, "Make a fiery serpent, and set it on a pole; and it shall be that everyone who is bitten, when he looks at it, shall live." So Moses made a bronze serpent, and put it on a pole; and so it was, if a serpent had bitten anyone, when he looked at the bronze serpent, he lived* (Numbers 21:6-9 NKJV).

Prayer today is a form of sacrifice to give up or offer up ourselves on behalf of someone else in exchange and in order for them to receive a healing. Intercession is taking to the Lord what someone is not able to do in their own strength, faith, or even spiritual condition in order for them to receive healing and restoration (see Job 42:8-10).

Samuel the prophet prayed to the Lord on behalf of the people. Intercession is innately within the function of the prophet. Prayer is the power behind the prophet's intercession and words. *Power prophecy* is saturated in prayer and intercession according to First Samuel 7:5 (NKJV): *"Samuel said, 'Gather all Israel to Mizpah, and I will pray to the LORD for you.'"*

David as a king and prophet understood the power of intercession that produced healing holistically in his reign in the following verses:

O LORD my God, I cried to You, and You healed me... (Psalm 30:2-3 NKJV).

Who forgives all your iniquities, who heals all your diseases... (Psalm 103:3-4 NKJV).

He heals the brokenhearted and binds up their wounds (Psalm 147:3 NKJV).

FORGIVING HEALING POWER

Forgiveness is another form of releasing healing; while on the other hand, unforgiveness can hinder, stop, or prolong healing. What is forgiveness in simpler terms? Forgiveness is defined as letting go of past grudges or lingering anger against a person or persons. When you are angry at someone but you then accept his or her apology and are no longer upset, this is an example of forgiveness.

As you minister in the area of healing, it is important to genuinely forgive all those who have ever hurt, crossed, wronged, and offended you in any form—or you will become ineffective in releasing healing to someone or even receiving healing for yourself.

Personal forgiveness of sins and trespasses causes a person to be a channel and vessel of the healing anointing flowing through them. Unrepented sins, offenses, and any form of unforgiveness are to be repented, dealt with, resolved, and forgiven immediately as ministers of healing in order to lay hands on the sick and speak the word of healing at a moment's notice.

Unforgiveness through offense snares and entraps us from freeing others when we are ourselves are bound (see Luke 17:1-4). We even as ministers of the prophetic believers in Christ must continually forgive others, ourselves, and minister forgiveness as part of healing and deliverance.

Unforgiveness can even hinder and restrict revelation to flow into our hearts to minister healing to others. Unforgiveness limits revelatory healing to be released from a prophet. Revelatory healing is the healing revealed by the Spirit that is needed.

One of the keys to ministering healing to someone or unlocking the power of healing in your life is first you may need to ask the person to whom you are ministering if there is unforgiveness in their heart toward anyone. Most of the time if someone you are ministering healing to cannot get healed, ensuring that they release those who wronged or offended or hurt them in any way will free them from the prison of offense, sickness, pain, and death. Renouncing, revoking, and breaking any New Age, occultic, or demonic allegiance, covenants, vows will bring healing.

Some are offended and carry the spirit of offense toward their pastor or leader yet don't realize it—and some are offended toward leaders they have never met just because of their teachings, style of dress, gossip, or rumors. Some are angry or offended at their local church. The Bible declares in Proverbs 18:19 (NLT), *"An offended friend is harder to win back than a fortified city. Arguments separate friends like a gate locked with bars."* The spirit of offense creates a stronghold and imprisonment to receive healing.

Prophets have the ability to discern if there is unforgiveness, unrepented sins, inner hurt, and offense that is hindering a person from their healing and deliverance. Forgiveness is a power key to unlock healing, and unforgiveness is a powerful key to lock up and shut out healing in our lives. Unforgiveness hinders prayers of healing to be heard from God. Unforgiveness and offense hinders and stymies the flow of the anointing on our life and can cause hindered prayers for us not to be forgiven when we pray.

Consider the following Scriptures by Jesus on the subject of forgiveness:

Whenever you stand praying, if you have anything against anyone, forgive him [drop the issue, let it go], so that your Father who is in heaven will also forgive you your transgressions and wrongdoings [against Him and others] (Mark 11:25 AMP).

For if you forgive other people when they sin against you, your heavenly Father will also forgive you. But if you do not forgive others their sins, your Father will not forgive your sins (Matthew 6:14-15 NIV).

Then Peter came to Him and said, "Lord, how often shall my brother sin against me, and I forgive him? Up to seven times?" Jesus said to him, "I do not say to you, up to seven times, but up to seventy times seven" (Matthew 18:21-22 NKJV).

OLD TESTAMENT DISTANT HEALING

In the following two case studies in the Old Testament Scriptures, you will discover that two of the most powerful men in their nation came to the prophet Elisha regarding their health and to experience *prophetic healing*:

1. *Commander of the Army—Naaman the Syrian*

Elisha had such a good reputation as a prophet of healing that Naaman was referred to go to him in Samaria by a young girl from Israel who was his wife's maid. She knew that if Naaman was in the very proximity of Elisha the prophet and the word of God, that he would be cured of his leprosy:

Now Naaman, commander of the army of the king of Syria, was a great and honorable man in the eyes of his master, because by him the LORD had given victory to Syria. He was also a mighty man of valor, but a leper. And the Syrians had gone out on raids, and had brought back captive a young girl from the land of Israel. She waited on Naaman's wife. Then she said to her mistress, "If only my master were with the prophet who is in Samaria! For he would heal him of his leprosy" (2 Kings 5:1-3 NKJV).

There was such a prophetic anointing on Elisha to the measure that he did not necessarily have to leave his house; or even better, Naaman in this case did not have to be in the same room, proximity, or presence of the prophet to be healed. The prophet healed him through prophesying, sending officially a word even from a distance. In other words, the prophet sent a prophecy from inside his house to Naaman. This is another example of *power prophecy!*

Naaman, a commander of the army of Syria, sought the prophet of Israel to be healed by the consent and permission of the king of Syria via a letter to the king of Israel:

And Naaman went in and told his master, saying, "Thus and thus said the girl who is from the land of Israel." Then the king of Syria said, "Go now, and I will send a letter to the king of Israel." So he departed and took with him ten talents of silver, six thousand shekels of gold, and ten changes of clothing. Then he brought the letter to the king of Israel, which said, Now be advised, when this letter comes to you, that I have sent Naaman my servant to you, that you may heal him of his leprosy (2 Kings 5:4-6 NKJV).

Culture of Honor Releases Power

Naaman the Syrian was a great and honorable man in which the Lord gave victory to the Syrian army through his command. He was a value and treasure to the king of Syria and it would have been such a great blessing to be healed of his leprosy by God's holy prophet. The key to receiving *prophetic healing* is to get around the presence of a credible prophet of Christ. Today, prophets while teaching, ministering, praying, and prophesying in word will invoke, summon, and release the presence and power of the Lord to heal (Luke 5:17).

In like manner, the prophet of God was honorable, powerful in character and deed, and a true treasure to God and to Israel, especially in wartimes. I believe strongly if the church would truly honor the office of the prophet in the same manner we honor our senior and pastoral leadership, we could genuinely benefit from the full scope of the prophetic office and ministry. God will send prophets to people outside the four walls of the church and the unsaved who desperately desire to be healed, delivered from demonic oppression, and salvation.

Prophetic healing is a powerful tool in evangelism. The prophetic anointing of healing is for the world to know that Jesus is alive and working actively in and through His heirs, believers, ministers, leaders, and for the sake of this book—*the prophets.* Jesus plainly describes the culture of the honor given to the prophet outside of their home, family, and friends versus the culture of dishonor among their own people in Luke 4:23-27 (NKJV):

> He [Jesus] *said to them, "You will surely say this proverb to Me, 'Physician, heal yourself! Whatever we have heard done in Capernaum, do also here in Your country.'" Then He said, "Assuredly, I say to you, no prophet is accepted in his own country. But I tell you truly, many widows were in Israel in the days of Elijah, when the heaven was shut up three years and six months, and there was a great famine throughout all the land; but to none of them was Elijah sent except to Zarephath, in the region of Sidon, to a woman who was a widow. And many lepers were in Israel*

in the time of Elisha the prophet, and none of them was cleansed except Naaman the Syrian."

There were many lepers in Israel, but the prophet Elisha was sent to Naaman to be healed. God will send prophets to people outside their church, family, and nation. Prophets are without honor and respect; even Jesus went to His own and they did not receive Him. Prophets are typically tolerated at home but celebrated away. In my prophetic school, I advise seasoned, emerging, or budding prophets to go where they are celebrated, not tolerated. It is important to understand that Jesus could not do any *"mighty work"* because of the people's unbelief, He could only heal *"a few sick people"* (Mark 6:5 NKJV). The lack of belief in the Prophet limited His ability to flow freely in the miraculous.

Prophets must also use wisdom in ministering in the prophetic in the face of emerging diseases, viruses, and calamities. It is incredibly important to hear from the Holy Spirit regarding administering healing by the laying on of hands and praying for people in close proximity especially with respect to the coronavirus disease (COVID-19), which is highly contagious and infectious. We can say that the coronavirus today could be considered in the same way as leprosy was in Naaman's day when *a distant healing* was the best response.

In another vein, the prophetic is just as contagious when you come in close contact or in the company of prophets prophesying—it will turn you into a different person, a prophet as well (1 Samuel 10:5-6 NLT).

In retrospect, Naaman tells the king of Syria of the news that he received from the young girl of a prophet having the power to heal him of his leprosy, so the king sent a letter to the king of Israel about sending Naaman to the prophet of Israel. It important to understand that the prophets of God in Israel had such reputation and notoriety in the known world in their day that even the enemies of God and Israel came to meet with them.

Kings, commanders of the army, high-ranking officials and those outside of Israel, especially opposing nations, respected the officers of the prophetic, the prophets of Yahweh. I believe that we will begin see the honor, respect, position, and relevance of the prophetic office in the world today be restored again as prophets emerge and are commissioned out from within the four walls of local assemblies and carry the raw power of the prophetic to nations of the world.

Elisha the prophet prophesied Naaman's healing. His healing was predicated and conditional on following every detail of the word of the prophet. Many do not receive *prophetic healing*—defined as healing that comes by way of prophecy, prophetic instruction, or by following any corresponding action or words of the prophet. Naaman's healing was in the mouth of Elisha. The king of Israel thought the letter from the king of Syrian regarding sending Naaman to Elisha to be healed was a plan to stir a fight or start a war with him, knowing he does not have the power to heal:

> *And when the king of Israel read the letter, he tore his clothes and said, "Am I God, to kill and to make alive, that this man sends word to me to cure a man of his leprosy? Only consider, and see how he is seeking a quarrel with me"* (2 Kings 5:7 ESV).

The king of Israel misinterpreted the intent of the king of Syrian unknowing that Naaman was seeking the prophet Elisha for healing. It would be quite easy to understand the thinking of the king knowing that the Syrian was one of his archenemies. Elisha the prophet got word of the king of Israel's concerns:

But when Elisha the man of God heard that the king of Israel had torn his clothes, he sent to the king, saying, "Why have you torn your clothes? Let him come now to me, that he may know that there is a prophet in Israel" (2 Kings 5:8 ESV).

Prophetic Counsel

There are those today who have never experienced being in the presence or room with a true spokesperson and statesman of God. Some are foreign to the prophetic anointing and ministry. In fact, there are many in the church today with cessationist views that says the ministry office, gift, and anointing of the prophet ceased with the canonization of the Bible and there is no need for active prophetic operations. In my opinion, these types of the teachings are counterproductive, especially coming from followers of Jesus who Himself set in His church today prophets, secondarily in rank, position, and order. The role and office of prophet was respected and relevant in Israel and to the world then—I believe that its relevancy is needed now more than any other time in history.

2. *King of Syria—Ben-Hadad*

The following is another case study in the Scriptures where the king of Syria is sick, seeking the counsel of the Lord from Elisha the prophet concerning his critical condition and if he would recover from the disease. The prophet revealed to the king's messenger to send word to the king that he would certainly recover from his sickness. However, the prophet only told the king's messenger what he saw by revelation—that the king would die, but not from the sickness. The prophet saw by the Lord an assassination by the hand of the king's messenger, so as to become the next king:

Then Elisha went to Damascus, and Ben-Hadad king of Syria was sick; and it was told him, saying, "The man of God has come here." And the king said to Hazael, "Take a present in your hand, and go to meet the man of God, and inquire of the Lord by him, saying, 'Shall I recover from this disease?'" So Hazael went to meet him and took a present with him, of every good thing of Damascus, forty camel-loads; and he came and stood before him, and said, "Your son Ben-Hadad king of Syria has sent me to you, saying, 'Shall I recover from this disease?' "

And Elisha said to him, "Go, say to him, 'You shall certainly recover.' However the Lord has shown me that he will really die" [not by this sickness]. *Then he set his countenance in a stare until he was ashamed; and the man of God wept. And Hazael said, "Why is my lord weeping?"*

He answered, "Because I know the evil that you will do to the children of Israel: Their strongholds you will set on fire, and their young men you will kill with the sword; and you will dash their children, and rip open their women with child" [murder mother and child]. *So Hazael said, "But what is your servant—a dog, that he should do this gross thing?" And Elisha answered, "The Lord has shown me that you will become king over Syria." Then he departed from Elisha, and came to his master, who said to him, "What did Elisha say to you?" And he answered, "He told me you would surely recover." But it happened on the next day that he took a thick cloth and dipped it in water, and spread it over his face* [suffocation] *so that he died; and Hazael reigned in his place (2 Kings 8:7-15 (NKJV).*

This biblical story proves how valuable the prophet and the prophetic is to us to reveal not only the will of God but exposing a hidden plan, plot, and ploy of the enemy designed to assassinate the purposes of God for our lives. We need a prophet who has our ear and we can trust. Prophets were notorious for exposing and revealing the hidden battle plans disclosed secretly in the king's bedchamber (see 2 Kings 6:8-20). The devil desires to cut off God's sons and daughters through premature death, sicknesses, diseases, and all types of secret or sneak attacks.

The ageless prophets were weapons and threats to the enemies of Israel; and the devil is fully aware of those same threats the prophetic poses against his agenda today. He is threatened by the power of the prophets then and now. He works endlessly and tirelessly to keep us from fulfilling the will and promises of God spoken by the prophets.

New Testament Distant Healing

The centurion answered and said, "Lord, I am not worthy that You should come under my roof. But only speak a word, and my servant will be healed" (Matthew 8:8 NKJV).

The Gospels contain many examples of people being healed by Jesus. Some came to Jesus on their own, crying out for Jesus to heal them. Some were brought by others before Jesus to be healed. Still more are healed as the result of when a loved one brought Jesus to the one who was afflicted. Now we examine three biblical accounts found in the Gospels, illustrating Jesus's healing from afar, by His words alone, at the request of someone whose loved one was suffering.

The following are synopses and scriptural accounts of Jesus healing from afar or from a distance through prophecy or the faith and intercession of someone else.

1. *The Syrophoenician Woman's Daughter*

In Mark 7:24-30 and Matthew 15:21-28, the Gospels share the story of a non-Jewish woman who came to Jesus pleading that He heal her demon-oppressed daughter. This woman had great faith, as she knew that even crumbs from the "bread of life" that Jesus was giving to His people, the Jews, would be enough to heal her daughter. Jesus did grant that healing, and commented on the great faith of the woman.

2. *The Centurion's Servant*

In Matthew 8:5-13 and Luke 7:1-10 the Bible gives the account of a centurion who approached Jesus because his servant was near the point of death. Jesus started to go to the centurion's house, but the centurion met him outside the house. He humbly told Jesus that he was not worthy to have Jesus come into his home. He also understood Jesus's authority, and that if He just spoke the word, the servant would be healed. Jesus, who pointed out the great faith of this man, said the word to bring healing to the servant. The centurion knew Jesus's word carried great power and authority to heal and that He could heal from where He was just by saying the word.

3. *The Capernaum Official's Son*

In John 4:46-54, an official came to see Jesus because his son was sick to the point of death. He asked Jesus to come before his son died. But instead of going with the man to heal the son—as Jesus often did with similar requests—Jesus simply told the man to "Go," and that his son would live. The man returned home and found his son was indeed healed at that very hour and time. In this story, the father is almost scolded by Jesus because the man's faith needed a sign. This man did not have great faith; he had just enough faith to come to Jesus.

In each of these examples, the person being healed received it through the petitioning, imploring, and inquiring of Jesus. Active intercession on the behalf of others to Jesus produced their healing.

ONLY SPEAK A WORD

There is a powerful key of speaking, prophesying, and praying the word of God that tends to lend extraordinary results in manifesting healing. The following Scripture verses in my personal observation and opinion do not just provide us with a biblical example but more importantly a key for us to exercise and practice to unlock miraculous healings. Preaching the word of God releases miraculous healing as Jesus works with us to confirm His word: *"And they went out and preached everywhere, the Lord working with them and confirming the word through the accompanying signs. Amen"* (Mark 16:20 NKJV). The faith expressed in the text creates a blueprint and template of how to release the word of healing or healing Scriptures that we desire to see. Speaking the word only creates an opportunity to see the word manifest just as you speak it:

> *The centurion answered and said, "Lord, I am not worthy that You should come under my roof. But only speak a word, and my servant will be healed"* (Matthew 8:8 NKJV).
>
> *He sends out His commandment to the earth; His word runs very swiftly* (Psalm 147:15,19 NKJV).

Jesus demonstrates healing and deliverance with a word at Peter's house according to Matthew 8:15-17 (ESV):

> *He touched her hand, and the fever left her, and she rose and began to serve him. That evening they brought to him many who were oppressed by demons, and he cast out the spirits with a word and healed all who were sick. This was*

71

to fulfill what was spoken by the prophet Isaiah: "He took our illnesses and bore our diseases."

Jesus is the perfect living example of prophetic healing through intercession when Isaiah the prophet centuries beforehand prophesied that He would take up and bear our infirmities and sickness through God's love and passion on the Cross to release life and health to those who believe in Him.

The passion of Christ on the Cross was the ultimate sacrifice and physical demonstration of intercession—to die on behalf of someone so they may live. What was prophesied by Isaiah about Jesus Christ was prophetic intercession and healing in the perfect sense, in that by His stripes, we are healed (Isaiah 53:5).

God's word heals. You will see in the following verses of Scripture, the power of speaking, preaching, and prophesying the word of God. Power prophecy brings healing as prophets and prophetic believers learn how to send the word to heal:

- Psalm 107:20 (NIV)—*"He sent out his word and healed them."*
- Psalm 119:50 (NKJV)—*"This is my comfort in my affliction, for Your word has given me life."*
- Psalm 119:162 (NKJV)—*"I rejoice at Your word as one who finds great treasure."*
- Isaiah 55:11 (NKJV)—*"So shall My word be that goes forth from My mouth; it shall not return to Me void, but it shall accomplish what I please, and it shall prosper in the thing for which I sent it."*
- Ezekiel 12:25 (NKJV)—*"For I am the LORD. I speak, and the word which I speak will come to pass; it will no more be postponed; for in your days, O rebellious house, I will say the word and perform it,' says the Lord God."*

|| 3 ||

PROPHETIC DELIVERANCE

By a prophet the LORD brought Israel out
of Egypt, and by a prophet was he preserved.
—HOSEA 12:13 NKJV

The LORD sent a prophet to the Israelites. He
said, "This is what the LORD, the God of Israel,
says: I brought you up out of slavery in Egypt."
—JUDGES 6:8 NLT

This chapter is not intended to provide an exhaustive study or dissertation on the subject of the ministry of deliverance; but simply offers some key principles in the relationship of the prophetic and operating in deliverance. My goal is to show how you can operate in revelatory deliverance through the power of the prophetic.

Many are not aware that deliverance is more prophetic than they think. There is a prophetic anointing to bring preservation, deliverance, and breakthroughs into your life and the lives of others. The power of deliverance starts and ends with the prophets. God is preparing a catalyst of prophetic believers who will move in prophetic deliverance. We will see entire people, cities, regions, territories, and nations brought out, delivered, and preserved by prophets.

The ministry of deliverance is part of the prophetic function of a prophet of God. We can see that God used a prophet to bring deliverance of Israel out of Egypt according to Hosea 12:13: *"By a prophet* [Moses] *the Lord brought Israel out of Egypt, and by a prophet he was preserved."*

God used a prophet to bring deliverance and to also protect and guard Israel. Furthermore, the prophetic arm had guided and protected Israel throughout the period of their wilderness wanderings, providentially aided them in driving out the Canaanites, defended them against their enemies, preserved, and watched over them continually. Moses became the first prototype prophet of deliverance. He had a unique calling to deliverance. Deliverance was one of the primary prophetic functions as prophet to Israel. Prophets will to some degree operate in an aspect of deliverance in their ministry.

> *But when he was approaching the age of forty, it entered his mind to visit his countrymen, the sons of Israel. And when he saw one of them being treated unjustly, he defended and took vengeance for the oppressed man by fatally striking the Egyptian. And he thought that his brothers understood that God was granting them deliverance through him* [Moses]; *but they did not understand. And on the following day he appeared to them as they were fighting each other, and he tried to reconcile them to peace, by saying, "Men, you are brothers, why are you injuring each other?" But the one who was injuring his neighbor pushed him away, saying, "Who made you a ruler and judge over us? You do not intend to kill me as you killed the Egyptian yesterday, do you?" At this remark, Moses fled and became a stranger in the land of Midian, where he fathered two sons* (Acts 7:23-29 NASB).

DREAM DELIVERANCE

In Matthew 2:3, we see that Jesus's birth troubled and unnerved Herod the king and all of Jerusalem, which consequently set in motion a conspiracy-orchestrated assassination attempt on baby Jesus. God, through a prophetic dream, warned Joseph of Herod's plan to destroy the life of Jesus even at birth to keep Him from becoming the true King of the Jews.

In both Pharoah against Moses and Herod against Jesus, it was clearly the work of satan ultimately trying to alter the very trajectory of the future. God sends an angel in a prophetic dream to reveal the plans of Herod to kill Jesus (read Matthew 2:1-13). Matthew chapter 2 provides us with a better picture and understanding of how prophetic deliverance works even in prophetic dreams. This is another example of *prophetic deliverance.*

In the ministry of the Jesus, His primary function was the demonstration of two aspects among the people: 1) *deliverance,* and 2) *healing*. Moses had often reminded the people that God delivered them out of Egypt by the Lord displaying His unmatched power. God does not do anything unless He discloses it by His servants the prophets (Amos 3:7). I believe this is an aspect of revelatory deliverance where God will reveal His delivering power to His prophets.

> *And Moses said to the people, "Remember this day in which you departed from Egypt, from the house of slavery; for by a powerful hand the LORD brought you out from this place. And nothing with yeast shall be eaten"* (Exodus 13:3 NASB).

Prophets work with the powerful hand of God to bring people out of spiritual bondages, slavery, and captivity. Prophetic words have the power to deliver people out of demonic systems, mindsets, strongholds, fortresses, and imprisonments. The mouth and the ministry of the prophet is key to bringing deliverance and preservation (Hosea 12:13).

PROPHETIC DELIVERANCE

Jesus cast out the spirits with a single command. There is a correlation between the prophetic and deliverance that resulted in healing. We can speak and prophesy deliverance over people. There is power in prophesying the word of healing and deliverance. Power prophecy in the form of *prophetic deliverance* is any word of God sent or spoken forth by a prophet, leader or believer that will manifest physical healing and tangible deliverance. You can speak and send the word of God that will result in deliverance and healing interchangeably.

In the following Scripture verses, we see examples of Jesus sending the word of healing and deliverance:

> *He sent His word and healed them, and delivered them from their destructions* (Psalm 107:20 NKJV).
> *When evening came, many who were demon-possessed were brought to him, and he drove out the spirits with a word and healed all the sick. This was to fulfill what was spoken through the prophet Isaiah: "He took up our infirmities and bore our diseases"* (Matthew 8:16-17 NIV).

Moses was used as a prophet to bring deliverance to an entire nation of people. He carried prophetic power and authority as a deliverer of a nation. This reveals the measure of rulership in the prophetic realm to deliver a nation from under the ruling powers of many false gods or practices. Deliverance is not just the routing of demons or spirits out of people or the removal of demonic influences. However, prophetic deliverance has a lot to do with bringing or leading people out of bondage, slavery, strongholds, and entire demonically governed houses or infrastructures. Prophets reveal and expose demonically engineered works of the enemy in people, leadership, cities, regions, nations, and yes, even churches.

Prophets open our understanding through their teaching and preaching that causes people to recognize root issues, problems, and hidden agendas at work. There are times when spirits must be *cast* out; but in other instances, deliverances occur when some things need to be *taught* out. Prophetic teaching and preaching in the Spirit of Truth can bring deliverance. I have witnessed in my own ministry a great deal of spirit or demonic manifestations that happens as I am preaching and teaching truth. Demons cannot sit under sound teaching and truth. Deliverance is more than casting out evil spirits but rather holistic in nature.

One of the important keys to seeing healing and deliverance is to teach or preach it. In other words, whenever I preach on the Kingdom of God, the power of healing and deliverance manifests. When I preach on Jesus Christ, His presence manifests in the meeting to heal, save, set free, and deliver.

There are times I encounter a hard or barred atmosphere because of unbelief or demonic resistance. One of the ways that I infuse faith into that environment to make it conducive for the supernatural and the power of God is that I begin to prophesy. Therefore, if you want to see deliverance and healing manifest in your church, service, or meeting, you will have to teach and preach until deliverance and healing comes. When you want to see deliverance and breakthrough happen—preach and teach on it. If you teach on it, it will come. This is a key to deliverance in the prophetic.

Prophets must counter false doctrines and teachings of devils and people. We can see in the following biblical text that warns us prophetically that in the last days there are, in fact, doctrines of devils that will seduce and deceive many into apostasy or the falling away from the faith in Christ Jesus. First Timothy 4:1 (NASB) says, *"But the Spirit explicitly says that in later times some will fall away from the faith, paying attention to deceitful spirits and teachings of demons."*

WHAT IS PROPHETIC DELIVERANCE?

Prophetic deliverance is the revelatory art and rule of engagement that is communicated and inspired by the Holy Spirit in the overall extraction, removal, rooting out, routing and excommunication of fallen, intruding, and unearthly spirits. The ministry of deliverance needs the collaboration and correlation of the ministry of the prophetic to see a restoration and continuation of the power of God that we see in the Gospels and in the early church according to the book of the Acts.

Prophetic deliverance cuts to the root systems where demonic covenants, contracts, and curses are created through open doors. The way God works in prophetic deliverance is combining the ministry of the prophet and seer. Prophets are also commissioned by Christ to heal the sick and cast out devils. It was not optional—it was a commandment and charge spoken by our Lord Jesus Christ to New Covenant believers. Power is not an option; it's an opportunity! Jesus Christ gave His apostles the power and authority to heal the sick and to cast out demons in Mark 3:13-15 (NKJV):

> *And He went up on the mountain and called to Him those He Himself wanted. And they came to Him. Then He appointed twelve, that they might be with Him and that He might send them out to preach, and to have power to heal sicknesses and to cast out demons:*
>
> *And He called the twelve to Himself, and began to send them out two by two, and gave them power over unclean spirits (Mark 6:7 NKJV).*

COMMAND THE DEVIL OUT

There is an authority under the prophetic anointing to command demonic spirits out of people. I have commanded devils out of people under the prophetic anointing where I was easily able to identify what spirits were wreaking havoc in someone's life. I have also spoken corporately over entire meetings and congregations for demons to exit, go, and leave—and many would testify of being healed as a result. There have been times when I would prophesy or declare healing over someone as I am ministering, I could sense demonic resistance or objection to the word of the Lord because of spirits in them fighting the hearing of the word.

Therefore, I would bind and command the spirits as the Holy Spirit would reveal to go in Jesus's name, then the person received healing. I would prophesy the devil out of people—which is to speak boldly the word of God's truth over the person that counteracts the lies of the devil. Then suddenly there a breakthrough would come upon the person who would be either healed or delivered.

The devil does not want people to receive healing and deliverance, so the enemy lies and tells them that God does not love them and uses words of witchcraft, control, and manipulations spoken over them by a family member or words believed about themselves through shame, hurt, abuse, molestation, rape, and any trauma. I counteract those lies with God's opinion, mind, heart, and love. I prophesy people into deliverance through the power of love, by loving them into deliverance and healing.

PREACH OR TEACH PEOPLE INTO DELIVERANCE

Jesus is recorded and documented in the Gospels of Mark 1:21-28 and Luke 4:33-37 regarding His teaching and preaching in the synagogue. The people were unfamiliar with His teaching and were impressed with it. They were new to Jesus and His message. One day they saw that He preached and taught with such authority that it caused His preaching to be abruptly and loudly interrupted by a man possessed by a demonic spirit:

> *They went into Capernaum; and immediately on the Sabbath Jesus entered the synagogue and began to teach. And they were amazed at His teaching; for He was teaching them as one having authority, and not as the scribes. Just then there was a man in their synagogue with an unclean spirit; and he cried out, saying, "What business do you have with us, Jesus of Nazareth? Have You come to destroy us? I know who You are: the Holy One of God!" And Jesus rebuked him, saying, "Be quiet, and come out of him!" After throwing him into convulsions and crying out with a loud voice, the unclean spirit came out of him. And they were all amazed, so they debated among themselves, saying, "What is this? A new teaching with authority! He commands even the unclean spirits, and they obey Him." Immediately the news about Him spread everywhere into all the surrounding region of Galilee* (Mark 1:21-28 NASB).

At times this happens, due to the weight of authority and anointing of the word that manifests demons to react, or it can be a ploy that demons use to distract listeners from hearing and receiving the prophetic or preached word. I have experienced both in my meetings, and what I usually do is bind the spirits and prohibit it from speaking, or I continue to preach or teach the devil out of the person.

Philip the evangelist preached Christ to the people of Samaria and manifestations of miracles of healing and deliverance began to happen among them. Demonic spirits would cry out during his powerful preaching of Christ. Demonic manifestation in a person is a revelatory sign for deliverance and expulsion of demons. The following is an example of power preaching that manifested the supernatural through Philip:

> *Therefore those who were scattered went everywhere preaching the word. Then Philip went down to the city of Samaria and preached Christ to them. And the multitudes with one accord heeded the things spoken by Philip, hearing and seeing the miracles which he did. For unclean spirits, crying with a loud voice, came out of many who were possessed; and many who were paralyzed and lame were healed. And there was great joy in that city* (Acts 8:4-8 NKJV).

The audacity and the veracity of Philip preaching with miracles and signs caused a practicing sorcerer named Simon to encounter the power of God, causing him to eventually become a believer. I have encountered witches and warlocks and even psychics who follow my ministry because of the manifestation of the supernatural. Miracles, signs, and prominent prophetic ministry tends to attract false prophetic powers and people to the message and the messenger (see Acts 8:9-13).

True power is when you have sorcerers, witches, warlocks, psychics, false prophets, mediums, clairvoyants, satanists, and practitioners of darkness converted into believers by encountering the power of God. Through power prophecy many have been delivered and transferred from the kingdom of darkness into the Kingdom of marvelous light (see Colossians 1:13).

ARROW OF PROPHETIC DELIVERANCE

And he said, "Open the east window"; and he opened it. Then Elisha said, "Shoot"; and he shot. And he said, "The arrow of the LORD's deliverance and the arrow of deliverance from Syria; for you must strike the Syrians at Aphek till you have destroyed them" (2 Kings 13:17).

The *"arrow of the Lord's deliverance"* is a picture of the supernatural force behind the power of prophecy by the hand of the prophet. The hand of the prophet represented and was a depiction of the hand of the Lord upon His word. The prophet Elisha, who was dying from an illness, put his hands on the king's hand with regard to the arrow that would be used as a prophetic sign and act of the Lord's arrow.

This prophetic act of the arrow would serve as continual victories by the direction and strength behind the prophetic. There is an element of mystery in the ministry of the miraculous. The irony is that Elisha—the great prophet of God and champion of faith in the prophetic whom God had done twice as many miracles through his ministry than his predecessor Elijah (even one after his death in 2 Kings 13:21-22)—would himself die from an illness (see 2 Timothy 4:20).

However, before Elisha dies, he extended prophetic grace to King Jehoahaz an opportunity to participate in an enactment of his own prophecy that symbolized his future victories over the Syrians. There needed to be a partnership, alignment, and action with the word of the prophet for him to see his declaration of victory beforehand, even before the war happens. God declared victory through the prophetic release of the arrow before war. This was so prophetic. The king had an opportunity to declare in advance through this prophetic act the outcome of future wars.

The prophet's hand helped to guide and steady the hand of the king to provide accuracy of the arrow. The prophet working hand-and-hand with the power of the king to prophetically bring deliverance and victories in battle in warfare even after the prophet died. The prophetic act was done in correlation with the king's faith to bring prophetic deliverance to a nation. The king was a prophetic participant in his own prophetic word through the bow and arrow act by Elisha the prophet. He was going to determine the prophetic trajectory and prophetic outcome and result of the prophetic act that was essentially a prophecy.

The king was advised to keep striking the ground. That is prophetic deliverance which is to follow what the prophet or the Holy Spirit directs you to do in a season, during warfare or in a time of need. Spiritual warfare is a key part of prophetic ministry. This is what separates a prophet from one who has the gift of prophecy.

Prophets are called into spiritual warfare to advise, counsel, and provide strategies of victory.

Prophets and seers were advisors to kings in ancient Israel (see 1 Samuel 28; 2 Samuel 24:11-18; 1 Kings 22:1-38; 1 Chronicles 21:9,11-13; 1 Chronicles 29:29; 2 Chronicles 18:1-27, 29:25).

Prophets were powerful advisors to kings on the prophetic outcome of wars and provided strategies. We can learn from Jesus's dual healing and deliverance ministries as Physician and Commander in Chief that He was very decisive and tactical in His approach depending on the standard of care and mode of deliverance needed to be applied in a case-by-case scenario. Yes, we understand that there are injuries and casualties of warfare that will need a medical practitioner and a rescuer. Jesus was unapologetically led by the Holy Spirit, which is genuinely the art of war and *prophetic deliverance.*

The *"arrow of the Lord's deliverance"* is a profound and powerful prophetic act where we can participate in the outcome of our prophetic word. The prophet put his hands on the hand of the king to ensure the king accurately hits the target. The hand of the prophet on the arrow was instrumental in hitting the exact target of his enemy. It was important for the prophet to assist the king, who represents authority, and the prophetic providing precision. The hand of the king was guided by the hand and power of the prophetic to create the trajectory that the king wanted even in his deathbed. The total obedience to the word of the prophet would have guaranteed unlimited victories.

We all need the voice, power, and guidance of the prophetic ministry to give us a prophetic trajectory of our destiny. Each aspect ensures that what is released prophetically will hit the mark. Prophets are marksmen. The king needed the prophetic anointing behind the arrow as a sign that God was with him to ensure deliverance from his enemy. The king had already secured victories through spiritual air-strikes and ground strikes in the spirit and in the prophetic before any physical warfare occurred. This is a principle of prophetic inter-cession in spiritual warfare where you strike across enemy lines and territories with arrows to strike down, dismantle, and disarm oppo-sitional artilleries, weapons, and bases of operations. Most physical warfare can be won first in spiritual warfare.

In the prophetic, details matter and there is always a window of time and opportunity to obey the word of the prophet. Prophecy is time sensitive. The prophet instructed the king of Israel to open the east window and shoot the arrows out the window, which was a pro-phetic sign that he would be used as an arrow in the hand of the Lord to destroy Syrian opposition and to be used to bring prophetic deliv-erance to Israel from Syria successively.

UNSTOPPABLE VICTORY

The king of Israel, working hand in hand with the prophet, created future deliverance beyond what successive generations in Israel could comprehend. This is a primitive example of the power prophecy that brought prophetic deliverance. The arrow released by the king was twofold—a declaration of war and a decree of victory. It is by the power and authority of the king to declare war and to decree law. Therefore, the arrow was declarative in nature but legal in essence because it was by the power of the king to enforce and start it, but the power of the prophet to reinforce to finish it.

These two powerful teams reveal the supernatural relationship of kings and prophets. They are an unstoppable force against the enemies of God. Never underestimate, undervalue, or underweight the power of the prophetic and prophetic voice in your life. The prophet gave the king a prophecy and strategy in the prophetic act according to Second Kings 13:17 (NKJV) where he was to both do it first with arrows in the spirit and in the natural with the army against Syria.

> *And he said, "Open the east window"; and he opened it. Then Elisha said, "Shoot"; and he shot. And he said, "The arrow of the LORD's deliverance and the arrow of deliverance from Syria; for you must strike the Syrians at Aphek till you have destroyed them."*

The king of Israel limited his ability prophetically to destroy the Syrians due to his lack of faith and unwillingness to do something that may have seemed foolish by shooting arrows out the window (airstrikes or aerial) and striking the ground continually (ground strikes). He was told by the prophet to take the arrows—which I must add that the prophet did not tell the king how many arrows he should take or how many arrows he should shoot. He told the king to strike the ground and he only struck the ground three time and stopped, therefore angering the prophet because he stopped.

Look at what the prophet Elisha's prophecy to the king of Israel would have done if he would have not stopped striking the target:

> *Then he [Elisha] said, "Take the arrows;"; so he [the king] took them. And he said to the king of Israel, "Strike the*

ground"; so he struck three times, and stopped. And the man of God was angry with him, and said, "You should have struck five or six times; then you would have struck Syria till you had destroyed it! But now you will strike Syria only three times" (2 Kings 13:18-19 NKJV).

The king's prophecy in the form of the arrows was a weapon. The man of God never told the king to stop. This prophecy God put solely in the hands of the king to decide the number of victories over the Syrians. If the king would have unloaded and emptied the quiver, then God would have honored His word that was in the king's hands. The king only struck the ground three times, which unfortunately instead of unstoppable victories until his enemies were destroyed, he was limited to only three victories and temporary deliverance from Syria. How many times do we limit ourselves and allow others to say or dictate how far or how successful we can become in life?

God's the limit and we must not be afraid to do things that may seem foolish to others but produces extraordinary results. The key to deliverance is in the power of your hands to determine how great you will be in God. The arrow of the Lord's deliverance is in the power of your hand to become an unstoppable force against every demonic, diabolical, and satanic opposition against your life, purpose, and ultimately your destiny.

Paul declares that our prophecy is a weapon in times of warfare (1 Timothy 1:18). Today we must learn how to use our prophecy as a weapon in spiritual warfare. What do I mean? When you obey the word of the Lord over your life, no weapon formed against you will prosper against you according to the prophet Isaiah (Isaiah 54:17). No matter what you are going through, your prophecy has already guaranteed you victory even before the battle.

4

REVELATORY DELIVERANCE

He [Jesus] *said to him, "Come*
out of the man, unclean spirit!"
—Mark 5:8 NKJV

There is a correlation between prophetic healing and prophetic deliverance. The ministry of the prophetic can be vitally key in how we diagnose or identify the problem by essentially providing revelatory action that consequently brings healing and deliverance to a person.

Prophets have the revelatory ministry to see what the root problem is. This level of prophetic intelligent can aide deliverance ministers in revealing how to engage in spiritual warfare. The revelation of identifying what spirits or demons are at work is massively important in bringing deliverance, freedom, emancipation, and breakthrough.

The prophets of God in the Old Testament were used in times and seasons of war to provide kings with strategies and guidance. Therefore, we can today benefit from God's prophetic ministers to help us in the ministry of healing and deliverance. It is important to emphasize, for the purpose of this chapter, that everything we do is prophetic. Jesus, when ministering in deliverance, was able to identify and call out certain demonic spirits. One example is in Mark 5:8, *"Come out of the man, unclean spirit!"*

The prophetic is more than an oracle, vocal, and communicative gift; it is a demonstrative gift. If you have a ministry of healing, you need the prophet to see by revelation what sickness, disease, and/or spirit is in the person's body. Healing is administered through the prophetic. I say it all the time that if God reveals, God heals. In other words, if you get a word of knowledge about the person's condition by the Holy Spirit, you now have the licensure to be a prophetic practitioner to minister healing. If you see it, heal it. This revelation of sickness is done through revelatory healing and in the case of prophetic deliverance, it is done through *revelatory deliverance*.

Revelatory deliverance is done by revelation through the Holy Spirit or angels. Angels as messengers and ministering spirits will assist prophets in providing supernatural intelligence on demons, the individual they are ministering deliverance to, cities, regions, territory, and nations. Angelic partnership with the prophetic ministry is a powerful team. As the prophet is ministering deliverance, the Holy Spirit or angels of God are helping to communicate revelation into what to say or do. The power of the prophetic is hidden within everything we do in the supernatural.

Identifying the source or the root issues prophetically is part of bringing total healing and deliverance to the person. You will notice that I use the words *healing* and *deliverance* interchangeably in this chapter because they both are essentially healing through a different method. I would say that healing and deliverance are the same difference.

Identifying and recognizing various types of demonic, satanic, and unclean spirits through the manifestation gift of discerning of spirits is critically important. I would say that the gift of discerning of spirits can be modernly termed the gift of *identifying spirits*.

Spiritual warfare and the ministry of deliverance was one of the primary functions in the ministry of Jesus Christ. I believe that

Jesus being a Prophet played an enormous role in His ability to see demonic, diabolic, and satanic activity in the unseen realm by prophetic grace and anointing. Prophets are seers, so therefore it gives them a prophetic advantage in receiving and seeing intelligence in the enemy's camp.

DEMONIC ENTRANCE AND PRESENCE

Demons are believed to be able to enter a person's life in many ways. Some objects are believed, by their very nature, to harbor demons. For examples: certain types of literature, especially if it leads the reader to question their faith; fantasy/horror novels or films; monsters, vampires, werewolves, or other types of violent role-playing games; CD recordings of certain types of music; art with non-religious or blasphemous/sinful themes; and artifacts depicting pagan gods. Sacred texts or simple decorations from a non-Christian religion may also be a hiding place for demons. Another type of way demons may enter someone's life is having objects with a sinful history; for example, a piece of jewelry from an adulterous relationship, an object purchased with greed, etc.

Prophets can minister deliverance when they recognize various demonic entrances, gates, doors, and portals. The Holy Spirit provides the believer with powerful revelation into the doors or roots that creates legal rights for demonic occupation and residence. Prophets function innately in *revelatory deliverance*. It is imperative that you are prophetic to operate in the ministry of deliverance. Most deliverance ministers are very prophetic and often may not consider themselves prophets.

You cannot effectively operate in deliverance without being prophetic. Power prophecy is the power of exposing and calling spirits out of people. Routing demons is one of the primary functions of the prophetic ministry. Places, territories, cities, regions, and nations can also be reputed to contain demonic presences that can then enter the lives of people living or visiting there. Indian burial grounds and homes or rooms where violence or abuse occurred are said to be examples of this sort.

PROPHETIC DEMONIC DIAGNOSIS

Deliverance ministries focus on casting out the spirit or spirits believed to cause an affliction. The person must first be *diagnosed* with the presence/possession of an evil spirit, which often requires the participation of a person who is trained or experienced in this area.

The following are some of the ways to prophetically identify and diagnose demonic presence:

1. The deliverance minister may ask questions to learn about the person's life and try to discover if they have committed any sins that might invite a demonic presence; if they have, they must repent of that sin as part of the deliverance process.

2. The minister of deliverance might question the person about their relationships with their spouse, children, and friends, as poor close relationships may be evidence of a demonic presence.

3. They may also ask about their extended family and ancestors to determine if the demon might be the result of a family, hereditary, or generational curse.

4. They can attempt to discern if an object or a room is the source of the demonic activity and can help the person understand what may have attached the demon to that object or space. Some claim to "see"

demons (or vague impressions of them) or hear their names through the Holy Spirit. Once the source of the demonic presence is identified, the way to cast it out can be accurately determined.

Demonic diagnosis helps with dismantling demonic powers. Jesus healed a woman who sickness was due to the spirit of infirmity, which was the demonic spirit that caused the physical ailment. The evil spirit was the root cause of her sickness and infirmity. Jesus as a Prophet had the ability through spiritual and demonic recognition to accurately diagnosis the root cause, which was an unseen evil spirit at work. Once Jesus cast the spirit of infirmity out of the woman, she was immediately healed (Luke 13:10-21). Healing happens through the power of deliverance. Healing and deliverance work interchangeably.

Prophetic Intelligence

We see examples in the following Scriptures of ancient prophets receiving supernatural intel into what the enemy was plotting and planning in the biblical accounts:

1. Jeremiah the prophet was given revelation into the plots against him:

    Because the LORD revealed their plot to me, I knew it, for at that time he showed me what they were doing (Jeremiah 11:18 NIV).

2. Elisha the prophet warned the king of Israel and pointed out the precise place the Arameans were positioned against them.

    The man of God sent word to the king of Israel: "Beware of passing that place, because the Arameans are going down there." So the king of Israel checked on the place indicated by the man of God. Time and again Elisha warned the king, so that he was on his guard in such places (2 Kings 6:9-10 NIV).

"None of us, my lord the king," said one of his officers, "but Elisha, the prophet who is in Israel, tells the king of Israel the very words you speak in your bedroom" (2 Kings 6:12 NIV).

3. David inquired of the Lord to Samuel the prophet with regard to the plans of Saul, the citizens of Keilah and the outcome.

    "Will the citizens of Keilah surrender me to him? Will Saul come down, as your servant has heard? LORD, God of Israel, tell your servant." And the LORD said, "He will." Again David asked, "Will the citizens of Keilah surrender me and my men to Saul?" And the LORD said, "They will" (1 Samuel 23:11-12 NIV).

The following is a New Testament account of the revelation of Jesus given to His servants about what is to happen or come to pass. Prophets and apostles were given revelation through prophetic insight and/or angelic communication.

The Revelation of Jesus Christ, which God gave to Him to show His servants—things which must shortly take place. And He sent and signified it by His angel to His servant John (Revelation 1:1 NKJV).

These Scripture references best show supernatural communication that we are given today as prophetic believers in Christ regarding imminent things given to God's prophets and apostles according to the New Testament Scriptures. Prophets play a vital role in the church today, especially in the ministry of deliverance and spiritual warfare.

HEALING VERSUS DELIVERANCE

The difference between healing and deliverance is that healing refers to physical or emotional healing. Deliverance, the casting out of demons, suggests people being set free from demonic oppression. In the Bible, however, we can see Jesus healing people through such deliverance. Both healing and deliverance were primary practices of Jesus in His earthly ministry, and continued in and through His apostles, prophets, and in the early church.

Power and authority to heal the sick and cast out demons was a common theme and thread throughout the ministry of the supernatural. The integration of the prophetic, as you will see later, has it core relationship with both healing and deliverance.

In retrospect, healing is where God supernaturally restores the physical body; whereas deliverance is the restoration of the soul (or inner self) by the same God through the believer. In my experience and tenure in apostolic and prophetic ministry, both are essentially the same—in fact, a lot of physical proclivities, ailments, and sicknesses have spiritual demonic roots, as you will see later in this chapter.

I have discovered that as a prophet I relied heavily on the Holy Spirit to teach me the ministry of healing and deliverance firsthand. Interesting enough, I experienced quite a bit of healing and casting out spirits in my prophetic ministry, which at one point I questioned if I was really a prophet in the beginning of my ministry because I was functioning more in healing and deliverance than prophesying. Until I started to search and study the Scriptures as an officer in the prophetic, I discovered that I exercised more than the gift of prophecy but as an office prophet that I would exercise the power to heal and cast out demons.

The *office* of the prophet does more than prophesy; primarily functioning as a power prophet exercising and executing power and authority over demons, sicknesses, and all manner of diseases. The office of the prophet epitomes not just function but power. The mark of the prophethood is *power prophecy!*

Power prophecy is the reinforcement of Heaven backing up the prophetic release of the word of God with manifestation of signs, wonders and miracles in both healing and deliverance. I have learned that there are several demonic, diabolical, disembodied, and devilish spirits that attack us physically—and some healing cannot be used or taken in that regard but must be grappled or wrestled out of the grasps or holds of the demonic. God has called us as believers to the ministry of expelling, evicting, exterminating, and exorcising demons. You will find that the prophetic adds great value in ministering healing especially in deliverance.

HEALING AND DELIVERANCE DIFFERENCES

Let us examine the word *healing* first. According to the Merriam-Webster Dictionary, *healing* means "the process or period of gradually regaining one's health and strength." It is tending to cure disease or restore health or to bring about recovery from an illness, weakness, or sickness. It is important to understand that healing is a process, and it can be a gradual thing. In other words, healing will take some time for a person to be restored or regain their health, soundness, and strength. It is restorative.

Simply put, healing means being healed physically or emotionally. When we examine some of God's promises concerning healing, this meaning is reinforced. You can see in First Peter 2:24 that Peter recounts and confirms with the Old Testament promise made prophetically in Isaiah 53:5 that by Jesus's *"stripes we are healed."*

Let us look at the following Scriptures to illustrate what healing was in the Old Testament:

- In Exodus 15:26 (NKJV), God tells Israel that none of Egypt's diseases will come upon them if they obey Him. God declares, *"I am the LORD who heals you."*
- David prays in Psalm 103:3 (NKJV) and proclaims that it is God *"Who forgives all your iniquities, who heals all your diseases."*
- In Psalm 147:3 (NKJV), David goes on to mention God healing the emotions and the body: *"He heals the brokenhearted and binds up their wounds."*
- Psalm 34:18 (NKJV), God confirms that He *"is near to those who have a broken heart, and saves such as have a contrite spirit."*

As you see, these Scriptures clearly refer to physical and emotional healing only. It does not imply a relief of demonic oppression. You will see that healing and deliverance work interchangeably. Prophets have the supernatural faculty like Jesus to discern what method is needed in any given situation.

Jesus was able to recognize that some infirmities and sickness were a result of sin, demonic possession, not due to any sin or demonic possession but for the glory of God (John 11:4) and times when the devil found a foothold through anger. Scripture provides us with a snapshot, the vital importance of the prophetic playing a key role in ministering deliverance.

Therefore, you can see that we need the power of the prophetic through the spirit of prophecy, gift of prophecy, prophetic anointing, prophetic mantle, and prophetic office all at work in the believer to see the kind of healing through deliverance needed. Power prophecy also casts out demons through the power of prophecy. This is another dimension of power that is executed by the prophets. Moses delivered an entire nation through the empowerment of God (Yahweh), and Jesus rescued, saved, healed, and restored humanity through the power of love, which was beforehand spoken and written of Him by the prophets.

PARTNERSHIP BETWEEN HEALING AND DELIVERANCE

Throughout the Gospel according to Luke you can see that healing and deliverance are very distinctive yet closely related. Though there is a distinction between the ministry of healing and the ministry of deliverance, you can see how much they operate interchangeably and in partnership.

Definitively, the healing ministry primarily refers to the restoration or rehabilitation of the physical body back to full health and strength by the power of the Holy Spirit. Deliverance refers to casting out demonic evil spirits to free people from torment, sicknesses, bondage, and oppression. These two ministries go together without question.

The reason the Gospel of Luke is interesting and important to highlight for the purpose of this chapter is Luke's medical background as a physician in administering care to see healing, restoration of health and wholeness. Luke's detailed accounts in the Gospel shows us the connection and relation of healing and deliverance. Luke saw firsthand how Jesus the Physician wrought healing and deliverance with the laying on of hands and speaking a word. Luke, being a doctor of medicine, understands the various healing processes. He witnessed the baffling, instantaneous miracles done by Jesus Christ.

Consider the following four examples in the book of Luke as clear evidence of the close relationship between healing and deliverance. You will see that healing sickness and deliverance from evil spirits are mentioned in the same breath. These ministries are meant to go together and often intersect:

> *When the sun was setting, all those who had any that were sick with various diseases brought them to Him; and He laid His hands on every one of them and healed them. And demons also came out of many...* (Luke 4:40-41 NKJV).
>
> *...and a great multitude of people...who came to hear Him and be healed of their diseases, as well as those who were tormented with unclean spirits. And they were healed. And the whole multitude sought to touch Him, for power went out from Him and healed them all* (Luke 6:17-19 NKJV).
>
> *And that very hour He cured many of infirmities, afflictions, and evil spirits; and to many blind He gave sight* (Luke 7:21 NKJV).
>
> *And certain women who had been healed of evil spirits and infirmities—Mary called Magdalene, out of whom had come seven demons* (Luke 8:2).

There are more examples that could be given from the book of Luke, as well as various places in the New Testament. In the ministry of Jesus, healing and deliverance were the two most common supernatural signs. Demonstration of healing and deliverance followed Jesus's preaching and teaching. His words were reinforced with demonstrations. They were demonstrations of the message that Jesus preached: *"the kingdom of heaven is at hand."*

As the Kingdom of God advanced, healing the sick and casting out demons were absolute byproducts. Sometimes Jesus healed people by laying hands on them or speaking a word of command to them. Other times, healing was a direct result of a demon being cast out.

The New Testament Scriptures teach and reveal that evil spirits can cause sickness. The ministry of healing and deliverance continued even after Jesus went to Heaven through His apostles, prophets, and New Testament believers. The early church healed the sick and delivered the demonized in the same manner Jesus did.

Notice the similarity in the following description to those in the book of Luke: *"Also a multitude gathered from the surrounding cities to Jerusalem, bringing sick people and those who were tormented by unclean spirits, and they were all healed"* (Acts 5:16 NKJV).

We cannot necessarily discern when healing will manifest into deliverance or deliverance into healing. It is important that as we mature in the healing ministry we should also become more familiar and acquainted with the ministry of deliverance and vice versa, depending on what side of the same ministry you operate the most. Even though they are distinct and can function and operate independently, they are so closely associated that we should not completely isolate or treat them separately or apart from one another, but as complementary.

The following are examples of healing through the ministry of healing and deliverance in the New Testament:

- Demoniac in the synagogue healed—Mark 1:23-25; Luke 4:33-36

- Heals diseases in Galilee—Mark 1:34; Matthew 4:23-24

- Heals demoniacs—Matthew 8:16-17; Luke 4:40-41

- Heals a demoniac—Matthew 12:22-37; Mark 3:19-30; Luke 11:14-15, 17-23

- Demoniacs in Gadarenes healed—Matthew 8:28-34; Mark 5:1-20; Luke 8:26-39

- Devil cast out and mute man cured—Matthew 9:32-33
- Deaf person cured—Mark 7:31-37
- Demon-possessed child healed—Matthew 17:14-21; Mark 9:14-29; Luke 9:37-45
- Woman with the spirit of infirmity cured—Luke 13:10-17

‖ 5 ‖

MINISTRY OF SIGNS, WONDERS, AND MIRACLES

*For I will not venture to speak of anything except what
Christ has accomplished through me to bring the Gentiles
to obedience—by word and deed, by the power of signs
and wonders, by the power of the Spirit of God—so that
from Jerusalem and all the way around to Illyricum
I have fulfilled the ministry of the gospel of Christ.*
—ROMANS 15:18-19 ESV

*God also testified to it by signs, wonders
and various miracles, and by gifts of the
Holy Spirit distributed according to his will.*
—HEBREWS 2:4 NIV

This chapter reveals the new emerging prophetic ministry of the saints who will operate in revelatory miracles, which is the new era working through the ministry of signs, wonders, and diversities of miracles. The ministry of signs, wonders, and miracles is the demonstration of word and deed. The prophetic represents the ministry function of the word and the signs, wonders, and miracles represent the ministry function of deeds.

Power prophecy is the epitome of releasing and manifesting miracles through the power of the prophetic. The purpose and emphasis of this chapter and the book *Power Prophecy* at large is to lay down a carefully constructed biblical foundation for living and walking in the supernatural power of God through the power of prophecy. Every believer of Jesus Christ is called into the ministry of signs, wonders, and miracles.

According to the Merriam-Webster Dictionary, the word *ministry* means the office, duties, or functions of a minister or officer. One who is well prepared, equipped and trained to serve. Therefore, saints in Jesus Christ's ministry—office, duties, and function—are to serve as signs, wonders and miracles to unbelievers. All servants in Christ have been called into the office of the supernatural, manifesting signs, wonders, and miracles. We will begin to see miracles birthed through the power of prophecy. Prophecy will initiate and activate the manifestation of signs, wonders, and miracles. Part of the prophetic flow and anointing will be an Acts 2:18-19 (NLT) anointing: *"They will prophesy. And I will cause wonders in the heavens above and signs on the earth below."*

The prophetic ministry will be the forerunning gift that will reintroduce the ministry of signs, wonders, and miracles. There is an ancient anointing that Jesus imparted into His church to be a supernatural church and assembly of miracle workers. Miracles will be the new norm as it was in the ancient prophets' era. The ministry of the prophet and the ministry of signs, wonders, and miracles working synonymously together.

You cannot have the prophetic without signs and wonders. I have discovered in my prophetic ministry over the years that the prophetic flow has opened the heavens for the glory of God to manifest itself in the midst of the people. In most cases, you will notice that signs and wonders follow prophecy. Prophecy is one of the keys to opening the spirit realm for the supernatural. The ancient prophets were forerunners of the ministry of signs, wonders and wonders.

THE SIGNIFICANCE OF SIGNS, WONDERS, AND MIRACLES

The prophets of God in the Old Testament relied heavily on the power of God in order to contend and challenge the various so-called powers of polytheism, which is usually defined as the doctrine or belief in more than one god or many gods, powers of hell, demonic forces, evil kings, opposing and apostate nations. The ministry of signs and wonder is an intricate dimension of the ministers of the prophets. In fact, the prophets used the ministry of the signs and wonders to prove the emptiness of false gods. Signs and wonders were an important facet of the prophet's ministry.

We can see the significance of signs and wonders in the ministry of Elijah with the great clash and prophetic contest of the prophets on Mount Carmel with respect to showing which "god" is alive and true in First Kings 18:20. The miracle of Elijah on Mount Carmel causes the turning of the hearts of the people of Israel back to God again (1 Kings 18:36-39). The glory of God fell by fire as a sign that He was with the prayer and mouth of the prophet Elijah. Israel witnessed the display of power as an answer of the prophet's prayer.

Signs, wonders, and miracles are used to challenge false prophetic powers and false operations. Elijah prayed for rain and contended with a false prophet as part of his prophetic ministry (1 Kings 18:1-46; 19:8 and James 5:17). Prophets and prophetic believers will challenge, contend, and confront false prophetic activities in the spirit as part of their function.

God would often use signs or miracles in the Bible to authenticate His chosen messenger. God sent down fire on Elijah's altar during Elijah's contest with the prophets of baal (1 Kings 18:36-39). He performed this miracle to prove that the God of Israel was the one true God. Elijah proposes a direct test of prophetic powers versus the powers of baal and the God of Abraham, Isaac and Jacob. The people of Israel were limping and/or vacillating between beliefs and opinions about serving the true and living God or serving false, empty, and dead gods and deities. This contest on Mount Carmel featured in the presence of the people of Israel, 450 prophets of baal, and 400 prophets and priests of Asherah. Elijah summoned them to his duel that ultimately resulted in the prophet of Israel slaying by the sword all of the false prophets of baal and Asherah.

Prophets are to challenge, confront, and destroy counterfeit prophetic powers. The prophets through the spirit of their mouth will consume false prophetic spirits, gods, and prophets. We are to expose demonically engineered and inspired prophets and lying signs and wonders:

> *Let no one deceive you by any means; for that Day will not come unless the falling away comes first, and the man of sin is revealed, the son of perdition, who opposes and exalts himself above all that is called God or that is worshiped, so that he sits as God in the temple of God, showing himself that he is God. Do you not remember that when I was still with you I told you these things? And now you know what is restraining, that he may be revealed in his own time. For the mystery of lawlessness is already at work; only He who now restrains will do so until He is taken out of the way. And then the lawless one will be revealed, whom the Lord will consume with the breath of His mouth and destroy with the brightness of His coming. The coming of the lawless one is according to the working of Satan, with*

all power, signs, and lying wonders (2 Thessalonians 2:3-9 NKJV).

There are demonic spirits performing false signs sent into the worlds and to the kings and those of influence over nations:

For really they are the spirits of demons that perform signs (wonders, miracles). And they go forth to the rulers and leaders all over the world, to gather them together for war on the great day of God the Almighty (Revelation 16:14 AMPC).

Elijah—Signs of Fire

And you [prophets of baal] *call on the name of your god, and I* [Elijah] *will call upon the name of the LORD, and the God who answers by fire—he is God...* (1 Kings 18:24 NIV).

Elijah had a ministry of signs, wonders, and miracles as a prophet. He was considered what we call a "signs prophet." He was a prophet who carried the supernatural, as his ministry was marked by God answering his prayer. We will see that Elijah's prophetic ministry was marked by God answering his prayer primarily as a direct result from his ministry of prayer according to James 5:17-18 (NKJV):

Elijah was a man with a nature like ours, and he prayed earnestly that it would not rain; and it did not rain on the land for three years and six months. And he prayed again, and the heaven gave rain, and the earth produced its fruit.

It is important to understand that the ministry of signs and wonders must be developed and cultivated in a secret place of prayer. The secret to Elijah's miracle ministry was from the power of prayer. The foundation of a prophet's or a believer's ministry in the supernatural is rooted and grounded in being able to not only hear the voice of God as a prophet but essentially God can hear your voice in prayer as an intercessor.

Consider one of the following examples of God manifesting a miracle of raising the widow woman's son from the dead after hearing Elijah's voice in prayer and intercession:

> *And he stretched himself out on the child three times, and cried out to the LORD and said, "O LORD my God, I pray, let this child's soul come back to him." Then the LORD heard the voice of Elijah; and the soul of the child came back to him, and he revived* (1 Kings 17:21-22).

The miracle of raising the child from the dead was because Elijah had a voice in prayer that God heard and was in direct relationship. The prophetic is not just hearing the voice of God but in divine communication it's relationally God listening and hearing your voice to answer your prayer, intercession, petition, and request. It is interesting that when Elijah was mocking the 400 false prophets of baal and they were doing their religious rituals, sacrifices, and cutting themselves while calling out aloud on the name of their god baal, that the Bible says, "But there was no voice; no one answered, no one paid attention" (see 1 Kings 18:26-29).

Divine communication works mutually—when God speaks, prophets hear, and when we pray God responds. In other words, communication is hearing and listening to each other's voice. As prophets and prophetic believers, we must learn to intimately hear the voice of God in prayer; then out of that place we then prophesy (1 Kings 17:1). And when we pray to God, He hears our voice and answers.

Amos 3:7-8 (NKJV) declares:

Surely the Lord God does nothing, unless He reveals His secret to His servants the prophets. A lion has roared! Who will not fear? The Lord God has spoken! Who can but prophesy?

God is raising up prophetic voices of revival. Prophets will be revivalists and God will hear their voices in praying and interceding over churches, cities, regions, territories, and nations. Prophets are vocal gifts of revivals where their voices will carry attesting signs, wonders, and miracles to mark that God is with them.

> **PROPHETIC KEY:** Those who will walk in the ministry of signs, wonders, and miracles will have such a prophetic voice that God will hear their voices in prayer and respond.

REPAIRING THE PROPHETIC ALTARS— FOUNDATION OF PRAYER

Then Elijah said to all the people, "Come near to me." And all the people came near to him. And he repaired the altar of the LORD that had been thrown down. Elijah took twelve stones, according to the number of the tribes of the sons of Jacob, to whom the word of the LORD came, saying, "Israel shall be your name," and with the stones he built an altar in the name of the LORD..." (1 Kings 18:30-32 NKJV).

Prophets repair and rebuild proper altars while tearing down demonic altars in people, cities, regions, territories, and nations to manifest answered prayers, which allows the breaking forth of miraculous signs and manifestations of the glory of God. We need to repair broken altars and prayers that are not producing manifestations of the supernatural.

It is important that prophets and prophetic believers, by the leading of the Holy Spirit, cut off any and all illicit things that are of a dark nature or satanic practices and/or objects that create legal rights unknowingly to open portals, gateways, access points, and doors for demons, astral projections, and demonic activities. False and demonic altars are built through dark covenants and blood sacrifices that must be confronted and pushed back by Elijah-type prophets.

PROPHETIC FIRE

At the time of sacrifice, the prophet Elijah stepped forward and prayed: "LORD, the God of Abraham, Isaac and Israel, let it be known today that you are God in Israel and that I am your servant and have done all these things at your command. Answer me, Lord, answer me, so these people will know that you, LORD, are God, and that you are turning their hearts back again." Then the fire of the LORD fell and burned up the sacrifice, the wood, the stones and the soil, and also licked up the water in the trench. When all the people saw this, they fell prostrate and cried, "The LORD—he is God! The LORD—he is God!" Then Elijah commanded them, "Seize the prophets of Baal. Don't let anyone get away!" They seized them, and Elijah had them brought down to the Kishon Valley and slaughtered there (1 Kings 18:36-40 NIV).

Elijah clearly provided proof that the God of Abraham, Isaac, and Jacob (Israel) answers by fire, which validated that he was a true prophet of God, the God he serves is alive and real and that the prophets of baal and their god was dead, empty, and false. This contest put signs and wonder at the center of the match. The ministry of the prophets contends with false prophets, psychics, sorcerers, mediums, clairvoyants, witches, witchdoctors, warlocks, magicians, prognosticators, satanists, and every form and practice in the realm of darkness in their ministries.

The ministry of signs and wonders is a powerful tool and weapon in the hands of the prophetic to counter, combat, and confront darkness. The prophets of God are unmatched in the realms of the Spirit. They carry endowments that are directly from the God of creation. He is the Source of their godly powers.

The Lord provided Moses with several miraculous signs to prove to others that he was appointed by God (Exodus 4:5-9; 7:8-10;19-20).

MOSES—SIGNS OF MIRACULOUS PLAGUES

But the LORD said to Moses, "Pharaoh will not heed you, so that My wonders may be multiplied in the land of Egypt" (Exodus 11:9 NKJV).

This man [Moses] *led them out, performing wonders and signs in Egypt and at the Red Sea and in the wilderness for forty years* (Acts 7:36 ESV).

Moses, through the ministry of signs and wonders, discounted and disqualified the powers of the Egyptian magicians. He executed miracles through the power and ministry of signs and wonders on all the gods of Egypt. Pharoah did not listen to the voice of the prophets Moses and Aaron in letting the children of Israel go out of Egypt; therefore, a succession of judgments in the form of signs and wonders ensued. Moses had executive powers from God (Yahweh) whereby he executed judgment as he was led prophetically by God with every plague released. This was the final statement of God's power.

Miracles essentially make a statement. Just as prophecy speaks, so do miracles. God executed judgment through the prophetic. In the case with both prophetic ministries of Elijah and Moses, we learn that signs and wonders were used to expose, counter, and confront the powerless and invalidity of worshiping many gods or a false god (deity) to God's people in Egypt and in Israel.

We have to understand the reality that there are false gods, deities, fallen spirits, and powers: *"For even if there are so-called gods, whether in heaven or on earth (as there are many gods and many lords)"* (1 Corinthians 8:5 NKJV).

Jesus Himself performed many miracles or "signs" to demonstrate His power over nature (Matthew 4:23; Mark 6:30-44; Luke 8:22-24; John 6:16-24). There are signs that Jesus did in the presence of His students that are not recorded in the Scriptures. Keep in mind that this proves that every miracle or even unexplainable miracles that will be done by the believers, apostles, and prophets today will not be found in the Bible.

One of the most important indicators regarding signs is that the miraculous signs point to and reveal Jesus Christ who ultimately brings divine healing, deliverance from demonic spirits and conversion, and salvation as born-again believers.

> **PROPHETIC KEY:** We need to repair and build an altar of prayer to the Lord. Elijah understood the importance of building an altar upon the original foundation stones of the twelve tribes of Israel. He created an altar as a foundation and origin of everything prophetic that he did. The power of the altar was the key behind his power in the prophetic, where even David found deliverance, refuge, salvation, and God's strength (Psalm 18:2 and Luke 1:69).

JESUS CHRIST—SIGNS OF THE MESSIAH

And truly Jesus did many other signs in the presence of His disciples, which are not written in this book (John 20:30 NKJV).

Fellow Israelites, listen to this: Jesus of Nazareth was a man accredited by God to you by miracles, wonders and signs, which God did among you through him, as you yourselves know. This man was handed over to you by God's deliberate plan and foreknowledge; and you, with the help of wicked men, put him to death by nailing him to the cross. But God raised him from the dead, freeing him from the agony of death, because it was impossible for death to keep its hold on him (Acts 2:22-24 NIV).

Jesus prophesied His own miraculous resurrection. His resurrection was to be a prophetic sign revealing that He was the Christ, the Son of the living God, and the Messiah who came into the world to save us. The sign of His resurrection from the dead was to point back to what was prophesied, spoken, foretold, and written of Him by the prophet. His prophecy was revealing the miraculous sign of who He really was.

JONAH—SIGN OF THE RESURRECTION OF JESUS CHRIST

Then some of the scribes and Pharisees answered, saying, "Teacher, we want to see a sign from You." But He answered and said to them, "An evil and adulterous generation seeks after a sign, and no sign will be given to it except the sign of the prophet Jonah. For as Jonah was three days and three nights in the belly of the great fish, so will the Son of Man be three days and three nights in the heart of the earth. The men of Nineveh will rise up in the judgment with this generation and condemn it, because they repented at the preaching of Jonah; and indeed a greater than Jonah is here" (Matthew 12:38-41 NKJV).

The scribes and Pharisees asked for a sign or miraculous indicator in order for them to believe Him as a true prophet. The sign of

Jonah would turn out to be Jesus's greatest miracle of all. The *"sign of the prophet Jonah"* was to point prophetically to the resurrection of Jesus Christ. It is important for me to insert this statement here for us to understand that everything that a prophet does is prophetic and is a sign pointing to Christ. A genuine prophet is to always point us to the Christ, the Anointed One, the Messiah and God in Christ.

Prophets are signs just as Jonah was a sign that Jesus used in His discourse with the religious Pharisees who were questioning His prophetic and Messianic ministry. The sign I would say is the miracle of Jonah surviving in the belly of the great whale, which pointed to the resurrection of Christ, who was buried in the belly of the earth.

The greatest sign, wonder, and miracle of all time is Jesus raising up from the dead in three days (John 11:25-26). The greatest revelation of the prophets is making known, manifesting the activity, presence, and testimony of Christ Jesus through the power and spirit of prophecy according to Revelation 19:10 (ESV):

> *Then I fell down at his feet to worship him, but he said to me, "You must not do that! I am a fellow servant with you and your brothers who hold to the testimony of Jesus. Worship God." For the testimony of Jesus is the spirit of prophecy.*

To fully appreciate the answer that Jesus gave, we must go to the Old Testament book of Jonah. In the first chapter, we read that God commanded the prophet Jonah to go to the city of Nineveh and warn its people that He was going to destroy it for its wickedness. Jonah disobediently ran from the Lord and headed for the city of Tarshish by boat. The Lord then sent a severe storm that caused the crew of the ship to fear for their lives. Jonah was soon thrown overboard and swallowed by a great fish where he remained for *"three days and three nights*" (Jonah 1:15-17). After the three-day period, the Lord caused the great fish to vomit Jonah out onto dry land (Jonah 2:10).

These three days are what Jesus was referring to when He spoke of the sign of Jonah. Jesus had already been producing miracles that were witnessed by many. Jesus had just performed a great sign in the Pharisees' presence by healing a deaf man who was possessed by a demon. Rather than believe, they accused Jesus of doing this by the power of satan. Jesus recognized their hardness of heart and refused to give them further proof of His identity. However, He did say that there would be one further sign forthcoming—His resurrection from the dead. This would be their final opportunity to be convinced. Signs, wonders, and miracles ministries are to provide additional and substantial evidence of God's love toward us. It reveals the love of God to those we are ministering to.

Jesus's paralleling of the Pharisees with the people of Nineveh is telling. The people of Nineveh repented of their evil ways (Jonah 3:4-10) after hearing Jonah's call for repentance, while the Pharisees continued in their unbelief despite being eyewitnesses to the miracles of Jesus. Jesus was telling the Pharisees that they were culpable for their unbelief, given the conversion of the people of Nineveh, sinners who had received far less evidence than the Pharisees themselves had witnessed.

The Pharisees wanted a sign or miracle to prove His legitimacy as the Messiah, but the only indicator was Him pointing to His miraculous resurrection as confirmation of who He is:

> *Then some of the Pharisees and teachers of the law said to him, "Teacher, we want to see a sign from you." He answered, "A wicked and adulterous generation asks for a sign! But none will be given it except the sign of the prophet Jonah. For as Jonah was three days and three nights in the belly of a huge fish, so the Son of Man will be three*

days and three nights in the heart of the earth" (Matthew 12:38-40 NIV).

PROPHETIC KEY: We must be open to be used as a sign to others by pointing them to Christ Jesus. Prophets are not a substitute or replacement of the Holy Spirit, but are those who carry keys in our mouths to unlock truths to bring people to encounter the Spirit of Christ. We are not to look for miracles or signs as believers, we are to be a sign that people can see the salvation of the Lord and ask, "What must I do to be saved?" (Acts 2:38).

CREATIVE MIRACLES

Jesus, through His ministry, functioned unconventionally at times to bring forth healing and miracles as a prophet. He was recognized as a prophet with mighty deeds and He employed unusual and unconventional methods and practices to manifest creative miracles. As prophets and a prophetic people, are we willing to be foolish in front of others and put our personal reputation aside so that miracles are birthed? Regardless how crazy it may look to others watching, spectating, or judging the works of God through us, total trust, reliance, and obedience bring God-type results.

Let us examine the unusual, uncharacteristic, and unconventional creative elements of the miracles that Jesus produces in the following two biblical accounts in the Gospel of Mark where Jesus sticks His fingers in a deaf man's ears and put His spit on the man's tongue; He also put His spit on the eyes of a blind man:

Mark 7:32-36 NKJV—Deaf and Mute Creatively Healed

Then they brought to Him one who was deaf and had an impediment in his speech, and they begged Him to put

His hand on him. And He took him aside from the multitude, and put His fingers in his ears, and He spat and touched his tongue. Then, looking up to heaven, He sighed [expression of prayer and intercession], *and said to him, "Ephphatha," that is, "Be opened." Immediately his ears were opened, and the impediment of his tongue was loosed, and he spoke plainly. Then He commanded them that they should tell no one; but the more He commanded them, the more widely they proclaimed it.*

Mark 8:22-26 NKJV—A Blind Man Healed at Bethsaida

Then He came to Bethsaida; and they brought a blind man to Him, and begged Him to touch him. So He took the blind man by the hand and led him out of the town. And when He had spit on his eyes and put His hands on him, He asked him if he saw anything. And he looked up and said, "I see men like trees, walking." Then He put His hands on his eyes again and made him look up. And he was restored and saw everyone clearly. Then He sent him away to his house, saying, "Neither go into the town, nor tell anyone in the town."

The Lord showed me with these two creative miracles that Jesus used His own spittle (salvia) to administer healing in both cases. The spit came out of His mouth, which was used as a healing ointment that He applied to the men. Because salvia is in the mouth of the living Word of God, Jesus, so there is healing in the mouth of the prophet. Prophets can activate the healing anointing by applying the word of God to create the miracle you are looking for. God created man out of the dust of the ground (Genesis 2:7); therefore, this same creative power can be accessed to create new eyes, ears, and limbs by the power of our mouths.

Look at this *creative miracle* of Jesus's regarding the ear cut off by one of His followers in Luke 22:49-51 (NIV):

> *When Jesus' followers saw what was going to happen, they said, "Lord, should we strike with our swords?" And one of them struck the servant of the high priest, cutting off his right ear. But Jesus answered, "No more of this!" And he touched the man's ear and healed him.*

Jesus touched the high priest's servant's ear and performed a creative miracle by either creating a new right ear or He creatively caused the ear to reattach to his head, forming skin or renewing the skin around the ear like the miracle in Ezekiel 37 in the Valley of Dry Bones.

PROPHETIC KEY: Atmosphere and environment are extremely imperative for creative miracles.

You will find a key in what Jesus did in both accounts in Mark chapters 7 and 8 that produced the type of miracle needed. Two things could hinder or stop the miracles: 1) people; and 2) certain places, cities, regions, or atmospheres. An atmosphere where the people or the multitude is full of suspicion, doubt, and unbelief can limited God's creative power to be released (Mark 6:5).

In Matthew 13:58 (AMP) *"He did not do many miracles there [in Nazareth] because of their unbelief."* You will notice that in Mark 7:32-36 Jesus took aside the man who was deaf and had a speech impediment away from the multitude to put His fingers in his ears and to spit and touch his tongue. He removed the man from the presence of the people to work that creative miracle and to exercise with wisdom that method free from scrutiny, criticism, and offense. He did not want to hinder God's method of performing the miracle.

116

Ministering a creative miracle has to be led totally by the Spirit, and in most cases these miracles happen away from the crowd. Not every miracle is to be in front of an audience. Some creative miracles will happen privately and the Holy Spirit is sensitive about what method is best.

In the second account, in Mark 8:22-26, Jesus led the blind man out of town in the same fashion as leading the deaf man out of the presence of the people in order to practice a different divine method of manifesting a creative miracle. He removed and led the man out of Bethsaida because that particular town and place was full of doubt and unbelief.

It will sometimes take leading a person out of a place of doubt and unbelief into a place of faith and the supernatural for the miracle to occur. There are those like the deaf, blind, and mute men, who need a prophet to give them ears to hear, eyes to see, and a voice to speak. Prophets can be your eyes, ears, and voice of healing. There are certain places, territories, churches, cities, regions, and nations that are not open to the supernatural or the gospel of Jesus Christ.

Prophets can discern atmospheres and environments that are conducive and ripe for not only miracles but creative miracles. There are times when I was not led to minister healing or work a miracle in a certain city, but felt that I was only to pray for a few. The atmosphere hindered the type of miracle needed in that moment. I have seen more unusual and creative miracles in certain atmospheres or places or cities than in others.

When I am called to minister in a certain church or city, sometimes I pray even harder for God to open the heavens over that place because I know that either the church of unbelieving believers are not open to the healing, miracles, signs, and wonders—or they are sizing me up seeking a sign from me to prove I am a prophet of God. Both cases stop or limit the miraculous. Different atmospheres are conducive for unusual miracles.

SIGNS OF SPECIAL MIRACLES

God worked unusual [special] *miracles by the hands of Paul, so that even handkerchiefs or aprons were brought from his body to the sick, and the diseases left them and the evil spirits went out of them* (Acts 19:11-12 NKJV).

Paul, through his apostolic ministry, understood that the true mark of apostleship is the ministry of signs, wonders, and miracles. Apostles are ministers of the miraculous. True apostles demonstrate the supernatural to some degree, form, or measure. Yes, there are different types of apostles; however, the Scriptures are very clear in Paul's epistles, in the earthly ministry of Jesus the Apostle of our faith, and in the apostles He chose and sent with apostolic, miraculous power that you cannot be a genuine apostle if void of power to heal the sick, raise the dead, cast out demons, cleanse the leper and experience the supernaturalness of God.

The exhibition of miracles, signs, and wonders in the ministry of the apostles validated their true apostolic call, commissioning and appointment according to Second Corinthians 12:12 (NKJV): *"Truly the signs of an apostle were accomplished among you with all perseverance, in signs and wonders and mighty deeds."* Genuine apostles had a distinguishing mark that separated them from all other ministries, which was their spiritual capacity and faculty to work miracles. When there are true ministers of signs and wonders, we must be aware of lawless, demonic, and satanic activities that work against and refute the powers of God. In fact, Second Thessalonians 2:9 warns us of counteractive power and false signs and wonders.

God worked special and unusual miracles by the hands of Paul. This gave Paul apostolic validity against those who questioned his apostleship being that he was not one of the original apostles of the Lamb who walked with Jesus bodily. Paul encountered healing power through a disciple by the name of Ananias who received a prophetic vision from the Lord with detailed instructions and words of knowledge to heal Paul's blindness.

It is interesting to point out that this powerful vision was given to a disciple who was not identified as a prophet. Ananias was obviously prophetic being a certain disciple used to extraordinarily release healing through the power of prophecy. Therefore, the verses in Acts 9:1-19 should encourage any ordinary believer, follower, and minister of Christ that He can use you to function in the ministry of signs, wonders, and miracles.

Truthfully, the ministry of signs and wonders is not just for the prophets, senior leaders, or the fivefold ministry gifts, but to *all* New Testament believers according to First Corinthians 12:7-10 (NKJV):

> *But the manifestation of the Spirit is given to each one for the profit of all: for to one is given the word of wisdom through the Spirit, to another the word of knowledge through the same Spirit, to another faith by the same Spirit, to another gifts of healings by the same Spirit, to another the working of miracles, to another prophecy, to another discerning of spirits, to another different kinds of tongues, to another the interpretation of tongues.*

Ananias was used to minister prophetically to Paul regarding his blindness from his calling and encounter with Jesus Christ on the road to Damascus. Paul's healing came through the power of the prophetic. This better illustrates and explains how signs, wonders, and miracles work in correlation with the prophetic. God decided to exercise this method of healing through the prophetic for Paul, who was literally blind, to see the revelation.

This is a New Testament example of how the ministry of signs, wonders, and miracles has always been interwoven within the very fabric and culture of the prophets then, now, and for tomorrow. Prophets are cut from a different cloth. Signs, wonders, and miracles through the prophetic ministry is to ultimately reveal that God still speaks today and is active among us.

> **PROPHETIC KEY:** The key to unlock exceptional miracles is simply to activate and not neglect the manifestation gifts of the Spirit that has been imputed, imparted, and implanted by the Spirit at every believers' conversion in Christ Jesus. However, after you receive the initiation of the Spirit, the second miracle is the filling and evidence of power to act.

There is one baptism but many fillings, and we must act and be led by the Spirit of God to partner with what Heaven's desires to do in and through us. Mostly all miracles that happened on earth took place with God's partnership with a man or woman. The next act of the supernatural is resident in you, therefore use your key and unlock your God-given potency and potential. You host the presence and the power of God to release miracles through the power of prophecy.

MINISTRY OF THE APOSTOLIC

God did extraordinary miracles through Paul (Acts 19:11 NIV).

Miracles is a New Testament function of the church, the primary acts of the apostles to minister that Jesus Christ is alive and working in believers by the Holy Spirit. The book of Acts is historically named, The Acts of the Apostles. The entire book demonstrates the activity of supernatural signs, wonders, and miracles through the apostles and the church (believers) by the power of the Holy Spirit. Acts reveals the work of the ministry of the Holy Spirit in and through the believers. Paul tells the true essence of apostolic ministry in Second Corinthians 12:12 (ESV): *"The signs of a true apostle were performed among you with utmost patience, with signs and wonders and mighty works."*

The apostles of Christ and the Holy Spirit are models to us today to follow them in supernatural ministry. Paul defied the odds by the working of miracles. Apostles in the New Testament have a ministry of signs, wonders, and miracles. You cannot legitimately be an apostle apart from manifesting the supernatural. Some may argue against that statement but biblical apostles were marked with signs, wonders, and miracles. It was distinguishing mark of their ministry. There are those who may argue this.

Culturally, those of us who are ministers of signs and wonders will deal with various cultural mindsets pertaining to operating in both word and deed. We see that way of thinking in First Corinthians 1:22 (NIV): *"Jews demand signs and Greeks look for wisdom."* The Jews demanded the proof of signs—mighty deeds or miracles—while the Greeks sought wisdom, knowledge or word. This proves that those of us who embrace the full ministry of signs and wonders will bear witness to each other. We need both word and deed as undeniable and irrefutable proof to the different nations and cultures where we are sent. *Power prophecy* is the ministry of releasing the power of prophecy with the confirmation of signs, wonders, and miracles.

The ministry of signs, wonders, and miracles are not only for the prophets, apostolic leaders, senior and associate pastoral leadership, but truthfully for every believer. All Holy Spirit-filled believers in Christ have been called into the ministry of the signs, wonders, and miracles. Supernatural ministry is for the saints and the anointing and transference of power have been delegated from the pulpit to the pews. Paul miraculously raises Eutychus from the dead who had fallen three stories out of a window:

> *As Paul spoke on and on, a young man named Eutychus, sitting on the windowsill, became very drowsy. Finally, he fell sound asleep and dropped three stories to his death below. Paul went down, bent over him, and took him into his arms. "Don't worry," he said, "he's alive!" Then they all went back upstairs, shared in the Lord's Supper, and ate together. Paul continued talking to them until dawn, and then he left. Meanwhile, the young man was taken home alive and well, and everyone was greatly relieved* (Acts 20:9 NLT).

In the following Scripture, Paul writes to the Galatians about the supply of the Spirit to meet the demands of the working of miracles by hearing with faith instead by the works of the law. The working of miracles is done through faith, not by works of the law, merit, or religious traditions. God is working miracles amid the Galatians by the Holy Spirit through the ordinary believers, not just through the apostles according to Galatians 3:5 (NKJV): *"Therefore He who supplies the Spirit to you and works miracles among you, does He do it by the works of the law, or by the hearing of faith?"* The answer to Paul's rhetorical question is obvious.

The Galatians had received the Holy Spirit when they were saved (Romans 8:9; 1 Corinthians 12:13; 1 John 3:24; 4:13), not through keeping the law, but through the saving faith granted to them when hearing the gospel. Faith comes by hearing and hearing by the word of God (Romans 10:17), and how can anyone hear unless there is a preacher, and how can anyone preach unless they are sent

(Romans 10:14-15). Therefore, I say that the gift of working of miracles comes by faith and faith activates miracles in the believer, so how can anyone do miracles unless they are filled by the Spirit.

In the New Testament, we can see the working of miracles in Paul's ministry where he was bitten by a snake, and the deadly poisonous venom miraculously did not harm him—he literally shook off the poison and was viewed as a god to the locals in that part of the world:

> *When Paul had gathered a bundle of sticks and put them on the fire, a viper came out because of the heat and fastened on his hand. When the native people saw the creature hanging from his hand, they said to one another, "No doubt this man is a murderer. Though he has escaped from the sea, Justice has not allowed him to live." He, however, shook off the creature into the fire and suffered no harm. They were waiting for him to swell up or suddenly fall down dead. But when they had waited a long time and saw no misfortune come to him, they changed their minds and said that he was a god* (Acts 28:3-6 ESV).

Paul was supposedly stoned to death and miraculously survived it—rising up as if nothing happened:

> *Then Jews from Antioch and Iconium came there; and having persuaded the multitudes, and they stoned Paul and dragged him out of the city, supposing him to be dead. However, when the disciples gathered around him, he rose up and went into the city. And the next day he departed with Barnabas to Derbe* (Acts 14:19-20 NKJV).

The partnership between the ministry of signs, wonders, and miracles and the ministers of the prophetic will ultimately cause unbelievers, and those uninformed who experience the power of prophecy, to be convinced, convicted, and converted according to First Corinthians 14:24-25 (NKJV):

> *But if all prophesy, and an unbeliever or an uninformed person comes in, he is convinced by all, he is convicted by all. And thus the secrets of his heart are revealed; and so, falling down on his face, he will worship God and report that God is truly among you.*

Prophecy is a sign to believers that God is in their midst and bring conviction upon unbelievers, leading them to repentance. Moreover, tongues are a sign to unbelievers. In other words, tongues or unknown tongues or the power by the Holy Spirit to speak in foreign or heavenly languages is a sign *not* to those who believe (believers) but to unbelievers (unlearned); prophesying is *not* for unbelievers but for those who believe (read and study 1 Corinthians 14).

THE AGES OF SIGNS, WONDERS, AND MIRACLES

The following twelve Scriptures reveal the Old Testament ministry of signs, wonders, and miracles in the prophets and fathers of old times:

1. Exodus 4:30, *"Aaron spoke all the words that the LORD had spoken to Moses and did the signs in the sight of the people."*

2. Exodus 7:3, *"But I will harden Pharaoh's heart, and though I multiply my signs and wonders in the land of Egypt."*

3. Exodus 7:10-12, *"So Moses and Aaron went to Pharaoh and did just as the LORD commanded. Aaron cast down his staff before Pharaoh and his servants, and it became a serpent. Then Pharaoh summoned the*

wise men and the sorcerers, and they, the magicians of Egypt, also did the same by their secret arts. For each man cast down his staff, and they became serpents. But Aaron's staff swallowed up their staffs."

4. Exodus 14:31, *"Israel saw the great power that the Lord used against the Egyptians, so the people feared the LORD, and they believed in the Lord and in his servant Moses."*

5. Deuteronomy 6:22, *"And the LORD showed signs and wonders, great and grievous, against Egypt and against Pharaoh and all his household, before our eyes."*

6. Deuteronomy 13:1-3, *"If a prophet or a dreamer of dreams arises among you and gives you a sign or a wonder, and the sign or wonder that he tells you comes to pass, and if he says, 'Let us go after other gods,' which you have not known, 'and let us serve them,' you shall not listen to the words of that prophet or that dreamer of dreams. For the LORD your God is testing you, to know whether you love the LORD your God with all your heart and with all your soul."*

7. Deuteronomy 34:11, *"And there has not arisen a prophet since in Israel like Moses, whom the LORD knew face to face, 11 none like him for all the signs and the wonders that the LORD sent him to do in the land of Egypt, to Pharaoh and to all his servants and to all his land,"*

8. Daniel 4:2, *"It has seemed good to me [Daniel] to show the signs and wonders that the Most High God has done for me."*

9. Daniel 6:27, *"He delivers and rescues; he works signs and wonders in heaven and on earth, he who has saved Daniel from the power of the lions."*

10. Psalm 77:14, *"You are the God who works wonders; you have made known your might among the peoples."*

11. Psalm 105:27, *"They performed his signs among them and miracles in the land of Ham."*

12. Isaiah 8:18, *"Behold, I and the children whom the Lord has given me are signs and portents in Israel from the LORD of hosts, who dwells on Mount Zion."*

THE ACTS OF SIGNS, WONDERS, AND MIRACLES

The following twelve key Scriptures, from the English Standard Version of the Bible, specifically in the book of Acts reveal the New Testament ministry of signs, wonders and miracles active in the ministry of the apostles and the believers:

1. Acts 1:8, *"But you will receive power* [miraculous power] *when the Holy Spirit has come upon you, and you will be my witnesses in Jerusalem and in all Judea and Samaria, and to the end of the earth."*

2. Acts 2:19, *"And I will show wonders in the heavens above and signs on the earth below, blood, and fire, and vapor of smoke."*

3. Acts 2:43, *"And awe came upon every soul, and many wonders and signs were being done through the apostles."*

4. Acts 3:16, *"And his name—by faith in his name—has made this man strong whom you see and know, and*

the faith that is through Jesus has given the man this perfect health in the presence of you all."

5. Acts 4:16, "saying, *"What shall we do with these men? For that a notable sign has been performed through them is evident to all the inhabitants of Jerusalem, and we cannot deny it."*

6. Acts 4:30, *"While you stretch out your hand to heal, and signs and wonders are performed through the name of your holy servant Jesus."*

7. Acts 5:12, *"Now many signs and wonders were regularly done among the people by the hands of the apostles. And they were all together in Solomon's Portico."*

8. Acts 6:8, *"And Stephen, full of grace and power, was doing great wonders and signs among the people."*

9. Acts 8:6, *"And the crowds with one accord paid attention to what was being said by Philip, when they heard him and saw the signs that he did."*

10. Acts 8:13, *"Even Simon himself believed, and after being baptized he continued with Philip. And seeing signs and great miracles performed, he was amazed."*

11. Acts 9:34, *"And Peter said to him, 'Aeneas, Jesus Christ heals you; rise and make your bed.' And immediately he rose."*

12. Acts 14:3, *"So they remained for a long time, speaking boldly for the Lord, who bore witness to the word of his grace, granting signs and wonders to be done by their hands."*

NEW TESTAMENT BELIEVERS—SIGNS
OF MIRACULOUS TONGUES

When the Day of Pentecost had fully come, they [120 disciples] *were all with one accord in one place. And suddenly there came a sound from heaven, as of a rushing mighty wind, and it filled the whole house where they were sitting. Then there appeared to them divided tongues* [different languages], *as of fire, and one* [distributed and rested] *sat upon each of them. And they were all filled with the Holy Spirit and began to speak with other tongues* [foreign languages], *as the Spirit gave them utterance* (Acts 2:1-4 NKJV).

The first miraculous sign and wonder of the church was done through 120 believers in the Upper Room at Pentecost. This supernatural phenomenon caused Jewish men—from multiple nations who came to Jerusalem—dumbfounded, baffled, and perplexed to hear these Galileans speak fluently in their own native language. They were speaking corporately the same message regarding the works of God.

The evidence of these tongues were simply a sign that after the Holy Spirit has come upon them they were empowered to do signs, wonders, and miracles. The tongues were clearly miraculous. This marked the saints as supernatural believers. The believer is given power when the Holy Spirit comes upon and dwells actively in them to manifest miraculous signs and wonders as evidence to unbelievers. The saints are marked with power.

But you will receive power [miracles] *and ability when the Holy Spirit comes upon you; and you will be My* [Jesus] *witnesses* [to tell people about Me] *both in Jerusalem and in all Judea, and Samaria, and even to the ends of the earth* (Acts 1:8 AMP).

The following verses give us a better understanding of the ministry of signs, wonders, and miracles and how it impacts people from different nations, cultures, beliefs, ideologies, and philosophies.

MARVELED TONGUES OF POWER

And there were dwelling in Jerusalem Jews, devout men, from every nation under heaven. And when this sound occurred, the multitude came together, and were confused, because everyone heard them speak in his own language. Then they were all amazed and marveled, saying to one another, "Look, are not all these who speak Galileans? And how is it that we hear, each in our own language in which we were born?" (Acts 2:5-8 NKJV)

"Parthians and Medes and Elamites, those dwelling in Mesopotamia, Judea and Cappadocia, Pontus and Asia, Phrygia and Pamphylia, Egypt and the parts of Libya adjoining Cyrene, visitors from Rome, both Jews and proselytes, Cretans and Arabs—we hear them speaking in our own tongues the wonderful works of God." So they were all amazed and perplexed, saying to one another, "Whatever could this mean?" Others mocking said, "They are full of new wine" (Acts 2:9-13 NKJV).

PROPHETIC KEY: The key to operating in signs, wonders, and miraculous healing and breakthroughs is exercising and praying continually in the Holy Spirit. Praying in the Spirit for hours in worship, in your devotion, and even when fasting and reading the Word will unlock unearthly powers that will release the glory. Your prayer language is heavenly and the source of the Spirit's power to the believer. It will also open you up to apostolic and prophetic revelation. It will cause you to see in and step synchronized with the frequency, current, and rhythm of the Spirit.

SUPERNATURAL ACTIVITIES

Supernatural activities are tailored to captivate the attention of people while provoking questions and an interest to discover and hunger to know God intimately through that experience. The supernatural creates a crash course with reality to try to comprehend things that are beyond our understanding. The ministry of signs and wonders is simply a ministry of the unexplainable.

Acts 2:5-12 stirs a number of mixed emotions such as:

1) *confused*, because everyone was hearing these unlearned and untrained Galileans speaking in their own language and native dialect (verse 6);

2) all were *amazed* and *marveled* at what they were seeing and hearing from ordinary Galileans without any specialized training, known to be society's lower class, poor, not scholarly or intellectuals, uneducated, and had no social status, rank, prestige or influence (verse 7);

3) *perplexed*, wondering and questioning what the miracle could mean (verse 12).

It is important for me to define the emotions of all those who witnessed the first sign and miraculous act of speaking in other (foreign) languages at Pentecost as the Spirit gave them the utterance or abilities. This is done to fully capture and comprehend their experience:

- *Confused, syncheo* means "to be bewildered or confounded, to be in an uproar or to disturb the mind of one, to stir up to tumult or outbreak."

- *Amazed, existemi* means "to throw out of position, displace or wonderment." It also can define as to being out of one's mind, insane, or completely astonished or astounded.
- *Marveled, thaumazo* means "to wonder, admire or marvel at the wonderful thing or with great admiration."
- *Perplexed, diaporeo* means "to be entirely at loss, to be in perplexity or in doubt."

We can see a picture of the cultural thinking regarding Galileans by the socially powerful scholars and influential and religious leaders according to the text in Acts 4:13 (NASB):

> *Now as they observed the confidence of Peter and John and understood that they were uneducated and untrained men, they were amazed, and began to recognize them as having been with Jesus.*

Those who genuinely walk in the supernatural are always or entirely misunderstood, mocked, challenged, or attacked by those who cannot wrap their minds and scholarships around extraordinary acts and works of God through ordinary people. The supernatural ministry of signs and wonders is not prejudice, racist, discriminatory, or bias. It is for all who are in Christ Jesus. It does not matter your background, intellectual prowess, education, ethnicity or race, gender, city, state or nation, economic or social status or where you attend church, just to name a few. If you are a genuine follower of Christ, you carry the ministry of signs and wonders by default and DNA spiritually by birthright of being born again from above (read John 3).

Healings and miracles are spectacular affirmations and attesting signs that God is alive. There are instances that miracles or healings were not always done and some were not healed according to the following example of Paul leaving when someone was still sick, *"Erastus remained at Corinth, but I left Trophimus sick at Miletus"* (2 Timothy 4:20 NASB). Trophimus was one of the Ephesians who traveled with Paul on his third apostolic mission (Acts 20:4). It is important to note for the purpose and integrity of this chapter and book, *Power Prophecy*, that there are cases in the mystery of God concerning healing that is part of the believer's inheritance (see Matthew 8:14-17). Sometimes we are not healed even when we walk closely with an apostle, prophet, or minister of signs and wonders or pray fervently in faith confessing the word of God.

The fact that Second Timothy 4:20 shows that Paul's close companion was not healed of his sickness shows this reality existed from the early eras of the church. However, such a fact is not inserted to discourage or as an introduction of doubt in the miracle-working power of our praying, preaching, and prophesying. Rather, it should encourage and stir us to press in and walk closer with the Lord even more into the ministry of signs, wonders, and miracles until the Scripture and others testify of our works—until like Jesus all who are touched are healed.

We as believers in Christ are called into the *ministry of signs, wonders, and miracles* according to the following Scripture passages that are listed for your perusal, study, and empowerment:

- Matthew 17:20
- Mark 16:17-20
- John 14:12
- Acts 3:6
- Acts 14:10
- Acts 16:18

- Acts 19:6
- Acts 28:8-9
- Romans 15:19
- 1 Corinthians 12:8-10
- 2 Corinthians 12:12

‖ 6 ‖

MEASURES OF PROPHETIC REVELATION

Surely the Lord God does nothing, unless He
reveals His secret to His servants the prophets.
—Amos 3:7 NKJV

We will not boast beyond our measure, but within
the measure of the domain which God assigned
to us as a measure, to reach even as far as you.
—2 Corinthians 10:13 NASB

The revelatory realm is the primary function of the prophet and prophetic people. In this book, *Power Prophecy,* it is important to explore the measurements of revelation by which prophets progressively receive as they operate in the power of God.

As a prophet, I would like to take you into the developmental and maturation stages of the office of the prophet. This chapter provides you with a simplified snapshot on how to grow and develop your own prophetic capacity and faculties in the prophetic that will manifest prophetic powers to unlock miracles, signs, and wonders. Every measure of prophetic revelation will introduce you to a new realm of the supernatural.

THE PROPHET'S MEASURE OF RULERSHIP

Prophets have been given an area or sphere of influence, a specific domain, a space of grace in the prophetic and measure of rule in their governmental office. This area or sphere of prophetic influence is called a *measure of rule*. It speaks to the limits of a prophet's authority. Prophets also have a *measure of revelation* that they walk in according to their area of authority, assignment, anointing, and appointment. Revelation is the primary grace by which the prophetic function. God does nothing without revelation with His servants the prophets (Amos 3:7).

Everything that a prophet does is simply within their measure of rule, authority, and revelation. Revelation is the standard of the prophetic that manifests all things that God intends to do according to heart, mind, will, and purpose. Revelation is progressive in a prophet's ministry. The more powerful the revelation, the more powerful the prophecy.

Prophet's cannot minister beyond their limit, grace and sphere of revelation. Some prophets try to prophesy outside or beyond their limited understanding and depth of the Word of God. This would be prophets overextending and overreaching prophetically in a realm of revelation that they have not matriculated and graduated to. Those who are not office prophets may try to prophesy or minister beyond the prophetic limitation of exhortation, encouragement, and comfort (1 Corinthians 14:3).

> *We, however, will not boast beyond measure, but within the limits of the sphere which God appointed us—a sphere which especially includes you. For we are not overextending ourselves (as though our authority did not extend to you), for it was to you that we came with the gospel of Christ* (2 Corinthians 10:13-14 NKJV).

The Christian Standard Bible says it clearly in the same verse: "We, however, will not boast beyond measure but according to the measure of the area of ministry that God has assigned to us, which reaches even to you."

Paul is simply saying that he will not boast beyond his proper limit, but will keep or stay within the limits of his commission to the Gentiles, which is the territory and area of authority God has granted to him as a measure. He was given apostolic authority and ministry to the Gentiles by God; in other words, ministry to the Gentiles, the non-Jews, was in Paul's lane to operate. His measure of rule or authority was within the confines of the Gentiles—the Gentiles were within his area of rule, authority, ministry, and jurisdiction. He had full apostolic jurisdiction to operate within those limits and boundaries. Likewise, this same revelation is applicable to the ministry of the prophet. Prophets are also given prophetic jurisdiction.

A good example of this is when a visiting or itinerant prophet is ministering under the authority of the senior or pastoral leadership, he or she must respect and honor the order of the house. The prophet is given full authority to function in his or her prophetic office only under the permission of the set leader of the house, no matter how much revelation the prophet sees in the spirit. The pastor can either limit or give the prophet full authority to speak into his or her respective congregation.

It is the pastoral responsibility to protect the sheep from ravenous, false, and abusive prophets. The more authority that the apostle or pastor gives the prophet, the more freedom for the prophetic release. Prophets must learn to respectfully walk in humility when ministering under authority, because in all honesty, the pastor has more authority than the prophet. When he or she ministers, the congregation will obey the voice of the prophet of the hour because they believe the prophet's character, ministry, and background was properly vetted or verified as genuine by the pastor. Unfortunately, some pastoral leaders subject the house and their sheep to under-developed, immature, false, greedy, and abusive prophets because of popularity rather than authentic power.

POWER OVER POPULARITY

In hindsight, Paul was addressing his opponents in Corinth who were questioning and challenging his apostolic authority as a genuine ambassador of Christ. They were trying to point out that Paul lacked impressive, dramatic, entertaining, or engaging presentation in his speaking compared to the secular Greek orators who prided themselves on the eloquence of speech according to the standards of the Greek rhetorical style (1 Corinthians 2:1-5).

In other words, they were not impressed with Paul's preaching style. Does that sound like some of our preachers today who compare themselves with other preachers because the style of preaching or homiletics (art of preaching) is not quite entertaining, in fact, they are boring. Most of these who ridiculed Paul's preaching were questioning his authority on the basis of eloquence of speech, not on the sheer exhibition of power. Some young preachers I have witnessed are excellent preachers, orators, and homilists, but lack exhibiting power.

Paul's mission was nothing more than to reach the Corinthians with the gospel of Christ. He boasted in the power of God in him and his apostolic team and God's power for the Corinthians through them. Eloquence and braggadocious preaching points are pointless if lacking God's power.

Although captivating speakers, there was no weight, depth, or authority behind those intellectual, empty words. We as prophets, due to our extraordinary communicative abilities as spokespeople, must not get into these kinds of self-promoting activities of who is the "best" or your "favorite" preacher or prophet. Many I know judge not by the authentically, tenure, creditability, and affirming signs, wonders, and miracles of genuine prophetic or apostolic ministries. Rather, as in Paul's example, they judge by the votes of the peers within an organization, church, ministry, stream, or social media "likes" or "hearts."

Paul was saying basically he was not in a speaking competition being judged and approved by peers. He did not class, rank, or compare himself with those who commend or congratulate themselves. His was not a popularity contest. It was foolish for him to attempt to respond to his unwise critics to even participate in measuring up to the standards of the Greek society in this manner. He said the Greek orators were measuring themselves by themselves or by their own standards and comparing themselves among themselves, which was clearly unwise.

Self-commendation on their part was foolish and pointless; and in fact, Paul says plainly they are unapproved by God: *"For it is not the one who commends himself who is approved, but the one whom the Lord commends"* (2 Corinthians 10:18).

Paul's approval came from God and he did not boast or brag outside of his sphere of influence; he stayed within the bounds and limits approved by God. He stayed in his lane. An office prophet has what I call a "prophetic lane." His or her lane is their area of operation. God has also given prophets a measure of rule to exercise. Each prophet has a specific or specialized calling and is sent with full authority to execute and exercise power.

For example, Jeremiah had measure of rule to function as an appointed prophet *over* nations and kingdoms (see Jeremiah 1:1-10). His prophetic commission and area of ministry operation was over nations and kingdoms. He was not just *called to* nations and kingdoms—his measure and level of authority gave him *charge over* them. This gives us a picture of the weight and capacity embodied in the officer of supernatural communication. He carried prophetic authority as a prophet over nations.

SIX REVELATORY MEASURES OF THE PROPHET

Let us examine each of the revelatory measurements of the power of the prophetic. There are six measures of the prophet's level of development and maturation in myriad degrees of revelations. The levels of prophetic revelation unlock the supernatural. The following are the 6M's of the *Prophet's Revelatory Development*:

1. Milk
2. Meat
3. Mystery
4. Mountain
5. Manifestation
6. Miracle

1. *Milk of Revelation*

> *For though by this time you ought to be teachers, you need someone to teach you again the first principles of the oracles of God; and you have come to need milk and not solid food* [meat]. *For everyone who partakes only of milk is unskilled in the word of righteousness, for he is a babe* (Hebrews 5:12-13 NKJV).

The milk of revelation represents those who are spiritually immature, those who are unskillful in the Word of God. When we were born again, we were regenerated into God's spiritual family as newborns or babes in Christ. Just like in the natural, infants need to be cared for and fed milk for their physical growth and development. Jesus Christ then instructed us to drink milk so that we could grow out of infancy into adolescence, and then finally adulthood. Unfortunately, there are believers who are late bloomers or those with stunted growth spiritually who prefer to remain babes in Christ for all of their Christian journey.

Hebrews 5:12-13 (NKJV) speaks about spiritual immaturity. Paul is addressing the lack of spiritual growth and slothful hearing when the believers should have grown in spiritual maturity so they could digest, comprehend, and ultimately teach deeper truths and oracles of God. However, instead of becoming teachers of the oracles or prophetic oracle of revelation, they still needed to be taught as babes on the fundamental and elementary spiritual principles in Christ (Hebrews 6:1 NKJV). Paul is dealing with the peril of these believers not progressing in their faith. One of the many characteristics of babes in Christ is that babes are *"unskilled in the word of righteousness,"* or the Word of God. The word *unskilled* also means inexperienced, unaccustomed, or unacquainted with the Word. Babes, therefore, are inexperienced at understanding deep spiritual truths; consequently, they cannot skillfully put God's Word to work effectively.

For example, there are Christians who can only understand the message of repentance from sin because they still need to be reminded that sin is destructive. That is their level of understanding. If you teach them deeper truths about the mysteries of Christ, it may sound like fables to them. This is one of the signs of spiritual infancy.

The Bible contains truths for babes (milk) and truths for the mature ones (meat). Hence, Hebrews 5:14 (NKJV) says, *"But solid food belongs to those who are of full age, that is, those who by reason of use have their senses exercised to discern both good and evil."* Paul is saying that more advanced teachings, or doctrines, are adaptable to the mature believer and discernible in their understanding of dissecting truth.

Mature believers' spiritual senses are exercised to the degree to be able to discriminate in their hearing sound and unsound doctrine. Prophetic senses as prophets are to be activated and regularly exercised. I explain further how to exercise and activate your five prophetic senses in my book *Realms of the Prophetic* in Chapter 17 titled "Prophetic Communications, Channels, and Conduits."

Eventually in our spiritual growth there should be a hunger not to remain in the same place spiritually as when we first started. As we grow and experience the supernatural, and more advanced spiritual matters as we become leaders, there will be an insatiable hunger for more. I know I had that hunger when I started out in the prophetic. I committed myself to grow exponentially in the Word of God—reading and studying the Bible—and in prayer. There were entire seasons when I spent literally eight hours or more studying and combing through Scripture learning the spiritual principles and disciples as a young prophetic voice called to be a prophet. I knew it would be vitally important as a young, new emerging or budding prophet at age eighteen to be able to rightly and accurately apply and skillfully handle the Word of God.

> *Study and do your best to present yourself to God approved, a workman [tested by trial] who has no reason to be ashamed, accurately handling and skillfully teaching the word of truth* (2 Timothy 2:15 AMP).

God's desire as a Father is for all His sons and daughters to grow spiritually, just as every earthly parent wants to see their child grow. Spiritual growth starts with hunger and passion to desire the sincere milk of the word so that you may grow in it and then start eating meat. The word *milk* in Greek is *gala,* which represents less difficult

Christian truth. It means that someone who is on the milk of the Word has the ability to understand lesser Bible truths. The milk of the Word is not difficult to understand. It is easier, a beginner level of comprehension of spiritual truths.

Moreover, milk spiritually represents good nourishment, elementary teaching and understanding. This the elementary development stage of the prophet. Milk is also symbolic of foundation food, which is the first principle for the young (see 1 Corinthians 3:2; Hebrews 5:12-13 and 1 Peter 2:2). Growing in the capacity and consumption of God's Word, the Bible, is the most important part of an emerging prophet. He or she must be immersed in the Word. The Word and the prophet must become one. The messenger and the message must become inseparable.

Babes in the Prophetic

The prophet will be fed with fundamental revelation of the Word of God. He or she would be considered a babe in Christ or in the infancy stage of his prophetic ministry. This is the budding stage of the prophet office. The revelation and release of prophetic utterance will not be meaty or with substance. Prophets in this stage of their prophetic ministry are considered "budding prophets." Prophets in this stage of their spiritual development must stay intimately close and in the written Word of God, the Scriptures, just as it is important for a natural babe to stay close to the mother for nourishment and to development physically. It is critically imperative in this stage of prophetic development to attend a school of the prophet or get under the tutelage of a senior or master prophet (see 1 Samuel 19:18-24).

Schools, guilds, and companies of prophets were established by Samuel as training institutions for preparing students to become the voice of God to the people. Essentially, these institutions were to train people to hear the voice of God by learning how to minister with the Holy Spirit and allow His power to flow through them to those who need to hear God's voice. Historically, in Israel the school of the prophet was a society of prophets who were under the leadership of Samuel as their prophetic or spiritual father (1 Samuel 19:20).

Prophetic Mastery

The company of prophets were under the tutelage or charge of Samuel the "master" prophet. The word *master* or *mastery* means "having or showing very great skill or proficiency." *Mastery* is the acquirement of complete knowledge or skill in an accomplishment, technique, profession, field or art according to the Merriam-Webster Dictionary.

A master is an expert or has an expertise in an area of occupation, profession, or art. Samuel as a master prophet was not a celebrated title, it was an honor conferred on him for being nothing more than a senior prophet who had a school of prophets or disciples under his disciplines.

Again, a master prophet is simply a senior prophet with comprehensive knowledge or skill in the prophetic. Many today in various schools of thought, streams, and religious organizations have made such a fuss or stir over the term or title "master prophet" being used for prophets today. I have heard some argue that it is not a biblical title used for prophet; but there are a number of biblical references historically to prove that the sons of the prophets understood clearly what the title master meant honorably. It was a title or honor or respect of position similar to a doctor, or better yet a master martial artist.

The word *sensei* is Japanese and means teacher. A master in martial arts is a senior teacher. The title used to describe or address a senior or experienced martial artist. Typically, such titles as Master or Grandmaster are honorific in nature, meaning that they do not infer rank, but rather distinguishes the individual as very highly revered and respected in their school, system, or style. This honorific title of master is a distinguishable honor used for a senior or most experienced prophet in rank, office, and position.

As a Samuel-type prophet for my generation, it is my responsibility to reintroduce and reinstitute sound biblical truth in light of history pertaining to all things prophetic. The word "master" was used primarily by prophetic students or disciples under the provost, chancellorship, and scholarship. They were understudies of prophetic of higher learning. These pedagogy received extraordinary prophetic education, which is key to becoming teachers as disciples. In retrospect, Paul was essentially saying students should now become teachers. Disciples should develop into becoming masters. Paul was confirming Jesus's words when He said, *"The student is not above the teacher, but everyone who is fully trained will be like their teacher"* (Luke 6:40 NIV).

The Douay-Rheims Bible rendition of the same verse reads, *"The disciple is not above his master: but every one shall be perfect, if he be as his master."* In other words, the word *master* speaks relatively of someone who carries advanced knowledge, skill, and experience that is needed for the prophetic development of those who desire to grow powerfully in the ministry of the prophetic.

The following are a few examples of the company of the prophets calling their senior prophet, who they are under, "master":

> *And the sons of the prophets who were in Bethel came out to Elisha and said to him, "Do you know that today the Lord will take away your master from over you?" And he said, "Yes, I know it; keep quiet"* (2 Kings 2:3 ESV).

Elisha was successor, provost, and in charge of the sons of the prophets:

Now the sons of the prophets said to Elisha, "See, the place where we dwell under your charge is too small for us. Let us go to the Jordan and each of us get there a log and let us make a place for us to dwell there." And he answered, "Go." Then one of them said, "Be pleased to go with your servants." And he answered, "I will go." So he went with them. And when they came to the Jordan, they cut down trees. But as one was felling a log, his axe head fell into the water, and he cried out, "Alas, my master! It was borrowed." Then the man of God said, "Where did it fall?" When he showed him the place, he cut off a stick and threw it in there and made the iron float. And he said, "Take it up." So he reached out his hand and took it (2 Kings 6:2-7 ESV).

Consider the calling of Jeremiah as a prophet; he felt an inadequacy to speak for God duly because of his youth in Jeremiah 1:6 (ESV): *"Then I said, "Ah, Lord God! Behold, I do not know how to speak, for I am only a youth."*

The word *youth* in the Hebrew in this context is not referring to his chronological age, but his inexperience to be a prophet. He felt that he did not meet the qualification to be a prophetic voice and spokesman on behalf of God. Like Moses (Exodus 3:4), Jeremiah claimed inadequacy and inexperience (youth in the office), but God provided him with creditability, support, and His presence:

But the LORD said to me: "Do not say, 'I am a youth,' for you shall go to all to whom I send you, and whatever I command you, you shall speak. Do not be afraid of their faces, for I am with you to deliver you," says the LORD (Jeremiah 1:7-8).

In prophetic development there will be times when you will feel inadequate, but God will be with you and will have anointed your mouth to speak for Him no matter how inexperienced you are. God will accelerate your development and set you over nations and kingdoms in a moment as an established prophet without thirty or forty years of training (Jeremiah 1:9-10). It is critically important during this phase of the journey as a prophet to continue to feed on the Scripture through reading, studying, meditating, and reciting the written Word of God, the Bible. There must be insatiable hunger and thirst for the Word.

Prophets must fall in love with the Word of God, which exponentially causes them to grow in revelation and in understanding the Scriptures. It is recommended that at this stage to get into an excellent Bible study or Bible-teaching church and use study materials such as a concordance, Bible dictionaries, study Bibles, etc. The strength of the prophetic anointing increases as the prophet increases the level of understanding of the Word of God.

Babes in Christ, Newborn Revelation (Carnality)

And I, brethren, could not speak to you as to spiritual people but as to carnal, as to babes in Christ. I fed you with milk and not with solid food [meat]; *for until now you were not able to receive it, and even now you are still not able"* (1 Corinthians 3:1-2 NKJV).

Newborn Babes

Therefore, laying aside all malice, all deceit, hypocrisy, envy, and all evil speaking, as newborn babes, desire the pure milk of the word, that you may grow thereby, if indeed you have tasted that the Lord is gracious (1 Peter 2:1-3 NKJV).

PROPHETIC KEY: The key to unlocking and accessing prophetic revelation is to grow in the knowledge of the Word of God. Continue to drink, eat, and feed your spirit with the Scriptures and understanding the Gospels of Jesus Christ and study intensively the book of Acts. Understanding the elementary doctrines will build a strong Word foundation and base in you. This causes you to matriculate exponentially through schools of the prophetic thoughts to operate at higher degrees in prophetic operations. Revelation is cultivated and developed in the Word that creates a strong foundation as a prophetic minister. The stronger your Word level, the more potent your administration of power. God backs up His Word.

2. Meat of Revelation

The word *meat* in the Greek is *broma,* which means what is eaten, or food. Meat represents spiritual maturity. It also means strong doctrine or teaching. Meat is the second developmental stage of the prophet revelation. Prophets at this stage have grown up past the milk and elementary principles and doctrine of the Word to a more advanced level of understanding of the Word of God. They have matriculated into a higher level of revelation of the Scriptures. They are now hungry for more meat (substance) of the Word. These will minister in strong doctrinal teaching and have greater depth and understanding of the hard doctrines.

This stage of the prophetic office enables the prophet or prophetess to grasp and comprehend the Scripture. The Spirit will open their minds to understand Scriptures. Prophets who function in this realm of revelation will become inspired expounders and interpreters of the prophetic Scriptures in the Word of God. Strong meat is for spiritually and prophetically mature prophets who can skillfully and rightly divide—dissect or breakdown—the word of truth (see 2 Timothy 2:15).

Prophets in this stage have become studious and have studied to show themselves approved to God as prophetic workers who are not ashamed of their valuable time spent dissecting revelation in the Scriptures. The following are some "meat" Scriptures found in the Bible: John 4:34; 6:27; Psalm 42:3; 1 Corinthians 3:2; 10:3; Hebrews 5:12-14; Job 6:7; 20:14. I encourage you to seriously study and digest them.

Prophets are fed the meat of the Word of God that is strong enough and digestible. This level of revelation is to mature and help grow up the church. Some of what is released, preached, taught, and prophesied is not readily received or understood by everyone. They carry weighty words and they walk heavy in meaty revelation. It will satisfy the palates of the hungry. New Testament prophets' food (meat) is to do the will of the Christ and to finish His work: *"Jesus said to them, 'My food* [meat] *is to do the will of Him who sent Me, and to finish His work'"* (John 4:34 NKJV).

At this stage of their prophetic development, mature prophets will begin to exercise their spiritual senses, which is key to building spiritual muscle and power. Prophets must exercise their prophetic senses that sharpen not only their prophetic or spiritual senses but also their prophetic gifts. Exercise builds stamina, muscles, endurance, and strength. Meat is the protein of God's Word that builds muscle that equals strength and power. This stage is the exercising and putting into practice the Word of God.

Mature prophets eat the meat of the words that give them strength to discern accurately what they see, hear, taste, touch, and smell in the spirit. They are able to recognize and identify both good and evil— angelic and demonic activities.

Growth and Development—Maturity

In fact, though by this time you ought to be teachers, you need someone to teach you the elementary truths of God's word all over again. You need milk, not solid food! Anyone who lives on milk, being still an infant, is not acquainted with the teaching about righteousness. But solid food [meat] is for the mature, who by constant use have trained themselves to distinguish good from evil (Hebrews 5:12-14 NIV).

PROPHETIC KEY: The key in this stage is to now study more advanced Scriptures and learn how to digest and interpret sacred letters. Accurately and contextually study and interpret the Scriptures. What is the most important key in this stage is to now put into practice, live, and become not just a student of the Word but a practitioner of the Word. It is being a living epistle (2 Corinthians 3:1-3). This is going from a disciple of the Word of God, to minister, to ultimately becoming a master teacher.

3. *Mystery of Revelation*

The word *mystery* in the Greek is *mysterion,* which means a secret that comes from the idea to shut the mouth or hold a secret or the idea of silence. Mystery is a hidden thing or secret that is confided only to the initiated and not ordinary mortals. It is something that is not obviously understood. Prophets in this stage of revelation will receive hidden purposes or counsel of God. They will function in the realm of God counseling them with regard to His dealing with the affairs of His church, people, and the wicked.

In rabbinic writings, mystery denotes the mystic or hidden sense of an Old Testament saying or of an image or form seen in a vision.

Prophets will have a revelation of the image or form seen in a vision by the Spirit. The mystery of revelation is given to the prophet as his or her revelation is being developed in a vision, sense, or dream.

Prophets in this stage of prophetic measures of revelation will be given access to know intimately and by experience, the mysteries of the realms of God's rule. This is the unlocking of not only prophecies in the prophet, but also comprehension of mysteries. God will give prophets revelatory knowledge of the mystic or mysteries. Prophets will be known to some as mystics or mystical in essence. The realm of knowing mysteries of the Kingdom of Heaven (heavenly things) would be accessible to prophets of God into God's absolute power, and they will be able to minister in the mysteries of God and dispense it in the church.

> *He answered and said to them, "Because it has been given to you to know the mysteries of the kingdom of heaven, but to them it has not been given"* (Matthew 13:11 NKJV).

Prophets will have the ability by the spirit to see, hear, and understand parabolic, symbolic, and prophetic revelations. God will unlock and decode by revelation the realm of understanding parables and mysteries of God:

> *And He* [Jesus] *said, "To you it has been given to know the mysteries of the kingdom of God, but to the rest it is given in parables, that 'Seeing they may not see, and hearing they may not understand"* (Luke 8:10 NKJV).

Prophets in the mystery of revelation of their development will be able to understand various writings, literature, and hidden truths in the Holy Scriptures. This is similar to Daniel the prophet having the power and ability to interpret, understand, and comprehend the mysterious handwriting of God on the wall (read Daniel 5). Daniel-type prophets emerge and excel in this stage of revelation to minister to kings—powerful leaders—on earth.

These prophets will minister in global stages and arenas with presidents, prime ministers, heads of states, and governors what is the mind of God regarding their country, nation, or people.

Prophets are stewards of the mysteries of God. They will manage various revelations of God.

Faithfulness is a quality found in a prophet in this stage who is a proven voice to serve as a minister of the mysteries of Christ. God trusts prophets at this stage with secret, hidden, and incomprehensible things. Stewardship and faithfulness are qualifiers at this stage of prophetic development. Can God trust us with this measure of revelatory knowledge as stewards of mysteries?

> *This, then, is how you ought to regard us: as servants of Christ and as those entrusted with the mysteries God has revealed. Now it is required that those who have been given a trust must prove faithful* (1 Corinthians 4:1-2 NIV).

It is important to reveal that the gift of prophecy at this level takes on a revised and redefined meaning. It is not just words of edification, exhortation, and comfort, or simply receiving divinely inspired messages (1 Corinthians 12:7-10; 14:3-4, 24-25)—now it is the comprehensive knowledge of the mysteries.

It progresses from a miraculous special act and ability of intelligible communication, rooted in spontaneous, divine revelation that is empowered by the Holy Spirit—and moves into understanding all mysteries and all knowledge that can by faith move mountains:

> *And though I have the gift of prophecy, and understand all mysteries and all knowledge, and though I have all faith,*

so that I could remove mountains, but have not love, I am nothing (1 Corinthians 13:2 NKJV).

The realm of unlocking revelatory understanding and speaking to mountains and things by faith is the prophet's ability to speak prophetically by faith and see things obey—like Jesus speaking the impossible such as rebuking the wind and silencing the sea (see Mark 4:39).

Speaking and Receiving Mysteries—Secret Communication

For anyone who speaks in a tongue does not speak to people but to God. Indeed, no one understands them; they utter mysteries by the Spirit (1 Corinthians 14:2 NIV).

Prophets are given an ability to explain mysteries in a way that people can understand their revelatory knowledge of mysteries revealed in their age; God has given them by the dispensation of grace to impart revelation at this stage.

For this reason I, Paul, the prisoner of Christ Jesus for you Gentiles—if indeed you have heard of the dispensation of the grace of God which was given to me for you, how that by revelation He made known to me the mystery (as I have briefly written already, by which, when you read, you may understand my knowledge in the mystery of Christ) (Ephesians 3:1-4 NKJV).

A prophet's prayer in this stage of prophetic revelation will open doors of utterance to speak the mysteries. Prophets pray that God will give them doors of opportunity to speak and share the mysteries of Christ and that they may manifest it as they release it. Prophets will manifest the mysteries of God with powerful and convincing utterances and speech. Prophets will discern the right doors to share the revelation of the mysteries given to them by the Spirit of Christ.

Continue earnestly in prayer, being vigilant in it with thanksgiving; meanwhile praying also for us, that God would open to us a door for the word, to speak the mystery of Christ, for which I am also in chains, that I may make it manifest, as I ought to speak (Colossians 4:2-4 NKJV).

The following are a few more biblical examples of how prophets and prophetic ministers who have progressed in their prophetic maturation minister in different mysteries of revelation:

1. Prophets will understand the mystery of godliness of God that manifested in the flesh of Jesus Christ. Moving in the realm of the revelation of Christ and ministering about Him in light of Scripture: *"And without controversy great is the mystery of godliness: God was manifested in the flesh, justified in the Spirit, seen by angels, preached among the Gentiles, believed on in the world, received up in glory"* (1 Timothy 3:16 NKJV).

2. Prophets are ministers, messengers, and voices of the mystery of God: *"But in the days of the sounding of the seventh angel, when he is about to sound, the mystery of God would be finished, as He declared to His servants the prophets"* (Revelation 10:7 NKJV).

3. Prophets are spokespeople of the mystery of hidden wisdom of the ages: *"But we speak the wisdom of God in a mystery, the hidden wisdom which God ordained before the ages for our glory"* (1 Corinthians 2:7 NKJV).

4. Prophets have made known about God's purposes through the mystery of God's will: *"Having*

made known to us the mystery of His will, according to His good pleasure which He purposed in Himself" (Ephesians 1:9).

PROPHETIC KEY: Exercise your spiritual and prophetic senses (Hebrews 5:12-14) and practice using your prophetic gift. One way I strengthened my prophetic gifts was by faith I began to use them often and exercised them by continually prophesying. I would look for opportunities and pray that God would open doors of utterance to minister in personal prophecy. The more I was faithful in ministering prophetic words, impressions, visions, dreams, and inspired revelation to people or the church, the more God gave me more revelation. When you are faithful over a few, God will make you ruler of over much (Matthew 25:23). Prophetic faithfulness developed into prophetic rulership, prophetic authority (Luke 19:17). Find a place or a prophet you can serve in order for your prophetic gifts to be used and sharpened (Proverbs 27:17). Continue to serve and steward your prophetic gift and revelation. Faith in your faithfulness will elevate and unlock mountain-moving power.

4. *Mountain of Revelation*

The word *mountain* in the Greek is *oros,* which is an elevated place, high place, hill, or a place above or raised from the ground. A mountain represents spiritually a place of great power, authority and strength, whether good or bad. It can speak to majesty, stability, and a realm. The Kingdom of God, satan, or man can represent mountain. In other words, a mountain represents the Kingdom, a place of revelation or meeting with God or God's glory. A mountain can also mean an obstacle or difficulty. Importantly, a mountain symbolically and spiritually represents something *impossible*. It is the realm of the impossible from where someone can function.

Prophets in the Scripture found a commonplace in and on the mountains with regard to Moses, Elijah, and Jesus—all of whom operated in the realm of the supernatural power of signs, wonders, and miracles. We will discover that mountains were a place where prophets and even eagles—symbols of prophets—live in mountainous places. Moses was even hidden in the cleft of the mountain. Mountain is the realm of prayer for the office of the prophet. This stage of the prophetic revelation is where the prophet gains powerful revelations of God in this place.

It is interesting that when Saul was freshly anointed as the first king of Israel, he was instructed by the prophet Samuel to go and meet a guild or company of prophets at a high place or elevated place of worship. At once, Saul comes into contact with this company of prophets who were ministering with musical instruments and prophesying that he would be turned into another man.

Prophets of Transformation

> *...After that you will go to Gibeah of God, where there is a Philistine outpost. As you approach the town, you will meet a procession of prophets coming down from the high place* [hill] *with lyres, timbrels, pipes and harps being played before them, and they will be prophesying. The Spirit of the LORD will come powerfully upon you, and you will prophesy with them; and you will be changed into a different person* (1 Samuel 10:5-6 NIV).

Prophets will learn in this stage of their prophetic development how to change the atmosphere, spiritual climates, environments, and even alter the spiritual habitations. Prophetic worship is the most powerful component learned in this stage where what prophets receive in obscurity, hiding, or in secret with God on the mountain, hill, or high place, they will have the power to release and impart to others. The mountain is the place of the impossible and downloads. In other words, prophets on the mountain of revelation have the heavenly downloads, glory, and power to direct the very trajectory and existence of humanity.

The following are examples of prophets receiving mountain revelation:

- Abraham had an appearance and a number of visitations of the Lord on a mountain (Genesis 22:14).

- Moses received the pattern, blueprint, and heavenly template of the Tabernacle on the mountain. He also received the Ten Commandments or Edicts and revelation of the visible face and presence of the glory of God. Moses's countenance was telling and revealed that he was in the face of God (Exodus 25:40; 34:29-35; Hebrews 8:5).

- Elijah encountered the small, still voice of God on the mountain regarding the wind, earthquake, and fire of God (1 Kings 19:11-18). The mantle of Elijah produced revelation where the prophet needed not to see, feel, or smell the next move of God, but to hear revelation. The mantle wrapped around his face was full of revelation. The mantle of the prophet on the mountain awakened God's still small voice for the prophet to be a voice of revelation, not just in the outwardly manifestations of God.

- Jesus withdrew Himself a number of times to pray to God the Father in the wilderness, lonely places but definitely on the mountain. He chose and selected His apostles by revelation from a mountain (Matthew 14:23; Luke 5:15-16; 6:12-13; Mark 3:13; 6:46; Mark 3:13-19). The more you stay on the mountain spiritually with God, the more you will come from that high place with revelatory healing and deliverance (see Luke 6:12-19). The mountain of revelation caused Jesus to come down out of the place with renewed strength and power to heal and deliver the multitude. This is symbolic of believers who mount up with wings as eagles for renewal of strength as they wait on the Lord (Isaiah 40:31).

- Moses and Elijah were included in the visitation of Jesus on the mountain when Peter, James, and John saw the revelation of Jesus transfigured before them (Mark 9:2).

We need prophets who will dwell in the high place of worship, fellowship, and communion with God. Heavenly things are imparted in this realm of revelation spiritually. God is calling mountain climber and mountaineer prophets who will ascend the hill of God to hear from a higher realm. Psalm 24:3 (NLT) declares, *"Who may climb the mountain of the LORD? Who may stand in his holy place?"* The English Standard Version says it this way, *"Who shall ascend the hill of the LORD? And who shall stand in his holy place?"*

Prophets at this stage of revelation will have continual or frequent unexplainable visions with Christ. There will be heightened levels of visions, dreams, and prophetic revelation (read Numbers 12:6; Joel 2:26-32; Acts 2:15-21).

Mountain of Transfiguration—Revelation of Glory

In the Bible, God's presence is often shown by the cloud and fire. Mountaintops, peaks, or pinnacles were often the preferential choice for appearances of God. The special literal manifestation of the cloud or fire was called *shekinah* in Hebrew. Prophets will receive more revelation knowledge in the presence and glory of God on the mountain (high place of worship) as did Moses (Numbers 11:25 and Deuteronomy 5:22). In the New Testament, an example of the voice of God spoke out of the cloud on the mountain in Matthew 17:5:

> *Now after six days Jesus took Peter, James, and John his brother, led them up on a high mountain by themselves; and He was transfigured before them. His face shone like the sun, and His clothes became as white as the light. And behold, Moses and Elijah appeared to them, talking with Him. ...Now as they came down from the mountain, Jesus commanded them, saying, "Tell the vision to no one until the Son of Man is risen from the dead"* (Matthew 17:1-3,9).

The word *transfiguration* in Greek is *metamorphoo,* and is where we get the English word *metamorphosis*, which means "to transform, change of form or appearance." Jesus's appearance change on the mountain was a glimpse of revelation to the three disciples into the genuine essence and glory of Jesus as God in the flesh. Jesus's, similar to Moses's, face shined like the sun and His clothes became white as the light.

Prophets are changed, transformed, and transfigured when they encounter the very presence or literal visitation or appearance of Christ in a vision. Experiencing the tangible glory and presence of God causes alterations of your very existence and your life. The glory of God causes a metamorphosis. On this mountain, the selected disciples had revelation of transformation. Power prophecy has transformative revelation in its prophetic release.

Prophets who minister from the glory of God have power in their prophecy that brings literal transformation. Just as a caterpillar goes through various stages of transformation. This stage of revelation on the mountain will have to be processed in the presence and glory of God before it is released to the multitudes because of the measure and depth of insight.

Moses and Elijah both met God on Mount Sinai where one received the Law and other received the prophetic inner voice of God. Both visited Jesus on the Mount of Transfiguration believing and passing on all of the Law and the Prophets of the Old Testament to be fulfilled in the greater Moses and in the spirit and power of Elijah in the Person of Jesus Christ.

Jesus was building His church and raising up a new race and prophets of new glory. Jesus's disciples—Peter, James, and John—were so in awe at the glory of Moses and Elijah that was revealed in their sight that they didn't know what to do, and asked Jesus to build three tabernacles for all three of them (Matthew 17:4). They failed to understand that the glory will be *in* them as glory carriers.

The glory of Moses of the Old Testament was fading away (see 2 Corinthians 3:13-18). The following is the passing of the mantle and baton of the Old Testament to Jesus on the Mount Transfiguration according to Matthew 5:17-18 (NKJV):

> *Do not think that I came to destroy the Law or the Prophets. I did not come to destroy but to fulfill. For assuredly, I say to you, till heaven and earth pass away, one jot or one tittle will by no means pass from the law till all is fulfilled.*

- Moses—the Law
- Elijah—the Prophets
- Jesus—the fulfillment of the Law and the Prophets and the introduction of the New Testament

Prophetic Intercession

Prophets at this stage of prophetic development will teach the prophet the power of prayer and intercession that will increase their faith in God, manifest the impossible, and equip the prophetic in the supernatural and spiritual warfare. Prophetic intercession is the foundation of the prophet's ministry, and this stage teaches an advanced measure of praying from a realm of power and authority. It is praying from heavenly places seated in Christ that produce revelatory answers and solutions for churches, cities, regions, states, countries, and nations.

The following is the mountain of prophetic intercession where it is not ground or surface-level intercession; rather it is high-level praying on the behalf of God's will being done on earth as it presides in the heavens (Matthew 6:10-13).

1. Speak to the Mountain (Doubtless Praying): *"So Jesus answered and said to them, 'Have faith in God. For assuredly, I say to you, whoever says to this mountain, "Be removed and be cast into the sea," and does not doubt in his heart, but believes that those things he says will be done, he will have whatever he says. Therefore I say to you, whatever things you ask when you pray, believe that you receive them, and you will have them'"* (Mark 11:22-24 NKJV).

2. Nothing Will Be Impossible (These Kinds by Prayer and Fasting): *"So Jesus said to them, 'Because of your unbelief; for assuredly, I say to you, if you have faith as a mustard seed, you will say to this mountain, "Move from here to there," and it will move; and nothing will be impossible for you. However, this kind does not go out except by prayer and fasting'"* (Matthew 17:20-21 NKJV).

3. Mountain of Prayer and Intercession (Isolated Place to Pray to God): *"And when He had sent the multitudes away, He* [Jesus] *went up on the mountain by Himself to pray. Now when evening came, He was alone there"* (Matthew 14:23 NKJV).

Prophets will be given divine revelations, and God will use them to help the church understand the original plan of God and to come alongside senior leadership and apostles to encourage them not to deviate from the prophetic revelation that was given to them on the mountain, as in like manner God did with Moses.

4. Blueprints, templates, and patterns on the mountain are given to prophets:

Who serve the copy and shadow of the heavenly things, as Moses was divinely instructed when he was about to make the tabernacle. For He said, "See that you make all things according to the pattern shown you on the mountain" (Hebrews 8:5 NKJV).

And see to it that you make them according to the pattern which was shown you on the mountain (Exodus 25:40 NKJV).

5. Written Revelation and Commandments of God: *"Then the LORD said to Moses, 'Come up to Me* [God] *on the mountain and be there; and I will give you tablets of stone, and the law and commandments which I have written, that you may teach them'"* (Exodus 24:12 NKJV).

Elijah's contention and warfare with false prophets on Mount Carmel is part of the revelation of how to defeat false prophetic operations on the mountain. God gave His prophet exactly what to do as Elijah tore down faulty prophetic and prayer altars and repaired the altar of God to get answered prayers and manifestation of the glory of God by fire. The spiritual warfare mountain and keys to victory in the realm of the prophetic are revealed in First Kings 18:16-45.

Revelation regarding the plans, secrets, counsels, and purposes of God comes to us through prayer. Jesus gained that revelation when He went to a deserted place to pray (Luke 4:42-43). Peter went up on the housetop to pray while being very hungry, and there he fell into a trance and saw Heaven opened and God gave him revelation about his impartiality (see Acts 10:9-20).

Jesus left the multitudes that gathered to be healed by Him, and most of the signs, wonders, and miracles came as result of His revelation of prayers in different places according to the following verses:

- Matthew 14:23—mountain
- Mark 1:34-35—solitary place
- John 6:2-3—mountain
- John 6:15—mountain
- Luke 5:15-16—wilderness
- Luke 9:10—deserted place

PROPHETIC KEY: The most powerful keys to unlocking the mountain of revelation to do the impossible in this stage and see the manifestation of God are worship, fellowship, and prayer. You have to spend quality time in the presence of God in the word, prayer, and in worship. I have spent literally hours—almost all day and night—praying and worshipping in the spirit. I would have the most powerful dreams, visions, and encounters with the glory by experience. Luke 6:12 (NKJV) says,

"Now it came to pass in those days that He [Jesus] *went out to the mountain to pray, and continued all night in prayer to God."*

This is where prophets are trained and taught prophetic intercession and how to pray Heaven down by way of manifesting the glory and their revelation. The key is to build an altar, after which you will learn keys to release and manifest your prayers, power, and prophecy. Elijah spent time in prayer first before he was released to prophesy to Ahab and Jezebel. Prayer births the power of manifestation in the ministry of the prophet, intercessor, or believer. Prayer and worship are the most powerful keys, tools, and weaponry of the prophetic.

5. *Manifestation of Revelation*

The word *manifest* in Greek is *phaneroo,* which means "to render apparent, appearance and manifestly declare." It means to make visible or known what has been hidden or unknown whether by words, deeds, or in any other way. This realm of the prophet's revelation is to manifest what is hidden or make known through their teaching or preaching. They unlock what is hidden in the Scriptures that is not easily seen. Hidden truths and pearls in Scripture are being exposed and revealed. Prophets in the office will plainly and thoroughly understand the unknown. Prophets operate in the realm of manifestation. There are revelations that bring manifestations of God. Revelation is what causes manifestation of the supernatural (see Ephesians 1:17-23).

This stage of prophetic revelation is when prophets will move in manifesting their revelation. Prophets at this level will not speak or communicate revelation, but will demonstrate what they speak.

You will see their words of prophecy literally become flesh or take on form and shape—*prophetic manifestation.*

Prophets in the measure of manifestation of revelation will know how to operate and excel in the gifts of the Spirit. For whatever situation, the prophetic officer will know how to exercise and activate what manifestation of the Spirit is necessary to accomplish the assignment. Revelation requires corresponding action. Most all miracles in the Bible required action from the recipient.

Without revelation prophetically, it becomes difficult to release the manifestation of a thing revealed. We as believing sons and daughters of God must move from a place of personal revelation to corporate manifestation. Whatever is secret or hidden will be manifested and revealed; whatever is concealed will be disclosed (Luke 8:17 and Matthew 10:26). Prophets at this stage will know and understand their specific manifestation gifts and will manage them properly for the common good and not for self-gain.

Consider the following two biblical references when you move into the measure of manifestation:

1. Manifestation of the Spirit: *"But the manifestation of the Spirit is given to each one for the profit of all"* (1 Corinthians 12:7 NKJV).

2. Each person's work will manifest: *"Each one's work will become clear* [manifest]*; for the Day will declare it, because it will be revealed by fire; and the fire will test each one's work, of what sort it is"* (1 Corinthians 3:13 NKJV).

Prophets will manifest the works of Christ to counter, nullify, ward, push back darkness, and ultimately destroy the works of the devil. They will understand their full purpose as prophets, as this stage of revelation exposes the works of the devil and converts those to repentance. The Son of Man was manifested to destroy the works of the devil:

> *He who sins is of the devil, for the devil has sinned from the beginning. For this purpose the Son of God was manifested* [revealed], *that He might destroy the works of the devil* (1 John 3:8 NKJV).

Prophets at this stage will manifest the works of God through the ministry of signs, wonders, and miracles. This level of revelation is the training stage for teaching the prophet how to manifest what they see in the invisible realm. They learn how to understand and diagnose what is the root issue or the origin in order to manifest the healing. In the manifestation of revelation stage, a prophet practices how to display miracles. This is the stage before the last stage of the prophetic measures of revelation—*miracles of revelation.*

The works (miracles) of God are to be manifested for the glory of God through the prophet's ministry: *"Jesus answered, 'Neither this man nor his parents sinned, but that the works of God should be revealed* [manifested, displayed] *in him'"* (John 9:3 (NKJV).

Prophets in the office of the prophetic are given secrets and the counsel of God according to Amos 3:7; this stage teaches him or her how to manifest or make known or reveal secret or hidden things. A key function of prophets is to manifest secret or hidden things. These types of prophets are revealers of the secrets of people's hearts.

Secrets and hidden things are manifested: *"For nothing is secret, that shall not be made manifest; neither any thing hid, that shall not be known and come aboard"* (Luke 8:17 KJV).

Heart secrets are manifested by the prophets: *"And thus the secrets of his heart are revealed* [made manifest]*; and so, falling down on his* *face, he will worship God and report that God is truly among you"* (1 Corinthians 14:25 NKJV).

In the manifestation of the revelation stage, God will manifest Himself to prophets by various visual, audible, direct revelation, visitations, and/or theophanies (appearance). They will experience all sorts of prophetic encounters and manifestations of God in this stage of their revelatory development. In their meetings, others will see and experience encounters with the prophet. In fact, prophets at this stage will walk in a ministry of manifestations. People will recognize these are prophets of God because God is with them.

This level of revelation will lend the power to invoke manifestations of the presence and glory of God. The mark of these prophets will be the Presence—they will be able to host and reveal the glory of God. Through the ministry of love and obedience to God's commandments, God will show Himself to these prophets at this stage. God will manifest Himself: *"He who has My commandments and keeps them, it is he who loves Me. And he who loves Me will be loved by My Father, and I will love him and manifest Myself to him"* (John 14:21 NKJV).

Manifestation of the sons of God is having earnest expectation: *"For the earnest expectation of the creation eagerly waits for the revealing* [manifestation] *of the sons of God"* (Romans 8:19 NKJV).

Manifestation of Jesus in us: *"Always carrying about in the body the dying of the Lord Jesus, that the life of Jesus also may be manifested in our body"* (2 Corinthians 4:10 NKJV).

> **PROPHETIC KEY:** The key in this stage to unlock the ministry of miracles is simply to work or labor in manifesting your revelation. This is work by faith; put in radical or bold action the word of faith, prayer, and revelation. In other words, this is basically stepping out in

faith and laboring in praying for the sick until you see it manifest. Jesus continually activated His total reliance and obedience in God to work the miracles that He wanted to see happen. For example, when God gives me a healing revelation healing or reveal by revelation how to administer healing, I do it, practice it, and work that revelation until I see it. I teach the revelation until it manifests.

The key to opening the door to the miraculous takes continual laboring in revelation. There was a time when I had prayed for more than hundred people before the first miracle manifested. I had to be bold and had to persevere and labor until miracles became a normal practice or second nature by faith. The apostles in the Bible all persevered in signs, wonders, and miracles in their apostolic ministry (2 Corinthians 12:12). Simply, you have to continue unapologetically manifesting your revelation by faith, which will be the key to opening the door of miracles.

6. Miracles of Revelation

The word *miracle* in the Greek is *seneuion* and means "a sign, mark, or token." A miracle is a symbol of supernatural power. The revelation realm in this stage of the prophetic office is manifesting the supernatural power of God where they speak and prophesy what is literally unexplainable. They will prophesy against the odds that will reveal the God of miracles. Creative miracles will be demonstrated through the inspired utterance of the prophet. This area of revelation that the prophet moves into is a distinctive mark and token of the supernatural power upon his or her prophetic office.

Miracles is one of the signs and revelation of God that the prophet will make known. The prophet functions in the realm of revealing the unexplainable. The prophet who operates in this realm of revelation is considered a "sign prophet," as signs, wonders, and miracles in the heavens and on earth appear as they minister, preach, teach, and prophesy. Miracles will accompany their ministry, message, and prophecy. These types of prophets walk with signs that confirm and validate the authenticity of their prophetic office. There will be unusual occurrences transcending the common course of nature, even changes in weather patterns.

Sons of Thunder—Wonders in the Heavens

For example, it is interesting that my twin brother and I would see sudden and unusual changes in the weather forecast when we ministered as prophets in different regions, cities, territories, and places. We noticed a supernatural pattern of rain and thunderstorms that seemingly came out of nowhere when we ministered. I remember one time especially when my brother immediately sensed spiritually what was happening in the spirit realm—that the rain was a sign from Heaven, indicating God's blessings and affirmation that He had sent us. Many times it would either rain before, while, or after we ministered together.

Joel the prophet prophesied that when God pours out His prophetic Spirit, there will be wonders in the heavens and signs on the earth below (see Joel 2:30 and Acts 2:19). Two sons of a man named Zebedee (James and John) were disciples and fishermen who were called by Jesus and given the title *"sons of thunder"* (Mark 1:17-20; 3:17 NIV). The title suited them as they possessed thunder-like qualities because of their vocal audacity, fervency, passionate, fiery nature, and powerful voices against injustice (see Luke 9:54).

My twin brother and I are both prophets and are also regarded like the sons of Zebedee as sons of thunder because of our thunderous voices when we preach and prophesy, accompanied with powerful displays of supernatural manifestations of signs, wonders, and miracles of the glory that happen when we minister. A common manifestation of God that confirms the coining of that title in our ministry as sign prophets is that it either rains before, during, and/or after our meetings. It is a prophetic sign that indicates God is with us and in the meeting.

As twins, we would bear witness to each other. Many times I would prophesy to someone in an entirely different meeting, and my brother would prophesy to the person later, or vice-versa and he would confirm verbatim the exact prophetic words as a witness that God has spoken it. We would have the same dreams where we would be able to finish with explicit details our dreams when we were growing in the prophetic. As twins, we minister as a prophetic team across the country and around the world, with signs and witnesses that God still speaks today.

I was honestly annoyed because there were some amazing places where we had ministered and there was strong prophetic inclination that it would rain. One day it clicked that God was validating our team ministry as prophetic witnesses as twins, symbolically representing *thunder and lightning*, and it makes sense why our ministry is commonly coined as a modern-day "Sons of Thunder," representing the biblical brothers. Jesus gave James and John, the two sons of Zebedee, the name "Sons of Thunder" in Mark 3:17 (NKJV): *"James the son of Zebedee and John the brother of James, to whom He* [Jesus] *gave the name Boanerges, that is, "Sons of Thunder."*

Miracles manifest the glory of God: *"This beginning of signs* [miracles] *Jesus did in Cana of Galilee, and manifested His glory; and His disciples believed in Him"* (John 2:11 NKJV).

Notable Miracle Manifestations

Now when they saw the boldness of Peter and John, and perceived that they were uneducated and untrained men, they marveled. And they realized that they had been with Jesus. And seeing the man who had been healed standing with them, they could say nothing against it. But when they had commanded them to go aside out of the council, they conferred among themselves, saying, "What shall we do to these men? For, indeed, that a notable miracle has been done through them is evident to all who dwell in Jerusalem, and we cannot deny it. But so that it spreads no further among the people, let us severely threaten them, that from now on they speak to no man in this name" (Acts 4:13-17 NKJV).

Prophets will move into this realm of revelations and evidences of signs, wonders, and notable miracles that will undeniably confirm that they have been with and sent by Jesus Christ. These prophets will walk in th e manifestation of miracles. They will be sign prophets.

God confirms the message by giving signs, wonders, various miracles and gifts of the Holy Spirit: *"God also testified to it by signs, wonders and various miracles, and by gifts of the Holy Spirit distributed according to his will"* (Hebrews 2:4 NIV).

PROPHETIC KEY: This last key in unlocking the miracle of revelation is to work the miracle. We must perform the works of God. This last stage of revelation is for us to become workers or laborers in miracles. Jesus performed the works of His Father (John 6:28), and He gave His disciples the key to Him working miracles in John 6—simply believe in Him.

The following example illustrates Jesus working a miracle by touching the blind man's eyes twice so he could see clearly:

Then He came to Bethsaida; and they brought a blind man to Him, and begged Him to touch him. So He took the blind man by the hand and led him out of the town. And when He had spit on his eyes and put His hands on him, He asked him if he saw anything. And he looked up and said, "I see men like trees, walking." Then He put His hands on his eyes again and made him look up. And he was restored and saw everyone clearly (Mark 8:22-25 NKJV).

Jesus worked the miracle by praying and touching the man's eyes until new eyes (creative miracle) or repaired vision (restored) happened. The nature of some miracles are unorthodox, radical, and even offensive to the person and/or onlookers. The key in this stage of miracles of revelation is to be radically bold and courageous as a miracle worker. People will not understand the revelation or even see the revelation of the miracle until you work it. We are called to be miracle workers and miracles take work (John 14:12; 1 Corinthians 12:29).

PART II

MANIFESTATION GIFTS

7

COMMUNICATIVE GIFTS

*There are, I suppose, a great many kinds of languages
in the world [unknown to us], and none is lacking
in meaning. But if I do not know the meaning of the
language, I will [appear to] be a foreigner to the one who
is speaking [since he knows exactly what he is saying], and
the one who is speaking will [appear to] be a foreigner to
me. So it is with you, since you are so very eager to have
spiritual gifts and manifestations of the Spirit, strive to
excel in ways that will build up the church [spiritually].*
—1 Corinthians 14:10-12 AMP

Throughout this chapter and the following two, I reveal how the prophetic is innately interwoven, interchangeable, and integrated with the manifestation gifts of the Spirit to release the supernatural through believers. We will examine the diversity of gifts and collate each respectfully for the emphasis and purpose of "Part II: Manifestation Gifts."

I will give you a snapshot of the nine manifestation gifts of the Spirit with a prophetic emphasis as it pertains to the gift of prophecy, prophets, and the diversity of the prophetic expressed. You will learn that there are different levels, dimensions, degrees, and realms of walking in the supernatural and the prophetic.

For the purpose and emphasis of this chapter we will discuss in detail the three *communicative gifts* of the Holy Spirit which are: 1) *prophecy*; 2) *diversities of tongues (languages)*; and 3) *interpretation of tongues (languages)*. However, it is imperative to first examine and understand key points as I lay a foundation to where we are going in the next two chapters regarding the *manifestation gifts*:

Key points:

- Defining the manifestation gifts
- Diversity of gifts, ministries, and prophetic operations
- Prophetic chemistry
- Keys to unlock the prophetic in each manifestation gift

DEFINING MANIFESTATION GIFTS

There are diversities [various kinds] *of gifts, but the same Spirit. There are differences of ministries, but the same Lord. And there are diversities of activities, but it is the same God who works all in all. But the manifestation of the Spirit is given to each one for the profit of all* (1 Corinthians 12:4-7 NKJV).

For to one is given the word of wisdom through the Spirit, to another the word of knowledge through the same Spirit, to another faith by the same Spirit, to another gifts of healings by the same Spirit, to another the working of miracles, to another prophecy, to another discerning of spirits, to another different kinds of tongues, to another the interpretation of tongues. But one and the same Spirit works all these things, distributing to each one individually as He wills (1 Corinthians 12:8-11 NKJV).

Manifestation and exhibition of the Spirit is when the nine gifts of the Spirit are evident and demonstrated in the life, ministry, and culture of the believers. This is the exhibition of the gifts of the Spirit. The gifts of the Spirit are the manifestation of the Spirit. The Holy Spirit is manifested when the gifts of the Spirit are actively operating in a believer to help others. In other words, the Holy Spirit is revealed through the gifts of the Spirit. Believers are to exhibit the gifts of the Spirit to aid other people. Manifestation is the expression of a bestowment.

What are the nine gifts of the Holy Spirit?

1. Word of wisdom
2. Word of knowledge
3. Discerning of spirits
4. Gifts of healings
5. Working of miracles
6. Faith
7. Prophecy
8. Different kinds of tongues
9. Interpretation of tongues

DIVERSITY OF GIFTS, MINISTRIES, AND OPERATIONS

Throughout the entire chapter of First Corinthans 12, Paul teaches about the supernatural and lays a firm foundation declaring that he does not want us ignorant concerning the supernatural and spiritual gifts (1 Corinthians 12:1). He expounds holistically on the gifts, the ministries, the operations, and the inworking of God in the believer. Paul reveals the sciences behind the supernatural, but I want to focus intentionally on the prophetic.

There are three distinctions of the ministry of the Holy Spirit:

1. Varieties of Gifts—Same Spirit

2. Varieties of Ministries—Same Lord

3. Varieties of Effects—Same God

The Spirit works the gifts of the Spirit; the Lord works the varieties of ministries; and God the Father works the varieties of its effects and power. The same Spirit, same Lord, and same God work together and harmoniously to manifest and exhibit the Spirit.

The nine gifts of the Spirit fall into three distinct divisions:

1. Gifts of Revelation—Revelatory Realm

2. Gifts of Inspiration—Communicative Realm

3. Gifts of Divine Power—Miraculous Realm

Three distinct divisions of the Spirit:

1. Gifts—Enablement, allotment, endowment, empowerment, charisma, inspiration, divine gratuity

2. Administrations—Ministries, services, offices, and mantles

3. Operations—Activity, energy, effect, working, power

The management or managers of the gifts:

1. The Holy Spirit—Distributions of the gifts; diversities of gifts

2. The Lord Jesus Christ—Administrations of the gifts; differences of ministries

3. God the Father—Operations of the gift; diversities of operations, activities and effects

4. Spirit-filled Believers—Activate, employ, manifest and manage the gifts (1 Peter 4:10-11); stewardship of the gifts

PROPHETIC CHEMISTRY

Prophetic chemistry deals with prophetic sciences where you learn the various components, elements, and chemistries of the gifts of the Spirit working interchangeably with the prophetic and the gift of prophecy that produce the potency behind this extraordinary ministry of the prophet and those who manifest the prophetic in their personal life, the church, and to the world.

For the purpose and emphasis of this chapter, I want to explain the functionality of each allotment of the Spirit and how the gift of prophecy, various prophetic graces, and the office of the prophet work in concert with each enablement. Typically, to teach you how the spirit of the prophet and the gift of prophecy work with the other gifts of the Holy Spirit.

There are two key levels of prophecy that function with all the gifts of the Spirit to some degree. Prophetic operations go from basic to the most advanced levels, but no matter what degree of the prophetic you flow, function, and operate in, you will see that prophetic gift pioneers or activates the other gifts of the Spirit. Oftentimes, I will stir up the gift of prophecy in a meeting to open up the atmosphere of faith to believe, which tends to activate my other gifts. The gift of prophecy is a forerunning gift you can use to open the door for other supernatural functions.

There are two spiritual levels of prophetic operations:

1. Spirit of prophecy (Revelation 19:10 NKJV)—Lowest level of the prophetic realm: *"And I fell at his feet to worship him. But he said to me, 'See that you do not do that! I am your fellow servant, and*

of your brethren who have the testimony of Jesus. Worship God! For the testimony of Jesus is the spirit of prophecy.'"

2. Spirit of the prophet (1 Corinthians 14:32 and 2 Kings 5:25-26)—Highest level of prophetic realm: *"And the spirits of the prophets are subject to the prophets"* (1 Corinthians 14:32 NKJV). *"When he went in and stood before his master, Elisha asked him, 'Where have you been, Gehazi?' 'Your servant didn't go anywhere,' Gehazi answered. But Elisha said to him, 'Was not my spirit with you when the man got down from his chariot to meet you?...'"* (2 Kings 5:25-26 NIV).

There is prophetic chemistry with the gifts of the Holy Spirit. The spirit, gift, and office of the prophet works within the three distinct divisions of the Spirit, explained previously, which are again: 1) *gifts,* 2) *administrations,* and 3) *operations.* All of the gifts, offices, and workings of the Spirit function generally under those categories. The prophetic is one of the multiple manifestations of the Spirit that exists within all three of these categories of the supernatural covered in Paul's teachings in First Corinthans 12:4-7.

Just as we see that there are gifts, administrations, and operations, therefore, the prophetic functions in a realm of its own under these same categories. In other words, in the realms of the prophetic— those who are called to function in various dimensions—there are three similar categories: 1) *prophetic gifts,* 2) *prophetic administrations,* and 3) *prophetic operations.*

Prophets and prophetic people will be spiritually equipped out of these prophetic divisions. Similarly, if called into the realm of healing and the miraculous, they will be equipped with healing gifts, healing administrations, and healing operations, just to give you an idea of how the chemistry of the Spirit works. The supernatural realm is comprised of spiritual gifts, administrations, and operations. The prophetic, healing, deliverance, miracles, intercession, and etc. all fall under the three supernatural divisions.

Prophetic gifts, prophetic administration, and prophetic operation are the chemistry and elements that make up the *"prophetic realms"* of the supernatural—the world of the prophetic. The prophetic is supernatural with prophetic gifts (abilities), prophetic administration (ministries), and prophetic operations (activities, mighty powers, and miraculous faculties). It is best from a foundational standpoint to explore the operation and chemistry of the prophetic within each category of the supernatural realm.

THREE DIVISIONS OF THE PROPHETIC REALM

There are three distinct divisions of the prophetic realm:

1   Prophetic Gifts—gift of prophecy

2. Prophetic Administrations—ministry, service, mantle, and office of the prophet

3. Prophetic Operations—spirit, power, anointing, and activity of prophecy

The spirit and gift of prophecy is the lower and developmental level of prophetic operations. As powerful and encouraging as the gift of prophecy is to the church, it is the lower degree of the prophetic because all believers can prophesy; and yes, there are those who prophesy more regularly and it is more active in some than others. Therefore, personal prophecy is the lowest dimension of the prophetic. In fact, personal prophecy is the least function of the office of the prophet. When people think of a prophet or prophetess in the church, many are under the impression that all prophets do is prophesy and give individual prophecy to people. The office, function, and seat of the prophet is greater than in responsibility.

A prophet functions primarily out of their *office* than out of the *gift* of prophecy. Prophets can function in all of the prophetic realms. They know when to activate their prophetic gift and when to stand in their office and manifest various prophetic capacities. They are not limited to words of edification, exhortation, or comfort. The prophet is the epitome of the prophetic. The prophet encompasses the entire realms of the prophetic and are given access to impart gifts, identify, and anoint ministry offices and exhibit prophetic activities. Each prophet is given a realm of the prophetic to walk in.

Likewise, operating in the spiritual gifts is the lowest level of the supernatural realm; in retrospect, operating in personal and individual prophecy is the lowest level of the prophetic realm. Functioning and desiring to manifest the spiritual gifts is most certainly something we should begin to want to do but we should also desire to move and mature into higher dimensions of spiritual operations. It is more than being spiritually gifted.

The Corinthian church was a very charismatic people who were extremely spiritual. They were defined as "spirituals," but Paul spoke of them as being babes in Christ—still yet carnal people (see 1 Corinthians 3:3). They lacked spiritual maturity; though they were spiritually gifted, there was among them envy, strife, and divisions like many of the cliques we see in today's churches and ministries. Today, there are very highly gifted churches, ministries, and believers—but there are also levels of spiritual immaturity and characteristics that are worldly, carnal, and even demonic.

What is Paul saying to the Corinthian church? I believe he is saying to them and to us: You can be spiritually gifted, anointed, and called—but you can also be carnal in your behaviors. Many of them were drawing divisions among themselves with competition, jealousy, strife, petty and frivolous arguments, elitism, and divisions by saying, *"I follow Paul,"* and another, *"I follow Apollos"* (see

1 Corinthians 3:1-4 NIV). We see this behavior today where people compare their leader to another leader in the body of Christ. There is a sense of entitlement and their level of identity is more associated to a person, tribe, network, fellowship, circle, stream, ethnic group, denomination, school of seminary, and various doctrinal views or leanings. The highest level of the supernatural realm is to be like Jesus Christ and to do the works, and greater, that He has done (John 14:12).

SPIRITUAL GIFTS VERSUS SPIRITUAL MATURITY

Spiritual giftedness does not equate spiritual maturity. I know some of the most powerfully gifted prophets and ministers of the gospel who are very fleshly, carnal, and worldly. They are public successes but private failures—their character does not match or even supersede their level of gifting. We see believers today who follow and are drawn to ministries with exemplary gifts; but unfortunately they do not have extraordinary characters. I say it all the time that yes the anointing makes the difference, but character and integrity will keep you in places that the anointing will take you. Gifts will open doors, but character will keep you in them. Therefore, the capacity to function in all of the gifts of the Spirit should not be something foreign to our understanding as believers.

All of the gifts of the Spirit are accessible and available to all believers today. It is not a thing, phenomenon, or activity of the past. It is the heart of God that His abilities and gifts flow through us bodily whenever the Spirit needs. We are encouraged to desire spiritual gifts where there is no limitation. Though there are certain gifts given severally by the Spirit, we can desire to expand and enlarge our spiritual capacities (see 1 Corinthians 12:31). There are leaders who teach and even discourage operating in spiritual gifts today; but the Scriptures are clear that we are to desire spiritual gifts, especially that we may prophesy and seek gifts that edify the church.

Paul thanked God for the grace of God given to the Corinthians believers, that they were enriched in everything by Him in all utterance and all knowledge. In other words, they were enriched fully in all utterances and knowledge. They were spiritually gifted in the language of the supernatural, which was speaking in tongues and prophecy. They were also a prophetic church that manifested the language of God. The first miracle and manifestation of the Spirit given to the new converts in Jerusalem during Pentecost was supernatural language—there was an exhibition of prophecy spoken in tongues that was unfamiliar to them but familiar to people from other nations who gathered there (read Acts 2).

According to the following example, Paul reveals that it is God's will that we never come short or get behind in any gift of the Spirit where we can be enriched with inspired prophetic utterances and supernatural languages:

> *I thank my God always concerning you for the grace of God which was given to you by Christ Jesus, that you were enriched in everything by Him in all utterance and all knowledge, even as the testimony of Christ was confirmed in you, so that you come short in no gift, eagerly waiting for the revelation of our Lord Jesus Christ* (1 Corinthians 1:4-7 NKJV).

There are some powerful revelations in this text of Scripture regarding the spiritual gifts at Corinth that we should know. The following are some keys that I have extracted from First Corinthans 1:4-7 about spiritual gifts in the believers:

- The grace of God is given to believers by Christ Jesus.

- Believers are enriched in everything by Christ in all utterance and all knowledge.

- Jesus has given us all the language and knowledge of the supernatural.

- The testimony of Christ is confirmed in us, which is the spirit of prophecy. All believers in Jesus Christ possess the spirit of prophecy.

- All believers are fully equipped spiritually by the Lord so that we do not come short in any gift.

- Jesus Christ is the greatest revelatory knowledge of believers.

- The spiritual gifts are used to testify, reveal, manifest, make known, and prophesy of Jesus Christ.

NINE SUPERNATURAL GIFTS OF THE SPIRIT

First Corinthians 12:8-10,28 is where the manifestation, supernatural, or spiritual gifts are often referred to as the "Nine Gifts of the Holy Spirit." These are supernatural gifts and, according to Scripture, are available to all Christians. The apostle Paul's teaching in the following biblical example in First Corinthans 12:1 (NKJV) is so the church would be aware of the supernatural and important spiritual gifts: *"Now concerning spiritual gifts, brethren, I do not want you to be ignorant."*

The purpose of this section of the chapter is to look at the multiplicity of ways the Holy Spirit works. There are many spiritual gifts; but importantly, there is only one Holy Spirit and the same Distributor of the gifts to the believers. The gift of prophecy is one of the gifts of the Holy Spirit, as you may already know at this point, however my intention is to emphasize the chemistry of the gift of prophecy and the prophetic anointing manifesting itself in many diversities of ways.

As we examine each gift of the Spirit, I will release the ancient secrets to unlocking the prophetic in greater capacity where you will not limit it to declaring the word of the Lord—but will see the prophetic operating in all nine of the different expressions of the Holy Spirit. Experiencing the prophetic is not just speaking, declaring, vocalizing, and communicating—I believe it is also God speaking through the other gifts.

I will show you how to unlock the prophetic in each of them and how to broaden, lengthen, and heighten your prophetic capacity and faculty to prophesy through the other gifts, and the ancient keys that the prophets and the apostles of God used to be supernaturally prophetic—to experience the God of the prophets.

Let's now take a closer look at and explore the realm of the gifts as it collates with the prophetic. As we look at each of the nine manifestation gifts of the Spirit, we will see the diversity of prophetic anointing operating differently in each gift, person, and for different purposes. Some people are gifted in various areas of the prophetic and possess different giftings than simply the gift of prophecy. Some are prophetic and their gift in the prophetic is stronger, a hybrid, or works uniquely with one or more expressions of the Spirit.

Not everyone is gifted or graced the same. God creates such peculiarity in gifts within the gift of prophecy, and other gifts are simply extraordinary. The prophetic gift typically clusters with other gifts of the Holy Spirt that release something new and fresh that we have not seen before.

You will discover how the gift of prophecy and other truths activate other gifts of the Spirit to accomplish God's purpose. I will share some biblical and a few of my personal experiences in activating the prophetic. The prophetic gift is one of the most powerful gifts that God has bestowed upon you and His church, and it is my heart to teach you how to fan into flames your full power of prophetic communication to exercise your voice every day.

Let's now examine the realm of the supernatural gifts. The nine manifestation gifts of the Spirit fall into three classifications or divisions: 1) *Revelatory,* 2) *Communicative,* and 3) *Power.*

The three classifications or subdivisions of the spiritual gifts are:

Communicative Gifts

1. Prophecy
2. Diversity of tongues (languages)
3. Interpretation of tongues (languages)

Revelatory Gifts

4. Word of Wisdom
5. Word of Knowledge
6. Discerning of Spirits

Power Gifts

7. Gift of Faith
8. Gifts of Healings
9. Working of Miracles

Prophets are not limited to only revelatory gifts. This the realm of gifts of the prophets you will see as more prevalent and evident in ministries. Whenever the gift of prophecy manifests, it is usually clustered and mixed alongside with one or more of the revelatory gifts of the Holy Spirit. This is maybe why many tend to confuse the gift of prophecy or prophesying with the revelatory gifts of the Spirit, which are word of wisdom, word of knowledge, and the discerning of Spirits.

The gift of prophecy is not a revelatory gift, it is classified as an inspiration gift. It is more inspired in function than revelatory. For example, some see a prophet operating in a word of knowledge, which we will examine further, and they tend to believe that they are prophesying, or it was a prophecy. Rather, it was not a prophecy but simply a word of *knowledge* or revelation of knowledge that was spoken by the prophet.

Prophecy and the word of knowledge are two separate functions. In fact, you can function fluently and heavily in the gift of prophecy and not be a prophet. On the contrary, you can function very strongly in the revelatory gift of word of knowledge with laser, forensic, and precise accuracy and still not be in the ministry office.

It is important for the church to understand that the prophetic gift gives us the ability to function as a prophet or like a prophet—but not to get function and office mixed up or confused. I know prophets who are office prophets, and they rarely function in the gift of prophecy. And some function in the gift of prophecy coupled with word of wisdom, not the word of knowledge. I heard a prophet say once, "The gifts do not define the office of the prophet but of the office the prophet most certainly defines the gifts."

In the next couple of chapters we examine each of the nine manifestation gifts of the Holy Spirit and particularly how they correlate and work specifically within the ministry of the prophetic. I will reveal how they are integrated prophetically in each manifestation of the Spirit. The *communicative gifts* are also known as the inspiration, vocal, or speaking gifts. The *revelatory gifts* are the three primary gifts of the prophets, which could be called prophetic gifts including the gift of prophecy. And finally, the *power gifts* are known also as demonstration or miraculous gifts of the Spirit.

1. Prophecy

Prophecy, the supernatural communicative and inspiration gift as we have covered extensively, is simply the ability through inspired utterance to speak plainly in the native language, or tongue, the words of God. In other words, it is the supernatural utterance or speech in the native tongue. It is a miracle of divine utterance, not conceived by human thought or reasoning. The gift of prophecy typically does not have a foretelling (future) element to it, but it has a forthtelling (present) flow to it. The gift of prophecy is the divine communication of God through humans to humans. Prophecy is for the purpose of speaking directly to build up people according to First Corinthans 14:3 (NIV): *"But the one who prophesies speaks to people for their strengthening, encouraging, and comfort."*

Prophecy is the gift that builds up others, especially believers. Prophecy is a sign for the believer in the same manner as speaking in different kinds of tongues is a sign for unbelievers (see 1 Corinthians 14:22). Tongues and interpretation of tongues, which will we examine shortly, coupled together is equivalent to prophecy. Therefore, when the gift of prophecy is activated, there is no need for diversities of tongues and interpretation of diversities of tongues.

Prophecy plainly utters by inspiration the mysteries, secrets, and hidden thoughts of God to those listening, while utterance in diversities of unknown tongues is speaking directly to God. Prophecy is for people, while tongues is for God. Tongues are for speaking various mysteries to God; but in diverse ways, God spoke in prophecy through His prophets.

The following are biblical accounts of prophecy through the prophets in ancient and ancestral times in Hebrews 1:1 (NKJV): *"In the past God spoke to our ancestors through the prophets at many times and in various ways."* The New Living Translation cites the same verse this way: *"Long ago God spoke many times and in many ways to our ancestors through the prophets."*

Prophecy Versus Tongues—Secrets Revealed Versus Secrets Concealed

The gift of prophecy is greater than tongues according to Paul when he wrote to the Corinthian church regarding the overemphasis, overarching, and over-spiritualization of speaking in all kinds and sorts of tongues. The gift of prophecy edifies, improves, and strengthens the church as a whole. Tongues is unfruitful to the church unless it is interpreted and translated. The following example helps us understand the greater usage of prophecy compared to speaking in *unknown* languages in the local church:

> *Now I wish that all of you spoke in unknown tongues, but even more [I wish] that you would prophesy. The one who prophesies is greater [and more useful] than the one who speaks in tongues, unless he translates or explains [what he says], so that the church may be edified [instructed, improved, and strengthened]* (1 Corinthians 14:5 AMP).

2. DIVERSITY OF TONGUES (LANGUAGES)

The gift of *diversities, divers* (KJV) and *different kinds of tongues (languages)* is the divine ability of God in a believer to speak languages that are spiritual, angelic, natural (native), mysterious, and unknown that are not learned or taught by the speaker. The extraordinary communicative gift of tongues is God's ability to give believers the utterance to speak in a variety of languages. In other words, it is the supernatural utterance in other languages that are not known to the speaker. It is important to understand that this gift is the endowment to speak all types of languages that were not previously learned.

The vocal gift of speaking with other tongues was the first manifestation of the Spirit's gifts of the believer. This first manifestation of the Spirit was demonstrated by the new converts on the Day of Pentecost. The early believers were inspired supernaturally with the ability to speak miraculously in foreign languages—different from their own native language. God will use prophets and believers to prophesy in diversities of tongues under the power of divine utterance.

Old Testament Example: Cradle of Diversities of Tongues

The first biblical mention of diversities of tongues in the Bible is found in Genesis 11, where God confused the tongue (language) of the people who had one tongue so that they could not communicate with or understand each other. Therefore, the building of the great tower of Babel had to stop, and humankind scattered around the earth establishing their own communities sharing the same tongue, language, and speech. All of the various, divers, different, and scattered languages spoken today worldwide originated because of this encounter:

> *But the Lord came down to see the city and the tower which the sons of men had built. And the Lord said, "Indeed the people are one and they all have one language, and this is what they begin to do; now nothing that they propose to do will be withheld from them. Come, let Us go down and there confuse their language, that they may not understand one another's speech"* (Genesis 11:5-7 NKJV).

New Testament Example: New Birth of Supernatural Diversities of Tongues

The following is the first New Testament example of this powerful vocal gift of speaking in different languages activated in the early church when the Holy Spirit gave them inspired foreign utterance in Acts 2:1-8 (NKJV):

When the Day of Pentecost had fully come, they were all with one accord in one place. And suddenly there came a sound from heaven, as of a rushing mighty wind, and it filled the whole house where they were sitting. Then there appeared to them divided tongues, as of fire, and one sat upon each of them. And they were all filled with the Holy Spirit and began to speak with other tongues, as the Spirit gave them utterance. And there were dwelling in Jerusalem Jews, devout men, from every nation under heaven. And when this sound occurred, the multitude came together, and were confused, because everyone heard them speak in his own language. Then they were all amazed and marveled, saying to one another, "Look, are not all these who speak Galileans? And how is it that we hear, each in our own language in which we were born?"

Supernatural Communication

The early believers were given miraculous languages that empowered them to speak in a foreign language they themselves were unfamiliar with. This was by far supernatural since they were Galileans and each one of them were given a separate language outside of their own to speak prophetically to all other nations gathered together in Jerusalem. The word *tongues* in the Greek is the word *dialekto,* which is where we get the word *dialect* transliterated in the English to mean conversation, speech, and discourse.

It is a tongue or language peculiar to any people. God has given believers, through the gift of diversities of tongues, supernatural abilities to speak in tongues. And more importantly for a spiritual purpose, the gift is a spiritual or heavenly language that is peculiar, unintelligible, and unknown to human interpretation or comprehension.

The heavenly dialect is foreign to humans. That is why critics and skeptics of this supernatural phenomenon call it foolish or that believers are speaking gibberish or babble or unintelligently when speaking in tongues. They do not understand its linguistics. The reason is simple—the language is not always intended to be understood by human understanding. It is a language that is out of our realm. Earth has languages peculiar to our way of communication and likewise Heaven has various languages and tongues peculiar to be understood only in the heavenly realm.

The realms of the spirit have a language in which believers can speak directly to God. This is clearly what sets believers apart from others—we have been given supernatural and secret communication that is very peculiar in itself. Even our own minds as human believers born again with another tongue spiritually, is what we are speaking in the spirit.

In fact, the ones in the upper room on the Day of Pentecost were speaking under the spirit of prophecy and those who heard them speaking in their own language were able to translate and interpret them testifying of the wonderful works of God, which is the spirit of prophecy. In other words, they prophesied and testified of God's works in a foreign language: *"...we hear them speaking in our own tongues* [languages] *the wonderful works of God"* (Acts 2:11 NKJV).

The *gift of tongues* can give you the ability to speak in an unlearned or untaught foreign language. God will give you inspired foreign language that will essentially cause others to be perplexed and confused to how you are able to do it, knowing that you have not learned or taken foreign language classes in school. How you are able to speak in unlearned foreign languages is simply supernatural. I oftentimes tell people jokingly, yet seriously, that I speak many languages. It is important to understand that this gift is not limited in scope. This first occurrence was needed to confirm the arrival and presence of the Holy Spirit filling and dwelling in believers with evidential manifestation.

There have been much debate and arguments regarding the baptism of the Spirit and whether a believer genuinely has the Spirit if the evidence of speaking in tongues is absent. I will not go further or add to this discussion other than to state my understanding is that all believers who have accepted Jesus Christ as Lord and Savior for the remission of their sins are given the gift of God, which is the Holy Spirit. All genuine believers have the Holy Spirit period.

On the other hand, there are those who are, after their initial conversion into Christ, then baptized or immersed by Jesus Christ into the power of the Spirit where we see the literal manifestation of the Spirit's power activated in the life of the believer.

Again, all believers have the Holy Spirit, which I believe is non-debatable—but not all believers are baptized into the power of the Spirit with accompanying signs of the believers according to Mark 16:16-18. Those who are genuine believers and followers of Christ will do the same things Jesus did. Today, more than ever, we must not only say what we believe, we must manifest and walk in what we believe.

Read carefully the *words* of Christ regarding the belief system of true believers and examples of what they *will do* as believers. We see that speaking with *"new tongues"* is one of signs of the believers:

> *He who believes and is baptized will be saved; but he who does not believe will be condemned. And these signs will follow those who believe: In My name the will cast out demons; they will speak with new tongues; they will take up serpents; and if they drink anything deadly, it*

*will by no means hurt them; they will lay hands on the
sick, and they will recover* (Mark 16:16-18 NKJV).

Clearly, the word of God declares that those who believe and are
baptized will be saved. That is guaranteed without a shadow of doubt.
It goes on to say that those who do not believe will be condemned.
This is equally correct as the previous statement. But the problem in
the church is that we know that both statements uttered by Christ are
true and sure, but as believers we stop at salvation and redemption
and never move ahead to empowerment and manifestation.

We have faith to believe in our salvation but struggle in many
churches, streams, and denominations to consider as truth today, not
only in the early church or first-century church with the apostles and
new converts or in the Old Testament with the prophets or specially
anointed men and women. As New Testament believers, the signs
and gifts of the Holy Spirit are active and alive in the saints today and
generations to come—that truth has not died. The Holy Spirit is not
dead, only dormant in some churches and ministries.

In retrospect, if we wholeheartedly believe in Christ, are baptized, and know we are saved—we must also believe His words that
the various signs will follow those who believe. If you do not believe
in the signs, they will not manifest in your life. If you believe the
signs were only for those in the past, they will just stay there. Signs
only manifest what you believe.

Therefore, it is critically important that we grasp and wrap our
faith around the mind of God that says we were born again and will
do signs, wonders, and miracles on earth in the now and Heaven has
given us a language of the supernatural in the manifestation of the
inspiration, vocal, and *communicative gifts of prophecy, diverse tongues,
and interpretation of tongues.*

Signs for the Unbeliever and Uninformed

Ancient tongues in Old Testament history.

The following examples in the Old Testament reveal that when the prophets understood Israel violated or rebelled against the Law, the covenant, and the words of the prophets, God would punish and chastise them by sending a foreign invading enemy to capture and punish them, speaking a foreign tongue or language. This confusing and confounding speech was a sign of judgment against a rebellious people. God's people in Israel who did not take seriously His Law, the prophets, and what they wrote and spoke, He would punish them with a foreign enemy who spoke another language.

They were hardheaded and stiff-necked people who had a hard time understanding God's plain language of the Law and by His prophets. So God basically said, "Okay, if you won't obey My simple instructions in a language that you know and understand, I'll punish you by allowing a foreign nation with a foreign language to conquer you." Israel would not obey God's simple instructions in their native tongue, so it would be almost impossible to obey an invading foreign enemy. What a punishment?

Isaiah reveals how the drunkards would not listen to God's prophet, therefore he responded to Israel by prophesying and predicting their subservience to Assyrian taskmasters and enemies:

> For with stammering lips and another tongue He will speak to this people (Isaiah 28:11 NKJV).

God warned His people Israel what would happen when they did not serve the Lord their God with joy and gladness of heart and ungratefulness:

> Therefore you shall serve your enemies, whom the LORD will send against you, in hunger, in thirst, in nakedness, and

in need of everything; and He will put a yoke of iron on your neck until He has destroyed you. The LORD will bring a nation against you from afar, from the end of the earth, as swift as the eagle flies, a nation whose language you will not understand (Deuteronomy 28:48-49 NKJV).

3. INTERPRETATION OF TONGUES (LANGUAGES)

The inspiration gift of *interpretation of tongues* is the divine capability to interpret and translate diverse languages. This is a powerful gift of the Holy Spirit that empowers a believer to supernaturally understand and interpret various languages both spiritually and naturally. In other words, the gift of interpretation of tongues is the supernatural ability to interpret in the native tongue, what is uttered in other languages not known by the one who interprets by the Spirit. The Holy Spirit prompts incredible and intelligible understanding in the minds of the believer who hears inspired foreign or unknown languages (angelic or secret) or the native earthly language.

Old Testament Examples—Ancient Interpretation of Tongues

Ezra 4:7 (KJV) provides an Old Testament account of interpretation of tongues: *"And in the days of Artaxerxes wrote Bisham, Mithredath, Tabeel, and the rest of their companions, unto Artaxerxes king of Persia; and the writing of the letter was written in the Syrian tongue, and interpreted in the Syrian tongue."*

Daniel was gifted spiritually in sacred letters and understanding sciences with the gift of interpretation prophetically according to Daniel 1:4 (KJV): *"Children in whom was no blemish, but well favoured, and skillful in all wisdom, and cunning in knowledge, and understanding science, and such as had ability in them to stand in the king's palace, and whom they might teach the learning and the tongue of the Chaldeans."*

In fact, God gave Daniel and the four young Hebrew boys, knowledge and skill in all literature and wisdom; and Daniel separately had understanding in all visions and dreams. He had the gift to read, interpret, and translate the writing on the wall that was written supernaturally by the hand of God. No one on earth had that ability to understand the language scribed by the hand of God.

Interpreting the Handwriting on the Wall

Daniel interprets the handwriting as recorded in Daniel 5:3-17 (ESV):

> Then they brought in the golden vessels that had been taken out of the temple, the house of God in Jerusalem, and the king and his lords, his wives, and his concubines drank from them. They drank wine and praised the gods of gold and silver, bronze, iron, wood, and stone.
>
> Immediately the fingers of a human hand appeared and wrote on the plaster of the wall of the king's palace, opposite the lampstand. And the king saw the hand as it wrote. Then the king's color changed, and his thoughts alarmed him; his limbs gave way, and his knees knocked together. The king called loudly to bring in the enchanters, the Chaldeans, and the astrologers. The king declared to the wise men of Babylon, "Whoever reads this writing, and shows me its interpretation, shall be clothed with purple and have a chain of gold around his neck and shall be the third ruler in the kingdom." Then all the king's wise men came in, but they could not read the writing or make known to the king the interpretation. Then King Belshazzar was greatly alarmed, and his color changed, and his lords were perplexed.

The queen, because of the words of the king and his lords, came into the banqueting hall, and the queen declared, "O king, live forever! Let not your thoughts alarm you or your color change. There is a man in your kingdom in whom is the spirit of the holy gods. In the days of your father, light and understanding and wisdom like the wisdom of the gods were found in him, and King Nebuchadnezzar, your father—your father the king—made him chief of the magicians, enchanters, Chaldeans, and astrologers, because an excellent spirit, knowledge, and understanding to interpret dreams, explain riddles, and solve problems were found in this Daniel, whom the king named Belteshazzar. Now let Daniel be called, and he will show the interpretation."

Then Daniel was brought in before the king. The king answered and said to Daniel, "You are that Daniel, one of the exiles of Judah, whom the king my father brought from Judah. I have heard of you that the spirit of the god is in you, and that light and understanding and excellent wisdom are found in you. Now the wise men, the enchanters, have been brought in before me to read this writing and make known to me its interpretation, but they could not show the interpretation of the matter. But I have heard that you can give interpretations and solve problems. Now if you can read the writing and make known to me its interpretation, you shall be clothed with purple and have a chain of gold around your neck and shall be the third ruler in the kingdom." Then Daniel answered and said before the king, "Let your gifts be for yourself, and give your rewards to another. Nevertheless, I will read the writing to the king and make known to him the interpretation."

New Testament Examples—Early Manifestation of Interpretation

The gift of interpretation of tongues is one of the nine manifestations of the Spirit given by the Holy Spirit to the believers: *"To another the working of miracles, to another prophecy, to another discerning of spirits, to another different kinds of tongues, to another the interpretation of tongues"* (1 Corinthians 12:10 NKJV).

The Spirit has graced some with the manifestation of the Spirit to interpret: "Are all apostles? Are all prophets? Are all teachers? Are all workers of miracles? Do all have gifts of healings? Do all speak with tongues? Do all interpret?" (see 1 Corinthians 12:29-30 NKJV).

The word *interpretation* in the Greek is *hermeneia* and means "to give interpretation of what has been spoken more or less obscurely by others." It comes from the root Greek etymology of the word *hermeneuo*, which is derived from the Greek god *Hermes*, messenger god of language, which means to explain in words, expound, or to interpret or translate what has been spoken or written in a foreign tongue into the vernacular. In other words, those who have the supernatural gift of interpretation of tongues have the ability through divine utterance and speech to explain and expound in plain or native words what is spoken or even written in a foreign language.

‖ 8 ‖

REVELATORY GIFTS

The secret things belong to the LORD our God, but
the things that are revealed belongs to us and to our
children forever, that we may do all the words of this law.
—Deuteronomy 29:29 ESV

This chapter continues to reveal how the prophetic is innately inter-woven, interchangeable, and integrated with the manifestation gifts of the Spirit to release prophetic revelation through the believers. We will discuss further in detail three more of the nine gifts of the Holy Spirit: 4) *word of wisdom*; 5) *word of knowledge*; and 6) *discerning of spirits—revelatory gifts.*

4. Word of Wisdom

The supernatural revelatory gift of *"word of wisdom"* is a supernatural endowment, allotment, and empowerment imparted by the Holy Spirit that gives a believer divine ability to release the very wisdom of God. The gift of word of wisdom is the divine revelation or instruction into the future plans, will, intention, and purpose of God.

This wisdom is not of human origin. It is a supernatural revelation or insight into the divine will and purpose, often given by the Spirit to solve complex and perplex problems, issues, crises, and situations.

This gift is activated to provide divine insight into the mind, will, counsel, and truth of God to execute sound judgment. This is one of the exercised gifts of the prophet to be able to provide solution, resolution, and even consultation regarding human affairs and matters. The word of wisdom is the supernatural wisdom of God.

This gift works effectively in "What to do" type of situations and circumstances where a word is offered that reveals how to handle things in a godly manner. It is an inspired utterance or message of wisdom supernaturally released to an individual. Paul defines wisdom as the knowledge of the mysteries unfolded by God (1 Corinthians 2; Ephesians 1:17).

5. WORD OF KNOWLEDGE

The supernatural revelatory gift of *"word of knowledge"* is the supernatural knowledge revealed by God by the Spirit that is not acquired or obtained by humans. It is the divine knowing of particular facts and specific details as opposed to acquired knowledge given by someone regarding a person, place, or thing. The gift of word of knowledge is divinely giving knowledge or insight in the divine mind, will, or plan of others and to know things that could not be known on his or her own accord. It is the supernatural ability in a believer to possess extraordinary knowledge of specific facts, information, and revelation about a person, place, thing, and/or situation that may have occurred in the past, present, and even in the future.

I know there are those in the prophetic who only associate the word of knowledge with the supernatural knowledge of confirmed specific things of past and present. But prophets in the Old Testament and even Jesus Himself gave very detailed words of knowledge of persons, places, and things in the future. Oftentimes future prophetic utterance is associated with the gift of word of wisdom, but I must say that word of knowledge of the unfolding of forensic prophetic details of the future should be directly related to the word of knowledge rather than the word of wisdom, though they both work hand in hand and interchangeably.

The gift of word of knowledge is a divine knowing that is given, inspired, and activated by the Holy Spirit without human assistance and/or resources. This non-human knowledge is what we call "the knower." When prophets function in this gift, there is a "knower" or "knowing" in them that cannot be explained by the prophet because this knowledge about a person's life, situation, event, or occurrence is divinely revealed. Prophets know it by the Spirit. They don't know how they know it, they just know it. They know it as if it was in their mind or memory and it comes up or comes to them as imparted knowledge of supernatural intelligence.

It is by divine intelligence that a prophet knows things. The Spirit gives those with the gift of knowledge the ability to know what they know without actually researching or someone telling them prior to witnessing and seeing evidence or even having prior encounter with a person, situation, place, thing, or etc. It is the knowledge of God regarding all things. God through this revelatory gift reveals all kinds of information to the believer and prophet.

The Word of Knowledge Defined

The apostle Paul defines the biblical gift of *word of knowledge,* which is a supernatural revelation by the Spirit about all things regarding people, places and things that is not received by any human sources:

> *But God has revealed them to us through His Spirit. For the Spirit searches all things, yes, the deep things of God. For what man knows the things of a man except the spirit of the man which is in him? Even so no one knows the*

things of God except the Spirit of God. Now we received, not the spirit of the world, but the Spirit who is from God, that we might know the things that have been freely given to us by God (1 Corinthians 2:10-12 NKJV).

Revelatory knowledge prophetically is given to us in parts or in pieces of revelation through the revelatory gifts and the gift of prophecy recorded in First Corinthans 13:9 (NKJV): *"For we know in part and we prophesy in part."*

6. DISCERNING OF SPIRITS

The extraordinary revelatory gift of *"discerning of spirits"* is the supernatural ability to determine and detect the operation of spiritual activities and their spirits. This gives a believer and/or prophet the spiritual detection and sensory to identify the realm of unseen activities of spirits. It is the ability to see into the unseen revealing spirits, motives, and hidden intentions and agendas.

Discerning of spirits is the supernatural ability to recognize, distinguish, and identify between various classifications of spirits:

- Holy Spirit—God realm
- Angelic Realm
- Fallen Angels—demonic, diabolical and satanic realm
- Human Spirit—soulish realm or human spirit

This is a supernatural revelation or insight into the realm of spirits to determine the source of the spiritual activity, to detect them and their plans, and to perceive the human mind. In other words, the manifestation of the Spirit of discerning of the spirits gives believes the capacity to discern, distinguish, or discriminate the source of a spiritual manifestation—whether it emanates from a good or evil spirit. This gift of the Spirit is a revelatory gift that opens the spiritual eyes and senses of the believer in the realms of the spirit. It is directly associated with prophecy as it would be necessary to know whether a prophetic utterance was genuinely inspired by God, conjured up by human spirits or spoken by demonic influence or possession of demons.

One thing to note is how this powerful gift collates with the prophetic and the prophets which also gives the prophet in the office the ability to discern and see mantles, genuine gifts of the Spirit, anointing, and graces. In other words, this allows the prophet to see genuine and false (pseudo) ministry. Prophets can see and identify specific gifts, graces, and spiritual characteristics in people's lives. The prophet can discern motives, characters, whether good and bad, and if they are demonically influenced or divinely inspired. This gift allows the prophet to judge properly various spiritual agents in action in a person, place, or thing. Prophets have the extraordinary ability to see in the realm of the spirit and distinguish through their spiritual vision.

To discern means to see, whether it be divine spirits, evil spirits, the human spirit, and even recognizing the very presence and manifestation of God. The gift of discerning of spirits gives insight into the spiritual world. The prophet has the ability to see in the spiritual realm with his or her spiritual senses. The word *discern* in the Merriam-Webster Dictionar means "to detect with the eyes, to distinguish, to recognize or identify as separate and distinct." It means also "to come to know or recognize mentally, differentiate and espy."

The gift of discerning of spirits gives the believer and the prophet or prophetic people the capability to make a distinction. In the realm of the spirit, it gives you the ability to grasp and comprehend what is obscure, hidden, and things behind the scene, a person, or thing.

Jesus Himself through this powerful prophetic gift discerned the work of satan in Peter who tried to rebuke Him:

> From that time Jesus began to show to His disciples that He must go to Jerusalem, and suffer many things from the elders and chief priests and scribes, and be killed, and be raised the third day. Then Peter took Him aside and began to rebuke Him, saying, "Far be it from You, Lord; this shall not happen to You!" But He turned and said to Peter, "Get behind Me, Satan! You are an offense to Me, for you are not mindful of the things of God, but the things of men" (Matthew 16:21-23 NKJV).

Just as our five natural senses—1) *sight,* 2) *smell,* 3) *taste,* 4) *touch,* and 5) *hearing*—help us to learn and understand the natural world, we also have the same *spiritual* senses to help us identify the spiritual world around us. The gift of discerning of spirits gives us the perceptivity and sensitivity to the prompting of the Lord as we yield our natural five senses to Him. The more the anointing of the Spirit comes upon our natural five senses, the more it makes us progressively sensitive to the impressions of God.

In my book *Realms of the Prophetic,* I explain how to activate your prophetic senses and how your senses are used interchangeably to provide prophetic intelligence and personal prophecy.

‖ 9 ‖

POWER GIFTS

But you will receive power when the
Holy Spirit has come upon you....
—Acts 1:8 ESV

And these signs will accompany those who believe...
then the disciples went out and preached everywhere,
and the Lord worked with them and confirmed
his word by the signs that accompanied it.
—Mark 16:17,20 NIV

This chapter continues to disclose and reveal that the prophetic is innately interwoven, interchangeable, and integrated with the manifestation gifts of the Spirit to release power and miraculous demonstrations through believers. We discuss further in detail the last three of the nine gifts of the Holy Spirit: 7) *gift of faith*; 8) *gifts of healings*; and 9) *working of miracles—power gifts*.

7. GIFT OF FAITH

The demonstration of the *"gift of faith"* is the supernatural ability to believe outside of our human will that empowers us to believe for the impossible. This is a supernatural ability to believe God without human doubt, unbelief, and reasoning. The Spirit will prompt a believer with a special grace to contend against human doubt, unbelief, fear, skepticism, and reasoning. This grace gives the believer confidence and unwavering trust and belief in God without a shadow of doubt. Different measures of faith are imparted to all believers in Christ. In fact, all believers are given a measure, proportion, or ratio of faith. There are various measures of faith allotted to each believer. Prophets functions regularly in the gift of faith in order to prophesy accurately and powerfully. All things prophetic flow out of the manifestation gift of faith.

There is a saving faith and measure of faith given to all Spirit-empowered believers; however, the *gift of faith* is the ability to function in the realm of the supernatural and to accomplish and overcome the odds against you or the faith that is against all odds. This faith operates when the probability ration is one billion to one of happening. This faith, in fact, activates when situations or circumstance demand supernatural intervention. The gift of faith is the belief in the ability of God in the believer to minister in all of the gifts of the Spirit and is the engineer behind manifesting the Spirit. This power gift allows the believer to function in the supernatural and literally stand up to do the impossible.

A realm of faith is activated in all believers to trust and have total belief in not only God to do it, but truthfully to believe that He has imparted and implanted His faith in all believers to do it. Many times we pray and believe God to do it, but fail to understand that He has given His supernatural faith for us to do so. There are things we are praying for that God has given us supernatural faith to do. This also gives us the faith to believe in prayer. Faith is the gateway to demonstrating the supernatural.

What Is Faith?

Faith refers to that strong or special faith that removes mountains, casts out devils (Matthew 17:19-20), and faces the cruelest martyrdom without flinching. This faith is distinguished from the "*saving*" Christian faith. This *gift of faith* activates all the other gifts of the Holy Spirit; but more particularly, it is the supernatural demonstration of the gift that unlocks the *gifts of healings* and the *gift of working of miracles,* which I will discuss next in this chapter.

The Christian faith is often discussed in terms of believing in God's promises, trusting in His faithfulness, and totally relying on God's character and faithfulness to act. Some of the definitions of "faith" in the history of Christianity have followed the biblical formulation in Hebrews 11:1 (NKJV): "*the substance of things hoped for, the evidence of things not seen.*"

The word *faith,* translated from the Greek is *pi'stis,* and was primarily used in the New Testament with the Greek perfect tense and translates as a noun-verb hybrid, which is not adequately conveyed by the English noun. The verb form of *pi'stis* is *pisteuo,* which is often translated into English versions of the New Testament as *believe.*

8. GIFTS OF HEALINGS

The power and demonstration of the "*gifts of healings*" is the supernatural power to heal without human assistance, medicine, and home remedies. It is the divine healing capacity to cure all manner of sickness, disease, virus, and physical ailments and proclivity by the Holy Spirit's power, without human aid or medicine. This manifestation of the Spirit is the healing power of God demonstrated through the manifestation of various kinds of healings.

It is significant to see that the words *gifts* and *healings* are plural, which implies there are multiple gifts and abilities of various kinds of healings. It is not a "gift of healing," rather, "gifts of healings" are given to believers. There are multiple supernatural abilities to heal different natures of sickness and disease. There are various manners of sickness and disease; therefore, there are various manners of gifts of healings to bring restoration of health.

Gifts of Healings Defined

The gifts of healings is the ability to supernaturally minister healing to others. The plural indicates the variety of sickness healed and the many forms the gift takes, such as healing by anointing with oil, by the laying on of hands, by saying the name of Jesus, or by the Cross. The demonstrative gifts of healings are among the spiritual gifts listed in First Corinthans 12. As an extraordinary charism (favor), gifts of healings are supernatural enablements given to a believer to minister various kinds of healing and restoration to individuals through the power of the Holy Spirit.

In the New Testament, both the words *gift* and *healing* are plural. In the Gospel of Mark chapter 16 account of the Great Commission, Jesus stated that one of the signs to follow believers in Him would be healing after the laying on of the hands and impartation.

Anointing with oil by the leadership of the church is involved with the laying on of hands and prayer over the sick. Healing can be released by laying on of hands in *prayer of faith* for someone who is sick, ill, or diseased. Leaders can impart healing and impart the gifts of healings to heal. These symbolize that believers are channels of divine power and that the healing was the work of the Holy Spirit. Healing is also connected with forgiveness of sins. The following is an example of laying hands on the sick with oil to impart healing by the eldership of the local church recorded in James 5:13-15 (NIV):

> *Is anyone among you in trouble? Let them pray. Is anyone happy? Let them sing songs of praise. Is anyone among you sick? Let them call the elders of the church to pray over*

them and anoint them with oil in the name of the Lord. And the prayer offered in faith will make the sick person well; the Lord will raise them up. If they have sinned, they will be forgiven.

Jesus sent His twelve disciples out two by two and gave them power over unclean spirits and to heal the sick with oil:

And He called the twelve to Himself, and began to send them out two by two, and gave them power over unclean spirits. ...So they went out and preached that people should repent. And they cast out many demons, and anointed with oil many who were sick, and healed them (Mark 6:7,12-13 NKJV).

The following are keys to what Jesus has given believers in the realm of healing and deliverance:

- Power and authority to heal the sick and cast out devils.
- Anointing to heal, pray, and lay hands on the sick—anointing is transferrable by the laying on of hands.
- Believers can activate the gifts of healings or pray to receive the gifts by the Holy Spirit.
- Elders and leadership in the local church should actively pray and release the anointing for the sick to be strengthened, restored, and healed. The presbytery, those who preside over the assemblies (churches) are ordained, licensed, consecrated, and anointed to pray for the sick—which should be an ongoing ministry of the eldership in the church.

- Prayer and faith unlock the anointing for healing and deliverance.

- Forgiveness releases the power of healing and repentance.

Old Testament Examples: God utters that He is the Lord who heals: *"...For I am the LORD, who heals you"* (Exodus 15:26 NKJV).

Abraham's Intercession Healed Barrenness

In the Bible, Abraham is the first one to be called a prophet. He had the ability to heal and break the barrenness of Abimelech the king through prayer and intercession. The first ministry of the prophet is *prayer* and *intercession*. The cradle of healing was developed in the intercession and prayers of the prophetic. The ancient secret of healing is released through the ministry of the prophet.

Prophetic intercession by Abraham the prophet unlocked the healing anointing for the king to be restored from barrenness:

> *Now therefore, restore the man's wife; for he is a prophet, and he will pray for you and you shall live. ...So Abraham prayed to God; and God healed Abimelech, his wife, and his female servants. Then they bore children; for the LORD had closed up all the wombs of the house of Abimelech because of Sarah, Abraham's wife* (Genesis 20:7,17-18 (NKJV).

Elisha Prophesied Healing of Leprosy

The supernatural ability to heal was active in the prophets of the Old Testament; they ministered in the arena of healing. One of many examples includes Naaman, a high-ranking commander of the king's army by whom the Lord had given victory to Syria. This commander was a leper. The prophet Elisha gave a prophetic word for Naaman to follow in order to receive his healing from leprosy. The healing was in the mouth of the prophet. Let's take a look at what occurred for the healing to be released supernaturally through the realm of the prophet in Second Kings 5 (NKJV):

Naaman was a man of great military status and rank but was a leper: *The Condition*

> *Now Naaman, commander of the army of the king of Syria, was a great and honorable man in the eyes of his master, but because by him the LORD had given victory to Syria. He was also a might many of valor, but a leper (2 Kings 5:1).*

The young girl from Israel recommended the prophet Elisha: *The Recommendation*

> *And the Syrian had gone out on a raids, and had brought back captive a young girl from the land of Israel. She waited on Naaman's wife. Then she said to her mistress, "If only my master were with the prophet who is in Samaria! For he would heal him of his leprosy"* (2 Kings 5:2-3).

There is an aspect of healing in the ministry of the prophets. The young girl understood the capacity and the result of being in the presence of the prophet. Elisha had the gift of healing evident in his prophetic ministry. He was a prophet who carried the ability to heal to such a degree that this young Israelite could make such a recommendation with certainty of faith that all Naaman had to do was be with the prophet, and he would be healed from his condition.

Oftentimes, our physical condition, sickness, or physical ailment needs to get into the presence of a man or woman of God carrying the anointing of healing upon their lives.

213

To enquire of the prophet is similar to seeking God Himself. Therefore, Naaman seeking the prophet to be healed in the Old Covenant paradigm was essentially him seeking the presence of God for healing. He believed the young girl's recommendation and he sought release from his master to go, and the king of Syria wrote a letter to the king of Israel. The king of Syria sent a letter to the king requesting that he heal Naaman of his leprosy. The king of Israel tore his clothes in lamentation knowing that he did not have the ability to heal Naaman. The king of Israel was grieved and distressed thinking the king of Syria was starting a war with Israel.

Elisha told the king to send Naaman to him for healing: *The Prophet*

> *And it happened, when the king of Israel read the letter, that he tore his clothes and said, "Am I God, to kill and make alive, that this man sends a man to me to heal him of his leprosy? Therefore please consider, and see how he seeks a quarrel with me." So it was, when Elisha the man of God heard that the king of Israel had torn his clothes, that he sent to the king, saying, "Why have you torn your clothes? Please let him come to me, and he shall know that there is a prophet in Israel"* (2 Kings 5:7-8).

Elisha knew he had the ability to heal Naaman from his condition. The presence of God was with the ancient prophets, allowing them to function in the realm of the supernatural.

Naaman made the journey and stood at the door of Elisha's house. The prophet sent a messenger to Naaman with instructions about what to do to be restored: *The Prescription*

> *Then Naaman went with his horses and chariot, and he stood at the door of Elisha's house. And Elisha sent a*

messenger to him, saying, "Go and wash in the Jordan seven times, and your flesh shall be restored to you, and you shall be clean" (2 Kings 5:9-10).

Healing of Prophecy

Naaman was furious at Elisha's prophetic instruction because he had a preconceived expectation of how the prophet Elisha would minister healing to him. Naaman thought Elisha would come out the door and greet him and wave his hand over him and heal the leprosy. He did not like that the prophet did not even come out of his house, but rather sent the word of prophecy and instruction via a messenger. Nevertheless, the healing was in the word of the Lord.

Moreover, Naaman did not like that the Jordan River was where he was instructed to wash, knowing that there were better bodies of water. God was challenging how desperate Naaman was for a healing and his servant said to him *My father, if the prophet had told you to do something great, would you not have done it? How much more then, when he says to you, 'Wash, and be clean'?"* (see 2 Kings 5:11-13).

Naaman obeyed the prophetic directive and he was restored, cleaned and healed: *The Healing*

> *So he went down and dipped seven times in the Jordan, according to the saying of the man of God; and his flesh was restored like the flesh of a little child, and he was clean. And he returned to the man of God, he and all his aides, and came and stood before him; and he said, "Indeed, now I know that there is no God in all the earth, except in Israel; now therefore, please take a gift from your servant"* (2 Kings 5:14-15).

It is important to understand that in the context of healing in the Old Testament, Elisha did not have to lay hands or do anything great, not even come out of his house to meet the commander of the army. He simply sent a prophetic prescription and Naaman's healing was in his obedience and faith in the word of the prophet of God. Naaman's faith without works would not have afforded the miracle he desperately needed.

We tend to sometimes have an expectation of how God will heal or how one man or woman of God will minister healing. Elisha showed a different administration of healing. We can even put healing in a box thinking that every prophet or person who has the gifts of healings will minister healing the same way or manner. Naaman's healing needed a different act of obedience.

This clearly shows us that there are various administrations of healings and different instructions for different physical conditions. Naaman wanted to wash in a better body or stream of water to be healed. This is another example of how we tend to want to pick and choose the method in which God should heal us. We want it to be pretty or suggest that we know a better way. It is the act of obedience to the prophet that is usually the issue of our faith when it comes to obeying the prophetic.

Obey the Prophet

I can recall a time when my twin brother, Hakeem, had prophetically advised a friend of his who had come to him about his grandmother who was suffering from a terminal illness. The friend was aware of the healing anointing that rested upon my brother's life as a prophet. Because of the distance, my brother gave him specific instructions for what he needed to do for his grandmother to be miraculously healed. My brother then mailed his personal prayer shawl that he used and witnessed miracles and healings administered by the shawl. He told the friend to take the prayer shawl and lay it over his grandmother on her deathbed for seven days. Then my brother began to prophesy that she would live and not die and be suddenly healed from her disease. Hakeem gave his friend clear prophetic instruction and told him that his grandmother's healing was in the concise execution and obedience of the word of the Lord in the mouth of His servant the prophet.

My brother had used his prophetic prayer shawl like Elijah the prophet who would wrap himself in fervent prayer and intercession for hours. There was anointing and gifts of healings evident in my brother's life and he would use this prayer shawl in his meetings where literal miracles took place when he would put it on someone or throw it on a sick person's body and they would be healed. This was not the first time he used his shawl; he had given similar instructions to our own grandmother who was healed from cancer through the Holy Spirit's power working through the office. Hakeem's shawl had a prophetic and healing reputation, and God brought special miracles by it—similar to Paul's handkerchief and aprons (see Acts 19:1-12).

After the prayer shawl was mailed to Hakeem's friend, all he had to do was follow and obey the instructions of the prophet. The young man gave the shawl to his grandmother and laid it on her for only a couple of days. Then the grandson noticed that the prayer shawl looked soiled because of all that was poured into it—it had been anointed with oil, was a covering for fervent prayers on the floor, dried the sweat and tears of intercession and ministry. My brother refused to wash it in order to preserve all of the supernatural essence and notable healings and miracles that God worked through it in his prophetic ministry. No matter how many times God uses a prophet in the miraculous, it is always the Holy Spirit that is working with and in the radical obedience and faith of the man or woman connecting to the faith of beneficiary of the miracle.

Unfortunately, the young man washed and dried the prayer shawl (the mantle) over the period of a day or two. Oh NO! This was not what the prophet had ordered—it was to remain on the gravely ill grandmother for a total of seven days. Consequently, a day or two elapsed before he laid it on his grandmother again. Sadly, after the seventh day window allotted for her miracle, the grandmother suddenly died.

Hakeem was devastated to learn of the passing of his friend's grandmother and he was equally as devastated to learn that the young man did not obey the prophetic instruction to the letter, and that the prayer shawl was washed without his permission. The point of this story is that some healings will be unlocked only by obeying the prophet with the healing in his or her mouth.

Ministry of Healing in the Gospels

There are a number of biblical accounts in the Gospels when Jesus healed all who encountered Him directly or indirectly. Typically the gifts of healings accompany the teaching, preaching, and declaring the word and the gospel of the Kingdom of God. There are times when healing was imparted with a touch, laying on of hands, or being in the presence (atmosphere) of the Lord. Healing was also released through prayer and intercession and even commanding healing through sending the word of the Lord.

The following are a number of Scriptures reflecting healing through the lens of the Gospels that will unlock the gifts of healings in your life. There is a key in each of the Scriptures that reveals the power of healing and deliverance.

Healing According to Matthew

Matthew 4:23-24 (NKJV): *"And Jesus went about all Galilee, teaching in their synagogues, preaching the gospel of the kingdom, and healing all kinds of sickness and all kinds of disease among the people. Then His fame went throughout all Syria; and they brought to Him all sick people who were afflicted with various diseases and torments, and those who were demon-possessed, epileptics and paralytics; and He healed them."*

Matthew 8:16 (NKJV): *"When evening had come, they brought to Him many who were demon-possessed. And He cast out the spirits with a word, and healed all who were sick."*

Matthew 9:35 (NKJV): *"Then Jesus went about all the cities and villages, teaching in their synagogues, preaching the gospel of the kingdom, and healing every sickness and every disease among the people."*

Matthew 12:15 (NKJV): *"But when Jesus knew it, He withdrew from there. And great multitudes followed Him, and He healed them all."*

Matthew 14:14 (NKJV): *"And when Jesus went out He saw a great multitude; and He was moved with compassion for them, and healed their sick."*

Matthew 14:35-36 (NKJV): *"And when the men of that place recognized Him, they sent out into all that surrounding region, brought to Him all who were sick, and begged Him that they might only touch the hem of His garment. And as many as touched it were made perfectly well."*

Matthew 21:14 (NKJV): *"Then the blind and the lame came to Him in the temple, and He healed them."*

Healing According to Mark

Mark 3:10: *"For He healed many, so that as many as had afflictions pressed about Him to touch Him."*

Mark 6:56: *"Whenever He entered, into villages, cities, or the country, they laid the sick in the marketplaces, and begged Him that they might just touch the hem of His garment. And as many as touched Him were made well."*

Healing According to Luke, the Physician

Luke 4:40: *"When the sun was setting, all those who had any that were sick with various diseases brought them to Him; and He laid His hands on every one of them and healed them."*

Luke 5:17: *"Now it happened on a certain day, as He was teaching, that there were Pharisees and teachers of the law sitting by, who had come out of every town of Galilee, Judea, and Jerusalem. And the power of the Lord was present to heal them."*

Luke 6:19: *"And the whole multitude sought to touch Him, for power went out from Him and healed them all."*

Luke 9:1: *"Then He called His twelve disciples together and gave them power and authority over all demons, and to cure diseases."*

Luke 9:11: *"But when the multitudes knew it, they followed Him; and He received them and spoke to them about the kingdom of God, and healed those who had need of healing."*

Healing According to John

John 14:12: *"Most assuredly, I say to you, he who believes in Me, the works that I do he will do also; and greater works than these he will do, because I go to My Father."*

Believers will walk in the ministry and gifts of healing (Mark 16:18). The following are additional biblical examples of the various types of gifts of healings demonstrated in the New Testament:

- Leper healed (Luke 17:11-19)
- The centurion servant was healed by the word of Jesus (Luke 7:1-10)
- Jesus spit on his eyes (Mark 8:23)
- Jesus speaks to the lame man (Acts 3)
- Jesus raises the dead (Luke 8:40-56, Luke 7:17-17 and John 11:17-44)
- Elders of the church praying for healing of sick with anointing oil (James 5:13-16)
- Jesus laid hands on the girl with a fever (Matthew 8:15 and Luke 4:39)
- Paul heals the father of the Publius (Acts 28:8)
- Paul had a vision of a man named Ananias, healing him from blindness (Acts 9:12-17)
- Those who touched Jesus's garment (mantle) were all healed (Luke 6:19)

9. WORKING OF MIRACLES

The last power and demonstration gift of *working of miracles* is the supernatural ability imparted to work the works of God that is outside the realm of natural explanation. It is the supernatural acts of God working through the believer giving him or her supernatural working of God's power to intervene in the ordinary course of nature and to counteract natural laws if necessary.

Incredibly it is the performance of deeds beyond ordinary human ability by the power of the Holy Spirit. The supernatural *gift of working of miracles* is among the spiritual gifts (*charismata*) mentioned by Paul in First Corinthans 12. This special gift is imparted to individual believers by the power of the Holy Spirit. The working of miracles is one of the most essential gifts for God to work through the ministry of believers to testify of Himself.

The following Old Testament Scripture reveals the incomprehensible nature of miracles by God: *"He performs wonders that cannot be fathomed, miracles that cannot be counted"* (Job 5:9 NIV).

The following New Testament Scripture reveals that God Himself testifies by the miraculous gifts of the Spirit in believers: *"God also testified to it by signs, wonders and various miracles, and by gifts of the Holy Spirit distributed according to his will"* (Hebrews 2:4 NIV).

Miracles, signs, and wonders through the acts of believers today is biblical and one of God's ways to testify of His glory. Miracles bear witness of the glory and presence of God. The word *miracle* in the Merriam-Webster Dictionary means "an extraordinary event manifesting divine intervention in human affairs." It is an unusual event, thing, or accomplishment that is a wonder and a marvel.

Simply put, a miracle is a wonder of God. It makes you marvel at the power of God that is unexplainable. When something is miraculous it is described to be phenomenal, superhuman, supernatural, uncanny, unearthly. It is marvelous, stupendous, stunning, astonishing, amazing, and sublime just to cite a few words. Some of these words are emphasized in the Scriptures, which clearly draws a distinction and clarity on the type of healings that took place with regard to healing versus a miracle, sign, or wonder.

Miracles Through the Ministry of Believers

All of the gifts of the Spirit are miraculous in essence, but the manifestation of the working of miracles is jaw dropping and eye popping in modern terms, when a miracle is performed. Miracles in the ministry of our Lord were common, as was the delegated power to do miracles that He granted to His apostles and His church to validate their message of Christ and themselves as special messengers of God. Special messengers with special miracles are common in the ministry of the apostles in the New Testament, as it was with the ministry of the prophets in the Old Testament. Miracles were an attesting sign of authenticity of the apostolic and prophetic.

Jesus has given to the ministry of the believers by the Spirit the power of working miracles, signs and wonder that was also evident in both the Old Testament ministry of the prophets and the New Testament ministry of Jesus, the apostles, and the church. The working of miracles was the earmark of Jesus's ministry both in healing and deliverance. His ministry was marked with the supernatural. This is Kingdom demonstration through the working of healing the sick, raising the dead, driving out demons, multiplying the food supply, and praying. Jesus's ministry with respect to all of these miracles was done in a superhuman realm; but the key is that He did not do these as God but as a man, which reveals to us that we can also do the same. My statement may go against popular beliefs that some miracles Jesus worked was done to prove His divinity, and not quite His humanity.

The gift of working of miracles works closely with the gifts of faith and the gifts of healings. The gift of working of miracles opens us to the realm of miracles collectively with the other gifts of the Spirit and more specifically with the power, demonstration, and manifestation gifts. Jesus is the Miracle Worker and He has imparted this measure and grace to some believers and those who operate in the fivefold ministry of apostles, prophets, evangelists, pastors, and teachers.

The gift of working of miracles superimposes any counteractive earthly and evil forces and powers. It is of a superior nature because it transcends beyond natural laws to fulfill God's purpose on earth. It is very pertinent to understand that Jesus was one with the Holy Spirit and anointed with the Spirit's miraculous power.

The Holy Spirit enabled, empowered, endowed, and energized Jesus to be able to work and function in the miracle realm. We need to see more of those in the church press into becoming workers of miracles, where the glory of God is revealed and Jesus Christ today is declared and made known. Jesus Christ is alive and still a Miracle Worker in and through His church and through us as sons and daughters of God.

Purpose of Miracles

Jesus Christ refused to do a miracle just to demonstrate His power and to reveal His identity. He called this tempting God in Matthew 4:7, when He was talking to the devil tempting Him in the wilderness. The devil tried to manipulate the Scriptures, tempting Jesus to demonstrate His power. There were a number of occasions where the religious Pharisees and scribes wanted Jesus to perform a miracle from Heaven (see Matthew 12:38 and John 6:30). Jesus displayed His power, signs, wonders, and miracles for His purposes only.

The following are seven keys revealing the purpose of miracles, signs, and wonders in the Bible:

1. Miracles of Awe—The Bible provides accounts of many men and women of God who experienced a *miracle of awe* supernaturally, intimately, and personally when the Lord called them to ministry or for a special purpose.

- Moses at the Burning Bush (Exodus 3:1-17)—Moses was required to remove his sandals because of the presence of God; and out of the burning bush he was called and commissioned to be a deliverer. Moses did not feel qualified to go to Pharaoh on behalf of God. However, God promised Moses that He would be with him and would work miracles, signs, and wonders through him (see Exodus 4:1-17). This is what God says to Moses to validate his ministry as a prophet of God to Pharaoh carrying the power of miraculous signs: *"Now you* [Aaron] *shall speak to him* [Moses] *and put the words in his mouth. And I* [God] *will be with your mouth and with his mouth, and I will teach you what you shall do. So he shall be your spokesman to the people. And he himself shall be as a mouth for you, and you shall be to him as God. And you shall take this rod in your hand, with which you shall do the signs"* (Exodus 4:15-17).

- Saul on the Road to Damascus (Acts 9)—Saul's encounter with Christ literally altered his life and revealed his rebellion against the church and ultimately called him to ministry after being struck with blindness for him to get the revelation. He needed to be blinded to his mission against the church to gain sight of a new revelation of his commission for the church as an apostle. His name was eventually changed from Saul to Paul.

2. Miracles of Provision—There are Bible accounts of when the people of God needed a *miracle of provision* that could not have been

met with natural means. God superimposed and intervened by providing and multiplying supernaturally.

- Elisha feeds one hundred men in 2 Kings 4:42-44 (ESV): *"A man came from Baal-shalishah, bringing the man of God bread of the firstfruits, twenty loaves of barley and fresh ears of grain in his sack. And Elisha said, 'Give to the men, that they may eat.' But his servant said, 'How can I set this before a hundred men?' So he repeated, 'Give them to the men, that they may eat, for thus says the LORD, "They shall eat and have some left."' So he set it before them. And they ate and had some left, according to the word of the LORD."*

- Jesus miraculously feeds five thousand in Matthew 14:16-21 (ESV): *"But Jesus said, 'They need not go away; you give them something to eat.' They said to him, 'We have only five loaves here and two fish.' And he said, 'Bring them here to me.' Then he ordered the crowds to sit down on the grass, and taking the five loaves and the two fish, he looked up to heaven and said a blessing. Then he broke the loaves and gave them to the disciples, and the disciples gave them to the crowds. And they all ate and were satisfied. And they took up twelve baskets full of the broken pieces left over. And those who ate were about five thousand men, besides women and children."*

- Provision of the manna to the Israelites in Exodus 16:35 (ESV): *"The people of Israel ate the manna forty years, till they came to a habitable land. They ate the manna till they came to the border of the land of Canaan."*

3. Miracles of Protection—There are times and seasons when God superimposed and divinely intervened through a *miracle of protection* for His people with prophetic warnings in a dream or angelic protections when they were in danger.

- Daniel in the lions' den (Daniel 6:1-16)
- Three Hebrew children in the fiery furnace (Daniel 3:1-23)
- Jesus as a baby divinely and prophetically protected from Herod by Joseph and the three wise men in a dream (Matthew 2:1-23)

4. Miracles of Deliverance—The New Testament provides extraordinary examples of a *miracle of deliverance*. We will discover that through prayer and worship and even through the power of angelic assistance, God's people were delivered from prison. God sent angelic messengers to warn His people of unseen or hidden danger of people or the enemy, whether human or demonic.

- Jesus miraculously received divine intelligence prophetically of the conspiracy and assassination attempts of the Pharisees and miraculously escaping (see Matthew 12:14-15; Mark 3:6-12 and Luke 6:11).
- Paul and Silas miraculously freed from prison through prayer and worship (Acts 16:16-34).
- Peter freed from prison by angelic reinforcement and prayers of the church (Acts 12:1-19).

5. Miracles of Healing and Deliverance—Old and New Testament Scriptures reveal examples of God's supernatural power to release a *miracle of healing and deliverance*. God's miracles healed His people

from all manner of sickness, disease, physical suffering, and those who were demonized, possessed by devils, and tormented by spirits.

- The following is an example of the apostle Paul imparting through articles of clothing special miracles demonstrated by his hands: *"And God wrought special miracles by the hands of Paul: So that from his body were brought unto the sick handkerchiefs or aprons, and the diseases departed from them, and the evil spirits went out of them"* (Acts 19:11-12 KJV).

- Miracles of healing and deliverance of people who were blind, lame, diseased, and sick by the apostles: examples found throughout the entire book of the "Acts" of the apostles.

- Jesus cast out a legion of demons into swine and the healing and deliverance of a man in Gadarenes (Luke 8:26-39; Matthew 8:28-34; Mark 5:1-20).

6. Miracles of Supernatural Revelation—There are biblical examples of a *miracle of supernatural revelation* when God gives divine understanding of His Word and His plans to His people, prophets, and apostles. God revealed His secret plans by revelation to His prophets as recorded in Amos 3:7 (NKJV): *"Surely the Lord God does nothing, unless He reveals His secret to His servants the prophet."*

- Jesus unlocks understanding of the Scriptures to His disciples in Luke 24:44-45 (NKJV): *"Then He said to them, 'These are the words which I spoke to you while I was still with you, that all things must be fulfilled which were written in the Law of Moses and the Prophets and the Psalms concerning Me.' And He*

opened their understanding, that they might compre-
hend the Scriptures."

- Revelation of the mysteries of God of the ages revealed to apostles and prophets of the New Testament in Ephesians 3:1-5 (NKJV): *"For this reason I, Paul, the prisoner of Christ Jesus for you Gentiles—if indeed you have heard of the dispensation of the grace of God which was given to me for you, how that by revelation He made known to me the mystery (as I have briefly written already, by which, when you read, you may understand my knowledge in the mystery of Christ), which in other ages was not made known to the sons of men, as it has now been revealed by the Spirit to His holy apostles and prophets.*"

- Daniel receives visions and revelation of the Glorious Man (Daniel 10).

7. Miracles of Authenticity—The following are additional examples of the purpose of miracles particularly in the New Testament where a *miracle of authenticity* confirms, validates, and certifies the anointed vessels of God, the divinity of Christ, and the Word of God. Miracles are attesting signs of God. Miracles of authenticity:

- Prove that Jesus is God (Acts 2:22)

- Accompany signs of the ministry of believers and confirm the word of God (Mark 16:17-20)

- Authenticate the ministry and message of the apostles (Acts 14:3)

- Validate the ministry and sign of an apostle (2 Corinthians 12:12)

- Confirm salvation and the gospel of Jesus Christ and authenticate the message was the purpose of such miraculous deeds (Hebrews 2:2-4)

Old Testament Definition of Miracles

The word *miracle* in the Old Testament is the Hebrew word *owth,* which means "a sign or signal or a distinguishing mark." It is a banner or remembrance. An ancient definition of *miracle* is given as a token, ensign, standard or proof. There are other synonyms to better describe a miracle in the Old Testament paradigm, which include omen or warning. The aspect of miracles in light of the Hebrews was a supernatural marker that was distinguishingly noticeable and memorable. Miracles were to be remembered in Israel generationally as a point of reference of when God by His mighty hand delivered them out of the house of the Egyptians and Pharaoh.

An example of this in found in Judges 6:13 (NKJV):

> Gideon to Him, "O my lord, if the LORD is with us, why then has all this happened to us? And where are all His miracles which our fathers told us about, saying, 'Did not the Lord bring us up from Egypt?' But now the Lord has forsaken us and delivered us into the hands of the Midianites."

God demonstrates and reveals His glory through the miracles through Moses according to Numbers 14:22 and through Jesus the greater Moses in John 2:11 (NKJV): *"This beginning of signs Jesus did in Cana of Galilee, and manifested His glory; and His disciples believed in Him."*

- Old Testament: *"Because all these men who have seen My glory and the signs which I did in Egypt and in the wilderness, and have put Me to the test now these ten times, and have not heeded My voice"* (Numbers 14:22 NKJV).

- New Testament: *"This miraculous sign at Cana in Galilee was the first time Jesus revealed his glory. And his disciples believed in him"* (John 2:11 NLT).

Cessationist Versus Continualist

The viewpoint of cessationism holds that the *charismata* (favors, gifts) were exclusively for the early church or apostolic age; therefore the gifts of working of miracles or miracles itself has ceased with the writing of the last book of the Bible or close of canon or the death of the last apostle, John. Essentially, cessationists say that the gifts died with the apostles and early believers. However, there are not two or three Scriptures in the New Testament that clear-cut support this theory.

In the viewpoint of continuationism, on the other hand, is that the gifts of the Spirit including the gift of working of miracles have continued throughout the history of Christianity, and have occurred ongoing after the early church or apostolic age, which gives us as believers today a prophetic advantage.

In modern Christianity, it is widely believed that God continues to operate this gift through believers interchangeably with the gift of faith. This gift gives someone the God-given ability to partner with the Holy Spirit with an emphasis on the power of God operating by the Spirit of God in and through the believers and His church. I believe it has always been the intent of God to signify or teach something with miraculous manifestations of signs, wonders, and miracles. Like other *charismata*, these are special and extraordinary powers bestowed by God only to a few, and primarily for the spiritual good of others rather than the recipient.

According to New Testament Scriptures, the manifestation of the Spirit in the form of the gifts of the Holy Spirit, especially the working of miracles, is to continue to work through the followers and believers of Christ until His return. The most powerful miracles are when the Holy Spirit resides in believers, empowering them to partner with the plan, will, and purpose of God to release the realm of God into the realm of earth. The supernatural is accessed through believers. God has given us His precious Spirit to work the works of Christ. The "greater works" responsibility has been transferred to the ministry of the believers.

New Testament Distinct Definitions of Miracles

There are four Greek words used in the New Testament to designate or describe *miracles*:

1. Sign—The Greek word *semeion* (Strong's Concordance #G4592) is sometimes translated as *sign* (Matthew 12:38-39, 16:1; Mark 8:11; Luke 11:16) and is used to validate a divine commission, to attest to a message from God, or bear witness of His presence.

2. Wonder—*Terata* or *teras* (Strong's #G5059), translated as *wonder* in some New Testament translations of Acts 2:19, denotes events, occurrences or phenomenal miracles that are astonishing for humans to see. This simply indicates something extraordinary.

3. Power—*Dunamis* (Strong's #G1411), another Greek word in the New Testament used to describe miracles, means force or power. It refers to events that are clearly caused by someone possessing superhuman power that is supernatural in origin (Romans 15:19; 2 Thessalonians 2:9). This is best defined as

miraculous power, exertion, thrust, or ability and simply means a mighty deed or act

4. Work—The last word in the New Testament used to refer to miracles in the Greek is *ergon* (Strong's #G2041). This word, often translated as *works*, refers to the deeds of Christ (Matthew 11:2, John 5:20,26; 7:3; 10:38).

Supernatural Miracles Workers

The following are a few biblical examples of those in the Old and New Testaments who worked in the realm of the miracles:

- God Himself—Isaiah 7:14; Psalm 77:14 (NIV) declares, *"You are the God who performs miracles; you display your power among the peoples."*
- Jesus Christ—Acts 2:22
- Believers—Mark 16:17-20; 1 Corinthians 12:10
- Prophets—Moses and Aaron: Exodus 7:3; Elijah: 1 Kings 17:9-16; Luke 4:26; 1 Kings 17:17-24; 1 Kings 18:41-45; 2 Kings 1:10-12; 2 Kings 2:8. Elisha: 2 Kings 2:19-22; 2 Kings 4; 2 Kings 5:26-27; 2 Kings 6:6,12; 2 Kings 13:21
- Apostles—By the hands of the apostles: Acts 2:43; 4:33; 5:12; 14:3,4; 19:11; Romans 15:19; 2 Corinthians 12:12. Received personally from the Lord Jesus: Matthew 10:1-2.
- The Seventy—Luke 10:17-20
- Paul—Acts 9:3-6, 16-17; 14:10; 16:18; 19:11; 20:9-12
- Other Disciples—Mark 9:39, John 14:12

- Deacons—By the first deacons (Acts 6:8; 8:5-7) who were given this power by the apostles (Acts 6:5-6)
- The false/anti-christ or ministers—Matthew 24:24; Revelation 13:11-15, and his "ministers" or "magicians" or "sorcerers" (Exodus 7:10-12)

Defying the Odds—Working of Miracles

There are several New Testament examples of the working of miracles through Paul the apostle. The first example is when Paul raised Eutychus miraculously from the dead after he had fallen three stories out a window.

> And a young man named Eutychus, sitting at the window, sank into a deep sleep as Paul talked still longer. And being overcome by sleep, he fell down from the third story and was taken up dead. But Paul went down and bent over him, and taking him in his arms, said, "Do not be alarmed, for his life is in him." And when Paul had gone up and had broken bread and eaten, he conversed with them a long while, until daybreak, and so departed. And they took the youth away alive, and were not a little comforted (Acts 20:9-12 ESV).

In the following Scripture Paul writes to the Galatians about how God supplies the Spirit to meet the demands through the working of miracles by hearing with faith instead of the works of the law. The working of miracles is done through faith, not by works of the law, merit, or religious traditions. God is working miracles in the midst of the Galatians by the Holy Spirit through ordinary believers, not just the apostles: *"Therefore He who supplies the Spirit to you and works miracles among you, does He do it by the works of the law, or by the hearing of faith?"* (Galatians 3:5 NKJV).

The answer to Paul's rhetorical question is obvious. The Galatians had received the Holy Spirit when they were saved (Romans 8:9; 1 Corinthians 12:13; 1 John 3:24; 4:13), not through keeping the law, but through the saving faith granted to them when hearing the gospel. Faith comes by hearing and hearing by the word of God (Romans 10:17) and how can one hear unless there be a preacher, and how can one preach unless they are sent (Romans 10:14-15). Therefore, I say that the gift of working of miracles comes by faith and faith activates miracles in the believer, so how can anyone do miracles unless they are filled by the Spirit.

In the New Testament, we see the working of miracles in the ministry of Paul when he was bitten by a snake and the deadly poisonous venom miraculously did not harm him. He literally shook off the poison and was viewed as a god to the locals in that part of the world:

> *When Paul had gathered a bundle of sticks and put them on the fire, a viper came out because of the heat and fastened on his hand. When the native people saw the creature hanging from his hand, they said to one another, "No doubt this man is a murderer. Though he has escaped from the sea, Justice has not allowed him to live." He, however, shook off the creature into the fire and suffered no harm. They were waiting for him to swell up or suddenly fall down dead. But when they had waited a long time and saw no misfortune come to him, they changed their minds and said that he was a god* (Acts 28:3-6 ESV).

Paul was supposedly stoned to death and miraculously survived it, rising up as if nothing happened:

> *Then Jews from Antioch and Iconium came there; and having persuaded the multitudes, and they stoned Paul and dragged him out of the city, supposing him to be dead.*

However, when the disciples gathered around him, he rose up and went into the city. And the next day he departed with Barnabas to Derbe (Acts 14:19-20 NKJV).

False Signs, Wonders, and Miracles

The Old and New Testaments reveal that false signs, wonders, and deceitful miracles will be performed by false christs and false prophets. There are a number of Scriptures in the Bible that reveal the practice of false (pseudo) miracles, signs, and wonders. We know there are authentic miracles, so the kingdom of satan will look to duplicate and deceive with lying signs, wonders, and miraculous practices. God has given us as believers the ability to operate in the realm of the supernatural. The Spirit of God has empowered us through gifts of working of miracles with the ability to function in the realm of the unexplained. As it is my intent to make us more aware of the realm of the miraculous, we must also beware of the realm of counterfeit miracles. The following biblical examples warn us of the false signs, wonders, and miracles in both the Old and New Testaments:

Old Testament Examples

When Pharaoh says to you, "Prove yourselves by working a miracle," then you shall say to Aaron, "Take your staff and cast it down before Pharaoh, that it may become a serpent." So Moses and Aaron went to Pharaoh and did just as the LORD commanded. Aaron cast down his staff before Pharaoh and his servants, and it became a serpent. Then Pharaoh summoned the wise men and the sorcerers, and they, the magicians of Egypt, also did the same by their secret arts. For each man cast down his staff, and they became serpents. But Aaron's staff swallowed up their staffs (Exodus 7:9-12 ESV).

If a prophet or a dreamer of dreams arises among you and gives you a sign or a wonder, and the sign or wonder that he tells you comes to pass, and if he says, "Let us go after other gods," which you have not known, "and let us serve them," you shall not listen to the words of that prophet or that dreamer of dreams. For the LORD your God is testing you, to know whether you love the LORD your God with all your heart and with all your soul. You shall walk after the LORD your God and fear him and keep his commandments and obey his voice, and you shall serve him and hold fast to him. But that prophet or that dreamer of dreams shall be put to death, because he has taught rebellion against the LORD your God, who brought you out of the land of Egypt and redeemed you out of the house of slavery, to make you leave the way in which the LORD your God commanded you to walk. So you shall purge the evil from your midst (Deuteronomy 13:1-5 ESV).

New Testament Examples

Here is an account of the devil tempting Jesus to perform a supernatural feat so people would be able to identify Him as the Son of God as recorded in Matthew 4:5-7 (NKJV):

Then the devil took Him up into the holy city, set Him on the pinnacle of the temple, and said to Him, "If You are the Son of God, throw Yourself down. For it is written: 'He shall give His angels charge over you,' and, 'In their hands they shall bear you up, lest you dash your foot against a stone.'" Jesus said to him, "It is written again, 'You shall not tempt the LORD your God.'"

False christs and prophets:

Then if anyone says to you, "Look, here is the Christ!" or, 'Look, He is there!" do not believe it. For false christs and false prophets will rise and show signs and wonders to deceive, if possible, even the elect. But take heed; see, I have told you all things beforehand (Mark 13:21-23 NKJV).

For false christs and false prophets will arise and perform great signs and wonders, so as to lead astray, if possible, even the elect. See, I have told you beforehand. So, if they say to you, "Look, he is in the wilderness," do not go out. If they say, "Look, he is in the inner rooms," do not believe it. For as the lightning comes from the east and shines as far as the west, so will be the coming of the Son of Man. Wherever the corpse is, there the vultures will gather (Matthew 24:24-28 ESV).

The coming of the lawless one is by the activity of Satan with all power and false signs and wonders, and with all wicked deception for those who are perishing, because they refused to love the truth and so be saved (2 Thessalonians 2:9-10 ESV).

And I saw three unclean spirits like frogs coming out of the mouth of the dragon, out of the mouth of the false prophet. For they are spirit of demons, performing signs, which go out to the kings of the earth and of the whole world, to gather them to the battle of the great day of God Almighty (Revelation 16:13-14 NKJV).

Prophets in this hour will have the supernatural power engineered, empowered, and enabled by the Spirit of God to counter and confront counterfeit signs, wonders, and miracles. Genuine prophetic ministry will be the conduit of the very God of miracles. The manifestation gifts of the supernatural are given to every believer in Christ to reveal, demonstrate, exhibit, and unearth the power of God. Power prophecy is activated through the power gifts. Power is irrevocably the distinguishing mark of genuine prophetic believers.

PART III

THE MINISTRY OF ANGELS

‖ 10 ‖

ANGELIC PARTNERSHIP

Praise the LORD, you his angels, you his mighty
ones who do his bidding, who obey his word.
—Psalm 103:20 NIV

Are not all angels ministering spirits sent
to serve those who will inherit salvation?
—Hebrews 1:14 NIV

The purpose of this chapter is not to be exhaustive or comprehensive, but simply to bring greater understanding and depth to believers, especially the prophetic type, on the reality and purpose of prophetic angels and how to partner with them in our prophetic ministry.

Since the beginning of time there has been a unique relationship of angels partnering with the affairs of humanity. This is not a formula but a scriptural study on the role and engagement of the prophetic and angelic. God is the Father of all spirits, and we have access through Christ to all that is made available to Christ. God talked to the prophets through angelic agency. God created the partnership between the angelic agency with His prophetic agents—the prophets.

Ancient prophets have always worked in divine partnership with angels. Angels are heavenly or unseen messengers of God, while prophets are earthly or seen messengers of God. The messengers of

God in Heaven through angels has been sent to work with the prophets of God on earth. Prophets not only receive direction and revelation by God through visions and dreams, but also through angels who carry messages from God. Angels speak to God's spokespeople.

This chapter explores the phenomenal relationship the ministry of angels have with the ministry of the prophetic. This angelic-prophetic partnership is simply supernatural. There are times when we are coexisting with angels unaware, not fully comprehending they live all around us. Some we have encountered and entertained because they have walked among us as strangers even in human form according to Hebrews 13:2 (NLT): *"Don't forget to show hospitality to strangers, for some who have done this have entertained angels without realizing it!"*

AN ANGEL AND PROPHET LINK?

As we explore the ministry of angels and the ministry of the prophetic, it is important to understand that God employs these two agencies to relay His messages between Heaven and earth. God's communicative agents, both visible and invisible, are essential to His purpose being executed on earth as it is already established in Heaven. Comprehending the reality of the angelic, the prophetic, and the supernatural has a lot to do with understanding the Kingdom of God, communicating His plan, and seeing Heaven on earth through what Jesus told His disciples how to pray, *"Your kingdom come. Your will be done on earth, as it is in heaven"* (Matthew 6:10). Comprehending the angelic agents' partnership with God's prophetic agents will give you a healthy perspective of their assignment, function, role, and purpose as messengers of God. There are more direct links with angels than we may realize.

The unique link between angels and the prophets is the extraordinary responsibility to carry the very word of God. It is impossible to fully understand the unseen realm, the power of God and revelations without first expounding and exploring revelatory connections between the angels and the mantle of the prophets. There are more than 300 biblical references of angels in the Bible. Angels are ancient in essence and are spoken of before the beginning of time, revealing their engagement in the affairs of humanity.

ANGELIC ACTIVITY ROLE

Angels have always played a major role in the eternal purpose of God, and their activity is more needed today than ever. The need for angelic partnership and angelic activity will increase as prophetic activity increases to accomplish the will and purposes of God. Angels act as messengers to the prophets. They take care of people. They record everything a person does, and this information is used on the Day of Judgment.

I will share some foundational knowledge of angels to broaden our perspective, but my goal is to show that God has sent us to partner with His unseen messengers to manifest the reality of Heaven. God's heavenly messengers are working on your behalf.

In Scripture, we are told that angels have many roles. A few of them include being God's messengers and holy warriors, watching history unfold, praising and worshipping God, and being guardian angels, protecting and directing people on God's behalf. The Bible tells us that God's angels are delivering messages, accompanying the lonely, granting protection, and even fighting His battles. Angels who were sent to deliver messages began by saying, *"Do not be afraid,"* or *"Do not fear,"* according to Luke 2:10. There are times or an urgency in which an angel of the Lord would appear or manifest to someone in natural form, which would bring awe, reverence, worship, and typically fear. The reaction or appearance of angels was a frightening encounter. The phrase *"Do not fear"* appears in the Bible about 58 times throughout both Old and New Testaments.

God's angels operate discretely and don't draw attention to themselves as they carry out the assignment given by God. While God has called His heavenly messengers to work on His behalf, He has also called angels to work in our lives.

The following are five basic roles and functions of angels partnering and working with us:

1. Angels provide angelic guardianship and protection. They are sent to guard and protect us. The Bible tells us, *"For He will order His angels to protect you wherever you go. They will hold you up with their hands so you won't even hurt your foot on a stone"* (Psalm 91:11-12 NLT). Angels can be regarded as our invisible and unseen bodyguards protecting us from things seen and unseen. Prophets are guarded and protected by angelic guardianship. We will see further in this chapter how this invisible agency works in relationship with God's prophetic spokespeople. Angels are also one of the unseen powers or phenomena behind the prophetic. Prophets have experienced the guardship of angels in the Bible. They protect as a duty to each believer in Christ as what we commonly call a "guardian angel."

For Daniel's protection, God sent His angel and shut the mouths of lions from killing His prophet. Divine protection accompanies the prophetic mantle. This is part of the angelic partnership that God initiates on behalf of His servants, the prophets.

> *My God sent His angel and shut the lions' mouths, so that they have not hurt me, because I was found innocent before Him; and also, O king, I have done no wrong before you* (Daniel 6:22 NKJV).

Angels are given charge over us as ministers of defense according to Psalm 91:11 (AMP): *"For He will command His angels in regard to you, to protect and defend and guard you in all your ways [of obedience and service]."* This translates literally to mean that God will instruct His angels to watch over individuals. God will give each of His angels a purpose: to guard His children. Those who are faithful will be under the constant care of His angels. Because of this specific role in our lives, they can warn and protect us from harm as part of their angelic duties (see Psalm 34:7; Matthew 18:10; Exodus 23:20).

> *For it is written, "He will command His angels concerning you to guard you carefully"* (Luke 4:10 NIV).

In Luke chapter 4, satan challenged Jesus to throw Himself off the highest point of the temple by citing that God would protect Jesus with His angels. However when citing Psalm 91:11, satan purposefully omitted *"in all your ways"* thus changing the meaning. The reality is that God sends His angels to protect those who have committed themselves to His loving care, not to those who want to put Him to the test.

2.   Angels are messengers of God that communicate His message to people and His prophets. Angels are communicators of God's message to us. Angels are one of God's ways He speaks to prophets, along with dreams and visions (Luke 1:19). Prophets and angels are partners in the communicative realm of the Kingdom of God. He will speak by way of angels or by prophets (or prophetic voices). Angels can speak to us in dreams (see Matthew 1:18-25). Angels in the ancient biblical text spoke directly to prophets in dreams (Daniel 8:15-26; 9:21-27). An angel warned Joseph in a dream regarding baby Jesus (see Matthew 2:12-23).

Moses received his prophetic calling directly from God through one of His angelic agents, an angel:

Old Testament: *"There the angel of the LORD appeared to him in flames of fire from within a bush. Moses saw that though the bush was on fire it did not burn up. So Moses thought, 'I will go over and see this strange sight—why the bush does not burn up.' When the LORD saw that he had gone over to look, God called to him from within the bush, 'Moses! Moses!' And Moses said, 'Here I am'"* (Exodus 3:2-4 NIV).

New Testament: *"And when forty years had passed, an Angel of the Lord appeared to him in a flame of fire in a bush, in the wilderness of Mount Sinai"* (Acts 7:30 NKJV).

The angel of the Lord appears to Moses in a flame in Exodus 3:2, and God speaks to Moses from the flame in Exodus 3:4, both instances referring to Himself in the first person as the Person calling him. A message from the angel of the Lord is a direct message from God. The same can be said about a message from God's prophets, that it is a message from the mouth of God since prophets are commonly known as *"mouthpieces"* or the *"mouth of God."*

3.   Angels observe and watch over us through angelic observation and surveillance. One of the duties of angels is to provide unseen surveillance and observation over us. This close observation is key in providing protection and watching for and against any diabolical, demonic, satanic, and harmful human activities or attacks against us. The Scripture declares to us, *"...We have been made a spectacle to the whole universe, and to angels as well as to human beings"* (1 Corinthians 4:9 NIV).

According to Scripture, many eyes are upon us, including the eyes of angels. But the implication is even greater than that. The Greek word in this passage translated as *spectacle* means "theater" or "public assembly." Angels gain pertinent knowledge through long observation, monitoring, and surveilling human activities. Unlike humans, angels do not have to study the past; they have experienced it. Therefore, they know how others have acted and reacted in critical situations and can predict with a great degree of accuracy how we may act in similar circumstances through historical observations.

4. Angels are ministers (ministering spirits) to us. Angels are sent to minister to and minister with believers. Prophets in particular were ministered to and received divine assistants. They are charged to tend to our care and welfare. Angels are actively involved in the lives of God's people. They have clear and specific functions; God sends them to respond in our specific times of need. One way God comes to our aide is through the ministry of angels. They are on earth right now, having been sent to minister to our needs as we are heirs of salvation. Prophets minister with angels in their prophetic ministries (Hebrews 1:14).

The following are Old and New Testament biblical references of angels as *ministering spirits* to believers:

- Psalm 104:4 (NASB), *"He makes the winds His messengers, flaming fire His ministers."*
- Hebrews 1:7 (NASB), *"And of the angels He says, 'Who makes His angels winds, and His ministers a flame of fire.'"*
- Hebrews 1:14 (AMP), *"Are not all the angels ministering spirits sent out [by God] to serve (accompany, protect) those who will inherit salvation? [Of course they are!]"*

The word *ministering* in the Greek is the word *leitourgikos,* meaning "the performance of service" according to Strong's Concordance. Ministering means employed in ministering. It comes from the root meaning to do a service or perform a work. Essentially, angels are employed to minister to us and to serve us. Angels are invisible ministers, attendants, and servants to believers and prophets. This is one of the functions of angels. God employs and deploys angels as a ministering agency. There is a ministry of angels according to the mentioned Scripture references.

Jesus, being hungry from fasting for forty days and forty nights, was ministered and attended to by angels after He was tempted continually by the devil in the wilderness: *"Then the devil left Him, and behold, angels came and were ministering to Him"* (Matthew 4:11 NKJV).

5. Angels are dispatched at the voice of God. Angelic dispatchment is activated with the command and prophetic release of the voice of God. Prophets are regarded as the voice of God on earth who speaks His word. They declare the word of God with their voice. Angels stand at attention, listening carefully for the voice of God. The word is what angels carry out. They do the Lord's bidding. Therefore, angels minister alongside prophets and prophetic voices to obey the voice of the Commander in Chief, who is Jesus Christ. Angels operate in rank and order under command. Angels are under the command of God and superior angelic officers.

Angels are dispatched by voice activations of the word of God. Therefore, because prophets of God are messengers of God on earth and are the voices that carry God's word or commands, angels are dispatched and deployed when prophets release divine utterances. Angels also obey the voice of the prophets who release the word of the Lord: *"Bless the Lord, O you his angels, you mighty ones who do his word, obeying the voice of his word!"* (Psalm 103:20 ESV).

Consider Daniel 10:12 (NKJV) where the angel responds to the words of Daniel the prophet saying: *"...Your words were heard; and I have come because of your words."* We can see that Daniel's words put the angel to work for him. Too many of our angels are unemployed because we do not pray, activate the word of God, or prophesy as the Spirit gives us divine utterances.

Prayers That Dispatch Angelic Arms

One of the many countless benefits we enjoy as sons and daughters of God and kings and priests in the Kingdom of God is the authority to dispatch angels through prayer. Prayer is the primary function of prophetic believers that releases angelic help in critical seasons. There are a number of Scriptures where God sends angels to help the prophets, forefathers, apostles, the church, and believers in Christ Jesus. This is one of the most important functions within the angelic partnership—we can activate angelic assistance through prayer, intercession, and the prophetic.

It is critically important for believers to know—your prayers and intercession cause God to send angelic reinforcement and enforcement to help you. Essentially, this is similar to when police officers or emergency medical services (EMS) personnel are dispatched when we call 9-1-1 for help. Prayer is calling on Heaven to send us help in handling our earthly affairs. Jesus declared on the Cross that He could dispatch twelve legions (72,000 to 120,000) of angels at His word or command through prayer to His Father (Matthew 26:53). An army of angels was at His disposal.

Mighty Chariotry of Angels

With mighty chariotry, twice ten thousand, thousands upon thousands, the Lord came from Sinai into the holy place (Psalm 68:17 New Revised Standard Version).

The *"mighty chariotry"* is a term for angels. The availability of angels is age-old and not specific to any covenant, but have always been in the unseen realms around servants of God as evidenced by this awesome display of warring angels around the prophet Elisha. In Second Kings 6, the Bible describes how God provides an army of angels leading horses and chariots of fire to protect the prophet Elisha and his servant, and opens the servant's eyes so he can see the angelic army encampment surrounding them.

The Bible describes a heavenly army of angels protecting the prophet Elisha and his servant from an earthly army. Elisha prayer that opened the spiritual eyes:

> *So he answered, "Do not fear, for those who are with us are more than those who are with them." And Elisha prayed, and said, "LORD, I pray, open his eyes that he may see." Then the LORD opened the eyes of the young man, and he saw. And behold, the mountain was full of horses and chariots of fire all around Elisha* (2 Kings 6:16-17 NKJV).

You only have to see them with your spiritual eyes to know it's true. That is what Elisha was telling his servant when they were surrounded by a large Syrian army. The servant was afraid, but Elisha said, *"Do not fear, for those who are with us are more than those who are with them"* (2 Kings 6:16 NKJV). When the servant opened his spiritual eyes, he saw an army of angels and chariots of fire surrounding the entire Syrian army. Imagine what that would be like in the unseen, invisible, and spirit realm seeing the extraordinary imagery of angels with fiery chariots.

Prophets are protected with angelic hosts (armies). Prophets were provided with full protection of God's invisible military armed forces due to the gravity and brevity of His carrier of His precious word. He guards His word-bearer with unseen soldiers.

The following is an example of angels being dispatched through the power of prayer as Jesus Christ spoke of dispatching of angels just after being betrayed and arrested: *"Or do you think that I cannot now pray to My Father, and He will provide Me with more than twelve legions of angels?"* (Matthew 26:53 NKJV).

Prophetic Breakthrough

Then he said to me, "Fear not, Daniel, for from the first day that you set your heart to understand and humbled yourself before your God, your words have been heard, and I have come because of your words" (Daniel 10:12 ESV).

Daniel prayed for twenty-one days and God sent the answer. There was contention between princes in the heavenly realm. Twenty-one is the number of breakthrough. The first day that Daniel had set in his heart to humble himself before God to pray and understand, God sent the answer. However, his prayer was held up or withheld by a principality over Persia that was delaying the answer. Continued praying in the spirit contends over answered prayers sent by God. Daniel's bombardment of prayer caused God to send archangel Michael, chief prince and warring angel, to fight on Daniel's behalf to get the prayers through. This was breakthrough prayer. This was *prophetic breakthrough* against spiritual princes.

Angelic princes were warring and battling in the heavenlies for twenty-one days as a result of the prayers of Daniel the prophet. He was anointed with breakthrough prayers that prevailed and contended in the spirit world until the answers broke through. There will be times when your prayers will be delayed due to principalities and powers in the heavens hindering your prayers. It is important to war over your prophecy and prayer (see 1 Timothy 1:18).

Daniel's words in prayer initiated angelic wars. Daniel's words in prayer were heard, and angels were sent because the power of prophecy is founded in the art of prayer and intercession. Prayer is interwoven with the prophetic word to release the supernatural to dispatch angels to help grapple your answers out of the hands and power of high-ranking spirits.

Power prophecy releases angels to bring breakthrough and answered prayers. Prophets are key to partnering with angels to get breakthrough and answers from God. The prayers of prophets contend with princes and principalities in the unseen realm. Daniel activated prevailing prayers to release answers through his continual, relentless praying for twenty-one days. I say to pray until something breaks.

There is an innumerable group of angels at our disposal to dispatch. The Scripture declares that there are so many that they cannot be counted: *"But you have come to Mount Zion and to the city of the living God, the heavenly Jerusalem, to an innumerable company of angels"* (Hebrews 12:22 NKJV).

ANGEL FOOD

Human beings ate the bread of angels; he [God] *sent them all the food they could eat* (Psalm 78:25 NIV).
Man did eat angels' food: he sent them meat to the full (Psalm 78:25 KJV).

Elijah was fed by an angel to receive supernatural strength. Prophets are ministered to by angels to gain natural and spiritual strength. Elijah was supernaturally strengthened by the food of angels in the wilderness:

Then he lay down under the broom tree and fell asleep. Suddenly an angel touched him and said, "Get up and eat." And he looked around, and there by his head was a cake of bread baked over hot coals, and a jar of water. So he ate and drank and lay down again. A second time the angel of the LORD returned and touched him, saying, "Get up and eat, or the journey will be too much for you" (1 Kings 19:5-7).

Jesus was ministered to by angels after His temptation by the devil in the wilderness. He was also given angel food: *"Then the devil left Him; and angels came and ministered to Him [bringing Him food and serving Him]"* (Matthew 4:11 AMP).

Jesus had fasted forty days and forty nights in the wilderness and was hungry—even the devil tempted Him to turn a stone into bread. Therefore, angels ministered and attended to Him, supplying an angelic meal prepared by His Father to renew His physical strength (see Luke 4:1-4). Prophets are not to live by bread alone but by every word (spiritual command) of God. Prophet food is to do the will of the Father who sends them (John 4:34).

Elisha even prayed that the eyes of his servant be opened to an army of angels (2 Kings 6:17-20). Prayer by the prophet revealed the angelic partnership relationship with the prophet to the angelic host in Elisha praying for servant Gehazi's spiritual eyes to be opened to the angelic realm. Prophets can see in the spirit realm and they can activate your spiritual eyes to be opened to a world in the spirit. Angels have the ability to impart to the prophet or believer in dreams (see Luke 1:26-35 and Revelation 10:8-11).

ANGELIC WARFARE

The apostle Paul understood angelic and unseen warfare and the wrestling in the spirit realm:

For we do not wrestle against flesh and blood, but against principalities, against powers, against the rulers of the darkness of this age, against spiritual hosts of wickedness in the heavenly places. Therefore take up the whole armor of

God, that you may be able to withstand in the evil day, and having done all, to stand (Ephesians 6:12-13 NKJV).

Prophets and believers in Christ have spiritual forces deployed on our behalf during times and seasons of spiritual and even physical warfare. The angelic warriors even assist our national armies just as they assisted Israel's army. Angels are special supernatural forces. Consider the following Scriptures that provide us with what angelic and invisible warfare looks like on earth. In spiritual warfare, God deploys angelic air strikes and ground attacks against our enemies:

These passages from the Bible are examples of *angels* killing and assisting us in battle and warfare, and in some instances wiping out opposing armies on our behalf:

And it came to pass on a certain night that the angel of the LORD went out, and killed in the camp of the Assyrians one hundred and eighty-five thousand; and when people arose early in the morning, there were the corpses—all dead (2 Kings 19:35 NKJV).

And the angel of the LORD went out and struck 185,000 in the camp of the Assyrians; and when the [surviving] men got up early the next morning, they saw all the dead (Isaiah 37:36 AMP).

For My angel will go before you and bring you in to the land of the Amorites, the Hittites, the Perizzites, the Canaanites, the Hivites and the Jebusites; and I will completely destroy them (Exodus 23:23 NASB).

But when we cried out to the LORD, He heard our voice and sent an angel and brought us out from Egypt; now behold, we are at Kadesh, a town on the edge of your territory (Numbers 20:16 NASB).

An example of a declaration of angelic wars in the heavens is recorded in Revelation 12:7. This is where the archangel, the general of the angelic army is warring with the great dragon (satan) and his angels: *"And there was war in heaven, Michael and his angels waging war with the dragon. The dragon and his angels waged war"* (Revelation 12:7 NASB).

|| 11 ||

ANGELIC HIERARCHY

ANGELIC HIERARCHY, CLASSES, AND GOVERNMENTAL STRUCTURE

The word *hierarchy* means "a system or organization in which people or groups are ranked one above the other according to status or authority" according to the Merriam-Webster Dictionary. It is an arrangement of classification of things according to relative importance or inclusiveness.

Angels are organized according to their rank, class, and grouping (choir). Angels are ministers on behalf of God and on our behalf as we are in the presence of God. Angels carry out various assignments, duties, and responsibilities according to the specific type of classification of angels they are. They serve in different categories within angelic hierarchy and structure.

One of the most interesting things about angels is that they function strictly within their rank and order. We will gain a greater understanding of this as we better comprehend the different functions, duties, and angelic job descriptions, as all of them are ministering spirits according to Hebrews 1:7,14.

We may be able to speak directly to God through prayer, but according to the Bible, He reaches us through a variety of angels, each with distinct duties. There are twelve types of angels within three major groups known as choirs. Regardless of where they are in the hierarchy, like us, they are individuals. Unlike us, because they are able to see far beyond a mortal timeline, they are extremely patient and forgiving. They are aware of our personal life goals and are assigned to assist us, but never interfere with our free will.

Let's examine and study for the purpose of understanding the angelic order, that each angel ministers within various classifications, ranks, and hierarchal structure.

CLASSES OF ANGELS

For by Him all things were created that are in heaven and that are on earth, visible and invisible, whether thrones or dominions or principalities or powers. All things were created through Him and for Him (Colossians 1:16 NKJV).

During my biblical research, I studied *twelve types or classes of angels* within the angelic structure, each with specific characteristics and virtues. I name the types/classes and then we will explore each one in-depth to better understand how angels partner with us prophetically:

1. Seraphim (Seraphs)
2. Cherubim (Plural of Cherub)—living creatures
3. Thrones (Elders)
4. Elect Angels
5. Ministering Spirits
6. Powers, Rulers and Authorities
7. Principalities
8. Archangels (Chief Prince or Prince)
9. Angels (Messengers)
10. Watchers
11. Hosts (Angelic Hosts or Armies)
12. Angelic Civilization

1. *Seraphim or Seraphs*

> *Above him stood the seraphim. Each had six wings: with two he covered his face, and with two he covered his feet, and with two he flew* (Isaiah 6:2 ESV).

Seraphim means "the fiery ones" or "burning ones." It is the plural of the word *seraph*. The Hebrew word *seraph* or *seraphim* is described as symbolic creature from their fiery copper color from the Hebrew etymology of their name. Seraphim are fiery, flying, talking, supernatural angelic-human type being and with their spare wings they cover their faces and feet. These angels are mentioned in the Bible as having faces, hands, and feet. Seraphs are the highest ranking celestial beings in the hierarchy of angels.

Each seraph has six wings, four of which they use to cover themselves in the presence of God as a sign of humility; the other two they use to fly. They cry out "Holy, holy, holy," and appear to worship God continuously. They are often depicted in religious art. As mentioned in Isaiah 6:1-7, seraphim is the most powerful class of angels.

They are the caretakers of the Almighty's throne and are known to continuously shout and shower praises over Him. Seraphim are known to guard over God's holiness. They are also described as being a majestic beings with six wings, human hands and voices, in attendance upon God. These angelic beings are burning or flaming angels. You can envision them burning or on fire or set on fire. The best imagery is someone set on fire or engulfed in flames. The prophet Isaiah gave us a revelation of seraphim in Isaiah chapter 6.

Seraphim are only mentioned once in the Bible. They appear in Isaiah 6:2-7, where they continually worship the Lord saying, *"Holy, Holy, Holy is the LORD of hosts; the whole earth is filled with His glory"* (Isaiah 6:3 AMP). Ancient prophets had visions of the angelic realm. They saw into the spirit, unseen, invisible, and supernatural realms. Prophets will have a number of encounters with God's angelic messengers in visions, dreams, and visitations. Revelations of angels is a function within the office of the prophet. Prophets were taken into heavenly visions or literally into the very presence of God and saw angelic activity. This was commonplace for the prophets and this reality of the supernatural is no different today.

2. *Cherubim (Plural of Cherubs)*

> *This is the living creature I saw under the God of Israel by the River Chebar, and I knew they were cherubim* (Ezekiel 10:20 NKJV).

The primary and primitive function of *cherubim* is to guard, protect, cover, and operate as chariot escorts for the glory of God and His throne. They are stationed as heavenly guards. They are guards in and around the abode and throne of God. They serve as covering the mercy seat (Exodus 25:18-20) and are guardians of God's presence. Cherubs come in pairs or chariots of two or four. They can be described as the heavenly body guards for the holiness and sacredness of heavenly things.

Angels are invisible spirits who attend to us daily though we are not able to see them. However, the presence of these invisible creatures coexists with humans knowingly or unknowingly.

Prophets are very aware of angelic presence. In my partnership with angels in my prophetic ministry, one way I sense the presence of angels in a meeting is when I feel in the spirit winds or a wind-like feeling blowing on or around me in the atmosphere (Psalm 104:4).

Living Creatures

In the books of Ezekiel and Revelation, other kinds of heavenly beings are mentioned, known as *"living creatures"* around God's throne (Ezekiel 1:5-14; Revelation 4:6-8). They appeared like a lion, an ox, a man, and an eagle, representing various parts of God's creation—wild beasts, domesticated animals, human beings, and birds. They, too, worship God continually: *"...Day and night they never cease to sing, 'Holy, holy, holy, is the Lord God Almighty, who was and is and is to come!'"* (Revelation 4:8 Revised Standard Version). We as prophetic worshippers can sing with angels. Worshippers are prophetic by default and will receive by revelation songs and messages in the form of lyrics from angels (Job 38:7; Zephaniah 3:17; Revelation 5:8-10).

David as king prophetically and by revelation saw that God used a cherub as one of His choice vehicles of transportation. He rides on a winged cherub and David saw the cherub as winds and flames of fire. Paul confirmed the words of David in Hebrews 1:7 (ESV): *"Of angels he says, "He makes his angels winds, and his ministers a flame of fire,"* confirming what it is said of Him in Psalm 104:4 (NIV): *"He makes the winds his messengers, flames of fire his servants."*

The ancient prophets revealed God riding on the cherubs or chariots of fire, as His chariot escorts and vehicles of transportation in true royal fashion as King of All in the biblical accounts:

He rode on a cherub and flew; He appeared upon the wings of the wind (2 Samuel 22:11 AMP).
For indeed, the Lord will come in fire, and His chariots will be like the stormy wind, to render His anger with rage, and His rebuke with flames of fire (Isaiah 66:15 AMP).

Chariots can come as a fiery storm or rushing whirlwind (smoking, lightning storm). God showed me that when His chariot of angels comes, it is like a powerful thunder and lightning storm or tornado. The chariot of angelic horses is blazing or engulfed in inconsumable flames. Ezekiel the prophet was taken into heavenly visions of God when the heavens were opened to him at the River of Chebar and he provides us with explicit, powerful details of cherubim as a whirlwind with a great cloud of raging fire engulfing it as God is riding on their wings (read Ezekiel 1).

In Ezekiel 1:12 (AMP), the cherubs went where the Spirit of God wanted to go. The Spirit of God drove the cherubs in whatever direction He wanted to go: *"And each went straight forward; wherever the spirit was about to go, they would go, without turning as they went."*

The angelic chariot is pictured with wheels full of eyes in Ezekiel 10:12 (NKJV): *"And their whole body, with their back, their hands, their wings, and the wheels that the four had, were full of eyes all around."*

Elisha actually saw his master prophet and spiritual father Elijah being escorted and taken up by cherubim into Heaven by supernatural transportation on a chariot of fire appearing with horses of fire as recorded in Second Kings 2:11-12 (NKJV):

> *Then it happened, as they continued on and talked, that suddenly a chariot of fire appeared with horses of fire, and separated the two of them; and Elijah went up by a whirlwind into heaven. And Elisha saw it, and he cried out, "My father, my father, the chariot of Israel and its horsemen!" So he saw him no more....*

Cherubim have four faces: one of a man, an ox, a lion, and an eagle. They have four conjoined wings covered with eyes though they are described as having six wings similar to the seraphim, a lion's body, and the feet of oxen. The first account in the Scriptures mentioning cherubim is in Genesis, they guarded the tree of life in the Garden of Eden and the throne of God in their active duties. Cherubim carry flaming swords in hand as you see in Genesis 3:24 (AMP) as they guard the Garden of Eden after Adam and Eve were driven out:

> *So God drove the man out; and at the east of the Garden of Eden He [permanently] stationed the cherubim and the sword with the flashing blade which turned round and round [in every direction] to protect and guard the way (entrance, access) to the tree of life.*

These angels are closest to God. They encircle His throne and emit an intense fiery light representing His love. There are only four of them and each has four faces and six wings. When they come to earth, they leave their serpent appearance behind, preferring tall, thin, clean-cut human embodiments. The following are Scripture references of cherubim in the Bible: Ezekiel 10:9-20 and 1 Kings 6:23-32.

Cherubim are mentioned in several other places throughout Scripture:

- They guarded the entrance to the Garden of Eden (Genesis 3:24).
- God is enthroned above them (Ezekiel 10:1-22).
- God rides on them (Psalm 18:10)
- Two golden figures of cherubim sit above the Ark of the Covenant, where God promised to dwell among His people (Exodus 25:22, see also verses 18-21).

Consider the description of the cherubim in the following Scriptures from the prophets:

- Cherubs with one face and two wings—Exodus 25:18:20

- Cherubs with one face (each) and six wings—Revelation 4:6-8
- Cherubs with two faces—Ezekiel 41:18
- Cherubs with four faces and four wings—Ezekiel 1:5-11

3. *Thrones (Elders)*

The word *throne* is the Greek word *thronos,* which means "a seat or position of power." It is a chair of state having a footstool. Thrones are angels God sits over and discharges His judgments through. They are celestial beings mentioned by Paul the apostle in Colossians 1:16. Thrones are also known as the "elders" that minister in the presence of the Lord. Elders with crowns serve and minister in God's heavenly courts and counsel. They serve God in Heaven and determine counsel regarding the affairs of humankind (see Acts 2:23).

Thrones represent positions of mastery and sovereign rulership from which law and judgment are administered and executed (see Daniel 7:25)—where even in the demonic kingdom (demonic elders) they think to change times and the law. The following Scriptures refer to thrones in the Bible: Daniel 7:9; Colossians 1:16; Revelation 20:4.

These elders sit on seats (thrones) in Heaven with God. John the apostle takes us into the heavenly realm and reveals with great detail that there are twenty-four thrones (seats) encircling a throne:

> *At once I was in [special communication with] the Spirit; and behold, a throne stood in heaven, with One seated on the throne. And He who sat there appeared like [the crystalline sparkle of a jasper stone and [the fiery redness of a sardius stone, and encircling the throne there was a rainbow that looked like [the color of an emerald. Twenty-four*

[other] thrones surrounded the throne; and seated on these
thrones were twenty-four elders dressed in white clothing,
with crowns of gold on their heads. ...the twenty-four elders
fall down before Him who sits on the throne, and they wor-
ship Him who lives forever and ever; and they throw down
their crowns before the throne... (Revelation 4:2-4,10
AMP).

4. Elect Angels

"I charge you before God and the Lord Jesus Christ and the
elect angels that you observe these things without prejudice,
doing nothing with partiality." (1 Timothy 5:21)

These specific angels are "chosen" angels of God that are sent on
special assignments designated by God. The word "elect" here in the
Greek is "eklektos" or "eklekton" which means to select or pick out
or chosen by God. It is to imply being God's choice angel or favorite ones to. These elect angels by virtue of their definition allows us
to understand to some degree what type of angels are they. The elect
angels have the special purpose of serving God and doing as He commands. Certain angels in Scripture are called "elect." Just as there are
elected officials, spiritual leaders and politicians, there is no difference as angels are by angelic and divine selection to govern, protect,
bring messages and carry out tasks.

The Greek word for *elect* found in First Timothy 5:21 refers to
being chosen or picked. This would indicate or infer that God chose
some angels not to fall with Satan and to carry out specialize tasks,
functions or missions. The same word in the verse, *eklekton,* is used
elsewhere for Christians who are elected and chosen by God in salvation (Romans 8:33; Titus 1:1). The word suggests that the elect

angels, like elect people, were chosen by God and cannot lose their elect position.

When God originally created the angels, they were all good just like the rest of creation (Genesis 1:31). Angels were created in a different class as holy and faithfully devoted to the Lord, but this changed in the heavens when Satan rebelled against God (Isaiah 14:12–15; Ezekiel 28:16). Consequently, a massive number of angels followed Satan's rebellion and thus became "fallen" angels, or demons (Matthew 25:41; Revelation 12:3–4). Contrarily, the angels who remained loyal and faithful to the Lord are known as "holy angels" or "elect angels" (Mark 8:38; 1 Timothy 5:21).

None of the elect angels will rebel against God or lose their chosen status, just as Christians cannot lose their salvation as God's elect children (John 10:28; Romans 8:38–39). There is divine security in their standing before the Lord as holy and elect angels who cannot sin or go against the commands of God. Biblically, there are no further information I was able to provide during my research concerning this particular angelic type and group.

5. *Ministering Spirits*

"And of the angels He says: 'Who make His angels spirits and His ministers a flame of fire." (Hebrews 1:7)

There are angels that are ministers. These types of angels are classified as "ministering spirits." They are assigned, sent as an envoy of messengers to minister to and with individuals. Ministering angels are tasked to minister, protect, serve and war alongside ministry gifts and humans. The prophet is not different where God will send a ministering spirit to tend to His spokesman. Ministering spirits are invisible ministers that can impart supernatural and physical strength to us Ministering spirits impart strength to us where we see in two biblical accounts with angels ministering strength to both Jesus in the wilderness (Matthew 4:11) and Daniel the prophet (Daniel 10:16-18). It is important to note that ministering spirits (angels) can appear as visible men and invisible spirits and oftentimes are unaware (Hebrews 13:2). Ministering spirits are dwell on the earth in an angelic community among man. These types of angels serves also as messengers and angelic elects (Daniel 7:10 and 1 Timothy 5:21).

Those who have regular encounters with angels understand this experientially and supernaturally. These types of divine spirits can appear and disappear at a moment notice but their primary function is to minister to you and I on a daily basis and are stationed here on earth with us. They carry more of an earthly responsibly in our daily and personal human affairs.

There is one familiar scripture text in the New Testament where we see an angelic phenomenon where healing was released as a result of angelic presence and stirring of the waters at the Pool of Bethesda in John 5:3-4:

"In these lay a great multitude of sick people, blind, lame, paralyzed, waiting for the moving of the water. For an angel went down at a certain time into the pool and stirred up the water; then whoever stepped in first, after the stirring of the water, was made well of whatever disease he had."

6. *Powers (Cosmic), Rulers (Ruling Spirits) and Authorities*

Then comes the end, when he delivers the kingdom to God the Father after destroying every rule and every authority and power (1 Corinthians 15:24 ESV).

For I am persuaded that neither death nor life, nor angels nor principalities nor powers [cosmic powers of angels], *nor things present nor things to come* (Romans 8:38 NKJV).

The word *powers* refers to "cosmic powers of angels." The word *powers* in the Greek is the word *exousia,* the ability or strength with which one is endued, possesses or exercises. It is the power to exercise authority or influence. Moreover, powers are the power of rule or government, which is simply within one's power or ability. The commands from those in power or authority must be submitted to by others and obeyed. We can see this principle exercised by Jesus from the recognition of His power and authority released with a word of healing for the centurion's servant (see Luke 7:1-10).

These are cosmic powers that rule in the cosmos, which is the universe. These are angelic beings that rule the orderly and harmonious universe or heavens. The rulers are essentially what their name denotes, they are ruling spirits that govern over lower class angelic spirits. This arrangement applies to both the angelic and demonic order. Though the fallen angels are no longer divine in essence, their powers remain the same in the order or hierarchy of satan's kingdom, so to speak. Power, ruling spirit, and authority are the same for God as they are with satan.

The name *powers* comes from the Latin word *potestas* (authority), which in turn comes from the Greek word *exousia* aforementioned, which refers to "someone whose will must be obeyed." These angels are given their name duly reflecting their power over evil forces, which is how the angels are able to restrain them from harm. They are said to give direct orders to the lower angels in warfare and spiritual battles against the forces of hell. Powers are historically known to record history and are overseers of the power human beings have been given in the world, such as kings, sovereigns, or lords. This can also apply to those who are modern rulers of nations.

Powers act as border patrol agents between Heaven and earth. Keep in mind that Jesus, and we as coheirs in Christ, are seated far above angels who are under the command of Christ and us as essentially *"little gods"* (Genesis 3:5; Psalm 82:6; John 10:34) or *"anointed ones"* (1 Chronicles 16:22; Psalm 105:15-17) or better *"sons of God"* (Romans 8:19). Though there are scholars or theologians that may argue that theological position of believers with respect to our spiritual position over angels. However, angels know our spiritual seat in Christ and as born-again believers who are born from above. I believe that we are more powerful than we know.

Consider this text regarding our seat of authority as coheirs and coregent and corulers with Jesus Christ over the heavenly realms in Ephesians 2:6 (NIV): *"And God raised us up with Christ and seated us with him in the heavenly realms in Christ Jesus."*

We are conquerors with Christ, and we have been given the right to sit with the King on His throne as a victorious church. We are currently spiritually seated on the throne ruling with Christ: *"To the one who is victorious, I will give the right to sit with me on my throne, just as I was victorious and sat down with my Father on his throne"* (Revelation 3:21 NIV).

Powers can also represent the following:

1. Authorities—1 Peter 3:22 (ESV), *"Who has gone into heaven and is at the right hand of God, with angels, authorities, and powers having been subjected to him."*

2. Rulers (Ruling spirits)—Ephesians 6:12 (ESV), *"For we do not wrestle against flesh and blood, but against the rulers, against the authorities, against the cosmic powers over this present darkness, against the spiritual forces of evil in the heavenly places."*

7. *Principalities*

> *...to the intent that now the manifold wisdom of God might be made known by the church to the principalities and powers in the heavenly places* (Ephesians 3:10 NKJV).

The word *principality* in the Greek is the word *arche,* which means "the first or chief in order, time, place, or rank." It is the first in position of rule and magistracy of angels and demons. This principality or prince or arch is to be chief, leader, and ruler of angels or demons (fallen angels) in the angelic order. Principalities operate from the heavenly places, abodes, or dwelling places. Principalities represent jurisdictional headship and do not exist without princes and delegated governing powers or deputies.

The third choir is best known to us because they are most like us with their vulnerability to the act of sinning. The following Scriptures refer to principalities in the Bible: Ephesians 3:10; 6:12.

8. *Archangels (Prince of Angels)*

> *But the prince of the kingdom of Persia withstood me twenty-one days; and behold, Michael, one of the chief princes, came to help me, for I had been left alone there with the kings of Persia. ...But I will tell you what is noted in the Scripture of Truth. (No one upholds me against these, except Michael your prince) (Daniel 10:13,21 NKJV).*
>
> *Yet Michael the archangel, in contending with the devil, when he disputed about the body of Moses, dared not bring against him a reviling accusation, but said, "The Lord rebuke you!" (Jude 9 NKJV)*

Each archangel has different roles, which include communicating the revelations and word of God to the prophets, glorifying God, and taking the soul of a person at the time of death, among other roles. These angelic beings are shaped like rays of light. Just like a principal in school, the principalities oversee everything. They guide our entire world—nations, cities, and towns. What's more, they are in charge of religion and politics. As if their plate is not full enough, they are also in charge of managing the earthly duties of the angels below them.

Archangels are not commonly called on and we are not taught to pray for them to help us personally; archangels respond best when dealing with matters involving all humankind. They are the first order of angels that appear only in human form.

This order is most commonly known because they are mentioned by name in the Bible:

- Michael—General in the angelic military forces
- Gabriel—Known by scholars and historians as the Chief Prince of the messenger angels. He is a special messenger of God.

9. *Angels (Messenger or Guardian Angels)*

These classifications of angels might just be called "messenger angels" or "regular angels." They are guardians of people and all things physical and are the most common type of angels. These angels are sent as messengers to humanity. Personal guardian angels come from this category. Angels may also protect and warn humans as well as act as warriors on behalf of God.

The word *angel* in the Greek is the word *malak,* which means "to dispatch as a deputy, a messenger specially of God." It means a representative and ambassador. Interestingly as I was studying, I discovered angels are defined naturally to be as a prophet, priest, or teacher. Prophets were like angels, divine messengers. Through angelic partnership, divine messages are exchanged between Heaven and earth.

The two following Scriptures in the New Testament help give us better understanding into the distinct types of angels and their specific activities roles, functions, and assignments in our invisible and visible partnership:

> *For by Him all things were created in heaven and on earth, [things] visible and invisible, whether thrones or dominions or rulers or authorities; all things were created and exist through Him [that is, by His activity] and for Him* (Colossians 1:16 AMP).

Paul the apostle, regarding unseen, invisible, and spiritual warfare, reveals the different types of fallen angelic opposition and arms against us as believers. This revelation in apostolic and prophetic warfare is extremely important as we gain further revelatory knowledge of our spiritual enemies and entities.

Ephesians 6:12-13 (AMP) says it like this:

> *For our struggle is not against flesh and blood [contending only with physical opponents], but against the rulers, against the powers, against the world forces of this [present] darkness, against the spiritual forces of wickedness in the heavenly (supernatural) places. Therefore, put on the complete armor of God, so that you will be able to [successfully] resist and stand your ground in the evil day [of danger], and having done everything [that the crisis demands], to stand firm [in your place, fully prepared, immovable, victorious].*

It is important for me to note here that though the *rulers,* aforementioned, in Ephesians chapter 6 are in essence demonic and opposing forces, we must understand the existence of angelic rulers were not all against God. There are angelic rulership that ministers for the Kingdom of God and there are those who are ministers of unrighteous for the kingdom of darkness. In other words, there are angels who are divine and there are fallen angels who are demonic.

There are two basic types of angels:

1. Angels—Divine
2. Fallen Angels—demonic or satanic

Jesus is the Head over everything, and we are joint-heirs in the hierarchy of the Kingdom of God; therefore we are also seated with Christ Jesus above the rank of angels:

> *...which He exerted in Christ when He raised Him from the dead and seated Him at His right hand in the heavenly realms, far above all rule and authority, power and dominion, and every name that is named, not only in the present age but also in the one to come. And God put everything under His feet and made Him head over everything for the church* (Ephesians 1:20-22 NIV).

The spirit of the ruler, prince, and power of the air, which is satan, works in the sons of disobedience. The spirit of disobedience is from the spirit of satan that influences those in the world against the spirit of God in obedience. The spirit of disobedience operates in sinners, but the spirit of obedience functions in the sons and daughters of Christ. Angels are obedient to God, and fallen angels (demonic spirits) are obedient to satan. Prophets of God are to be obedient to the Spirit of God in Christ, which is the Holy Spirit.

Ephesians 2:2 (NIV) says: *"in which you used to live when you followed the ways of this world and of the ruler of the kingdom of the air, the spirit who is now at work in those who are disobedient."*

10. *Watchers (Sentinel Angels or Angelic Watchers)*

I saw in the visions of my head as I lay in bed, and behold, a watcher, a holy one, came down from heaven. ...The sentence is by the decree of the watchers, the decision by the word of the holy ones, to the end that the living may know that the Most High rules the kingdom of men and gives it to whom he will and sets over it the lowliest of men (Daniel 4:13,17 ESV).

Watchers are sentinel angels, soldiers, and guards whose job is to stand and keep watch. These angelic beings are stationed on heavenly posts as supernatural guards and soldiers. They stand in position and on guard by a place to keep watch. They are the epitome of their name. According to Strong's Concordance a *watcher* means "an angel as a guardian or waking or wakeful one." Their primary function is to watch, and are reporters and messengers with direct tasks to report.

However, they are also protectors or guards as angelic soldiers in the angelic forces. These angelic beings are known as being the ones standing at portals where they watch and report heavenly and earthly activities between portals. They provide ongoing information of activities. Watchers do this through their powerful vision and opening of the eyes to see into multiple realms, both spiritual and natural. They are the most similar to prophets or watchman prophets who stand on post and watch for approaching enemies. They serve in the same capacities in the Kingdom of God. They are guards on posts watching demonic activities in the heavenlies and us as believers and humanity as a whole.

By definition, watchers are awake ones. They watch nonstop and do not sleep or slumber. They are also the angels with the Holy Spirit that awaken someone or stirs up the intercessors, prophets, and prayer warriors in times to intercede and pray during the most heavy demonic activities. In the stirring up to war or labor in spiritual warfare, these angels awaken believers and sound the alarm in the heavenly realm of pending enemy attacks. They give information to the prophets and prophetic intercessors about what to pray and what to watch for.

The changing-of-the-guards meaning is applied accurately to angel guards (watchers) and prophets during a transition and change in watchmen or watchers on their post for another to take their post during the night.

Watcher angels are mentioned in three Bible verses, each cited in a vision that King Nebuchadnezzar had (Daniel 4:13,17,23). Not all Bible translations use the term "watcher" angels. The English Standard Version, Common English Bible, and the King James Version speak of *"a watcher"* in Daniel 4:13, and the New American Standard Bible calls it *"an angelic watcher."* But the New International Version simply calls this being *"a messenger"* from Heaven. The New English Translation says that Nebuchadnezzar sees *"a holy sentinel."* Nevertheless, all these watcher angels are supernatural, celestial beings, or *"holy ones"* who come down from Heaven with authority to speak for God.

Watchers in Genesis

The term *watcher* is connected with biblical angels. They appear in singular and plural form in the book of Daniel. "The watchers" is also the name given to Nephilim (many translate as giant) mentioned in four verses in Genesis 6:1-4. A Nephilim is half human and half angel.

Regarding Nephilites, we are given a very brief description in Genesis of the causes of the great biblical Flood. This took place before Noah built his vessel, the great ark:

When human beings began to increase in number on the earth and daughters were born to them, the sons of God saw that the daughters of humans were beautiful, and they married any of them they chose. Then the LORD said, "My Spirit will not contend with humans forever, for they are mortal; their days will be a hundred and twenty years." The Nephilim were on the earth in those days—and also afterward—when the sons of God went to the daughters of humans and had children by them. They were the heroes of old, men of renown. The LORD saw how great the wickedness of the human race had become on the earth, and that every inclination of the thoughts of the human heart was only evil all the time (Genesis 6:1-5 NIV).

These *"sons of God"* were referred to in some Bible translations as supernatural beings. It can be assumed and even confirmed that these beings were watchers, and their offspring otherwise known as giants or old men of renowned. The Good News Bible calls the Nephilim *"great heroes and famous men."*

The following suggestions about who watchers could be:

- Godly descendants of Seth, the third son of Adam and Eve
- Angels
- Kings and rulers

The Hebrew word translated "watcher" in Daniel 4 comes from a root word meaning "wakeful one" and thus can mean watcher, sentinel, or guardian. The International Standard Bible Encyclopedia describes watcher angels as servants of God who "possess a certain joint authority to speak the decrees of God, and apparently form a heavenly council who listen to God's word and then act as divine messengers to bring these commands and revelations to human beings."

The watcher brings heavenly decrees from God. God decrees and decisions are released through the watchers according to Daniel 4:14,17.

Scripture affirms the concept of heavenly beings who watch the earth in Ezekiel 1:15-20 and are interested in the affairs of humans: *"...This Good News has been announced to you by those who preached in the power of the Holy Spirit sent from heaven. It is all so wonderful that even the angels are eagerly watching these things happen"* (1 Peter 1:12 NLT).

Since God's purpose is to use the church to display His wisdom to rulers and authorities in the heavenly realms (Ephesians 3:10), the idea of attentive watcher angels or guardians is biblically sound. Likewise, the Bible confirms the presence of angels who guard and protect humans: *"The angel of the LORD encamps around those who fear Him, and He delivers them"* (Psalm 34:7 NKJV; see also Matthew 18:10; Acts 12:9-15).

Just as there are watchmen or prophetic watchmen in the natural who serve the Lord in the ministry of intercession and prayer, these angelic watchers are watchers in the spirit world or angelic realm. They have power to establish, initiate, and mobilize things on earth according to God's will as we pray. They also are special messenger angels or sentinels empowered like an armed guard with a message, information, dream interpretation, revelation, and strategies that we need to fulfill our specific assignment on earth. They have a steadfast word in their mouths (Hebrews 2:2) as they work in the angelic partnership in the ministry of intercession and those who are prayer warriors.

11. Hosts (Angelic Forces)

And suddenly there was with the angel a multitude of the heavenly host praising God and saying (Luke 2:13 NKJV).

Praise Him, all His angels; praise Him, all His hosts! (Psalm 148:2)

The hosts, angelic (heavenly) hosts, is a group or army with heavenly power to assist God's people. The main purpose of heavenly hosts is to strengthen and comfort believers. The heavenly host is a group or army with heavenly power to assist God's people. Heavenly hosts are creations of God:

You are the LORD, you alone. You have made heaven, the heaven of heavens, with all their host... (Nehemiah 9:6 ESV).

Thus the heavens and the earth, and all the host of them, were finished (Genesis 2:1 NKJV).

Much of the confusion about hosts is due to the fact that celestial stars are sometimes referred to as *"sun, the moon, and the stars, all the host of heaven"* in Scripture (Deuteronomy 4:19 NKJV).

Lord of the Invisible Forces

George William Butler writes in his book published in 1878, *The Lord's Host,* "There are three *'Hosts of the Lord'*—the angels, the stars, and the church. The heavenly hosts protect a people from general ruin and destruction and enable the seed or remnant to be preserved. A 'host' contemplates a dual protection from both heaven and on earth."[1]

God is referred to as *"LORD of hosts,"* throughout Scripture (Haggai 2:4 NKJV; Psalm 24:10 NKJV), which is translated to *Jehovah-Sabaoth* or *Yahweh-Sabaoth* in Hebrew. *Yahweh-Sabaoth* means "Lord of Armies," which contemplates His righteousness and power over both spiritual and physical armies. God is the Lord of hosts. According to *MacLaren's Exposition*: "by that title, 'the Lord of hosts,' the prophets and psalmists meant to express the universal dominion of God over the whole universe in all its battalions and sections, which they conceived of as one ranked army, obedient to the voice of the great General and Ruler of them all."[2]

Jacob dreamed of a stairway with the angels of God ascending and descending from heaven and earth. When Jacob escaped from his father-in-law, he was joined by a host of angels and informed that his brother Esau was now in pursuit of him. Genesis 32:1-2 tells us that when Jacob met with the angels, he called the name of that place Mahanaim, which represents two hosts or armies.

12. *Angelic Civilization*

> *But you have come to Mount Zion and to the city of the living God, the heavenly Jerusalem, and to innumerable angels in festal gathering* (Hebrews 12:22 ESV).

There is a habitation of angels defined as an abode or dwelling place for angels. This means that the angelic realm is literally civilized. In the angelic realm as in the spiritual realm, there are multiplicity of realms, territories, communities, habitations, jurisdictions, and divisions of *"innumerable"* companies of angels. Though there is limited understanding and knowledge of the full extent of the reality of angels, we do know that angels operate and function in an organized civilization, in rank and order through a hierarchal structure, and sent on assignment by the power and authorities of the Commander in Chief. Simply put, the angelic realm is very organized and structured.

Jude 6 informs us that in the heavens there are habitations, dwellings, or estates that were specifically created for angelic living and residency.

ANGELIC RANK AND COMMAND

Now that we understand the reality of angels in the realms of the spirit and how they minister and engage among us and to the Lord, we must understand that these angelic beings exist and function in rank and in order. This rank and order is within a governmental structure according to Colossians 1:16. We discussed in previous references the ten hierarchal structures of angels. There is a chain of command within the hierarchy of angels. This is the order of angels that better helps us to understand the succession of authority among angels.

The demonic principalities and powers actually had their origin among an angelic hierarchy. They did not create anything new that had not already existed. After satan was banished from Heaven, he restructured his fallen angels in the very same rank and order as God in Christ had originally established. These fallen angels understood the power structure and the chain of command easily because they were originally part of the God's angelic hierarchy. As stated previously in this chapter, angels function and operate under command.

It is extremely important to comprehend two aspects of the angelic structure: 1) the order of principalities and powers are not demonic in nature; and 2) not all of the angelic ruling or governmental angels, authorities and powers rebelled with lucifer as part of the angels from Heaven (Revelation 12:4,9).

Note: Angels are called *"stars"* according to Revelation 12:4. There are spiritual powers and authorities that govern the natural or visible world from the invisible world. Just as we have mayors, heads of states, prime ministers, presidents, governors, and powerful leaders over city, states, territories, countries, and nations in the natural, there are also angels that operate as royal delegates having territorial, jurisdictional, and governmental authority that they rule from.

The following is a great biblical example of this where six angels called *"executioners"* had charge over a specific city where the idolaters were executed by God's judgment or judicial decision:

> *Then he cried in my ears with a loud voice, saying, "Bring near the executioners of the city, each with his destroying weapon in his hand." And behold, six men came from the direction of the upper gate, which faces north, each with his weapon for slaughter in his hand, and with them was a man clothed in linen, with a writing case at his waist. And they went in and stood beside the bronze altar. Now the glory of the God of Israel had gone up from the cherub on which it rested to the threshold of the house. And he called to the man clothed in linen, who had the writing case at his waist. And the LORD said to him, "Pass through the city, through Jerusalem, and put a mark on the foreheads of the men who sigh and groan over all the abominations that are committed in it"* (Ezekiel 9:1-4 ESV).

Unseen Powers Over the Elements

Jesus speaks to the winds (demonic spirits). We can see the power over the elements demonstrated by Jesus Christ speaking to a storm recorded in Mark 4:35-41 (ESV):

> *On that day, when evening had come, he said to them, "Let us go across to the other side." And leaving the crowd, they*

took him with them in the boat, just as he was. And other boats were with him. And a great windstorm arose, and the waves were breaking into the boat, so that the boat was already filling. But he was in the stern, asleep on the cushion. And they woke him and said to him, "Teacher, do you not care that we are perishing?" And he awoke and rebuked the wind and said to the sea, "Peace! Be still!" And the wind ceased, and there was a great calm. He said to them, "Why are you so afraid? Have you still no faith?" And they were filled with great fear and said to one another, "Who then is this, that even the wind and the sea obey him?"

Jesus spoke directly to the storm. Though this is a powerful phenomenon. Jesus did not speak peace or shalom to the tempest—rather, He rebuked the winds. Jesus rebuked the winds after He had recognized and discerned that He was dealing with more than a typical storm. He spoke directly to the source behind the storm.

In Mark 4:35-41, we can see two elements that Jesus deals with at sea in the ship:

- The winds (demonic winds)
- Water (sea or marine demons)

Jesus essentially spoke to the spirits behind the winds. He recognized that demonic and elemental powers created the windstorm to destroy Him. As prophets, we must be able to discern demonic elemental, environmental, and weather forecasts that are sent to kill and destroy lives, especially the anointed ones of God. There were demonic forces behind and in the wind. It was in the invisible realm. Prophets have the ability to speak by authority and faith to the elements. An example of prophetic prayer power regarding the elements is evident with Joshua's prayer and the sun stood still (read Joshua

10:1-15). *"There has never been a day like this one before or since, when the Lord answered such a prayer. Surely the Lord fought for Israel that day!"* (Joshua 10:14 NLT).

Jesus Confronts Legions in the Regions

Jesus was confronted by a man with a "legion" of demons inside. After Jesus rebuked the storm at sea, He and His disciples are immediately met by this man when they reach the shore. The man was possessed by an unclean spirit and legion of demons that no one had the strength or power to subdue him. Look at what happens after Jesus rebuked the spirits behind the storm—and what He encountered next:

> *They went across the lake to the region of the Gerasenes. When Jesus got out of the boat, a man with an impure spirit came from the tombs to meet him. This man lived in the tombs, and no one could bind him anymore, not even with a chain. For he had often been chained hand and foot, but he tore the chains apart and broke the irons on his feet. No one was strong enough to subdue him. Night and day among the tombs and in the hills he would cry out and cut himself with stones* (Mark 5:1-5 NIV).

This one man had the ability to control the atmosphere of the region by gripping the entire region with fear. It was no coincidence that the demon-possessed man was emboldened to meet Jesus immediately after He and His disciples departed the ship.

Jesus was confronted with several natural and spiritual elements of demonic possession and control that He demonstrated His power over:

- Land (atmospheric demonic or territorial spirits that control the land)
- Man (demonic possession of a person)
- Herd of pigs (animal possession)

Demonic power has a tendency to try to control entire cities, regions, territories, and entire nations through territorial spirits. You can see that this legion of demons in this territory and country of Gerasenes was extremely territorial, to the degree that people were afraid to enter that place around the tombs.

Recognition of Jesus's Power and Authority

When he saw Jesus from afar, he ran and worshiped Him. And he cried out with a loud voice and said, "What have I to do with You, Jesus, Son of the Most High God? I implore You by God that You do not torment me." For He said to him, "Come out of the man, unclean spirit!" Then He asked him, "What is your name?" And he answered, saying, "My name is Legion; for we are many." Also he begged Him earnestly that He would not send them out of the country (Mark 5:6-10 NKJV).

A legion of spirits is approximately between 6,000 to 10,000. That is how many spirits were driven out of the man and region and drowned in the sea—the same place where Jesus rebuked the winds and sea. There was definitely a link, a connection, with the demonic powers in the elements: wind, water, and land.

Now a large herd of swine was feeding there near the mountains. So all the demons begged Him, saying, "Send us to the swine, that we may enter them." And at once Jesus gave them permission. Then the unclean spirits went out and entered the swine (there were about two thousand)*; and the herd ran violently down the steep place into the sea, and drowned in the sea* (Mark 5:11-13 NKJV).

Jesus demonstrated elemental power over the demonic spirits in the wind, sea, and the land. Demonic, diabolical, and devilish powers behind the elements were trying to confront Jesus first in the ship at sea through the wind and the sea with water to hinder Him from bringing deliverance to that region. As we studied that there are powers over the weather elements, it is very possible and confirmed in Scripture that even principalities and powers at times are behind and will tamper with the elements of earth to cause various storms, earthquakes, fires, and other catastrophes.

Think about it, if fallen angel demons can do this, how much more can the angels of God do when employed and released through divine angelic reversal to halt, disrupt, and nullify the demonic plans of natural disasters. Or even more so, can you imagine the prophetic power in your mouth to speak with elemental power to the storms and command it to obey—a realm of prophetic power is tapped and released! This is *Power Prophecy!*

PROPHETIC REVELATION OF DEMONIC DISASTERS

As prophets and prophetic believers in Christ, forces will contend against us as we travel to try to hinder, stymie, derail, and destroy natural disasters. Paul encountered several shipwrecks and a poisonous snake because of his apostolic rank in the spirit (Acts 27:27-28,39-44; 28:5).

Let's examine the time when the apostle Paul was setting out on this voyage across the sea. He prophetically perceived that his journey would end with disaster, and I believe he sensed marine and sea demons would try to stop his forward progress:

Since much time had passed, and the voyage was now dangerous because even the Fast was already over, Paul advised them, saying, "Sirs, I perceive [prophetic revelation] that the voyage will be with injury and much loss, not only of the cargo and the ship, but also of our lives" (Acts 27:9-10 ESV).

Paul prophetically perceived the outcome of the voyage by the shipwreck caused by the tempest and demonic spirits at sea. Paul's prophetic revelation and advisement was pivotal to navigating around the projected tempest at sea by evil spirits to alter the weather patterns. Paul saw prophetically a spirit behind the tempest called Euroclydon, a northeaster that produces a southwest wind that stirs up broad and massive waves (see Acts 27:13-15). In the middle of the storm there stood an angel of the Lord, as Paul ensured they would survive the storm and accomplish their apostolic mission and purpose.

Angelic Intervention for Safe Transportation

For there stood by me this night an angel of the God to whom I belong and whom I serve, saying, "Do not be afraid, Paul; you must be brought before Caesar; and indeed God has granted you all those who sail with you" (Acts 27:23-24 NKJV).

Prophets and apostles carry prophetic rank, power, and authority that will warrant elemental warfare through demonic changes in the weather patterns or elements designed to stop any forms of healing, deliverance, and ultimately salvation to come to cities, regions, nations, and entire people.

Isaiah 28:2 (NKJV) speaks of a "mighty and strong one" having power over the elements: *"Behold, the Lord has a mighty and strong one, like a tempest of hail and a destroying storm, like a flood of mighty waters overflowing, who will bring them down to the earth with His hand."*

The ministry of angels is intimately involved in the ministry of the saints:

- Prayer—1 Corinthians 13:1; 14:2 and Revelation 8:1-6
- Healing and Deliverance—Psalm 107:20 and John 5:4
- Escorts and Transportation at death—Luke 16:22
- Evangelism—Mark 13:27; Hebrews 1:14 and Revelation 14:15
- Administering Judgments—Genesis 19:21-22 and Revelation 15:1
- Strengthening—1 Kings 19:4-5 and Matthew 4:11

NOTES

1. George William Butler, *The Lord's Host,* Edinburgh (1878). Can be downloaded by visiting: https://www.readbookpage.com/pdf/the-lord-s-host/; accessed February 7, 2022. Reprints on Amazon: https://www.amazon.com/Lords-Host-Lessons-Book-Joshua/dp/1163293814; accessed February 7, 2022.
2. *MacLaren's Expositions of Holy Scripture*; https://biblehub.com/library/maclaren/expositions_of_holy_scripture_j/the_lord_of_hosts_the.htm; accessed February 22, 2022.

PART IV

MIRACULOUS DNA

|| 12 ||

THE FINGER OF GOD

But when the magicians tried to produce gnats by their
secret arts, they could not. Since the gnats were on people
and animals everywhere, the magicians said to Pharaoh,
"This is the finger of God." But Pharaoh's heart was
hard and he would not listen, just as the Lord had said.
—Exodus 8:18-19 NIV

But if I drive out demons by the finger of God,
then the kingdom of God has come upon you.
—Luke 11:20 NIV

The miraculous demonstration of signs and wonders at times in the Old and New Testament Scriptures were referred to and confirmed as the *"finger of God."* The finger of God speaks relatively to the authenticity of God's supernatural power. It is imperative as believers to comprehend that the supernatural is simply manifesting signs, wonders, and miracles. The phrase *"finger of God"* is an anthropomorphism terminology used by the Egyptian magicians to describe the supernatural act of God (Exodus 8:16-20).

In Exodus 31:18 and Deuteronomy 9:10, the phrase refers to the method by which the Ten Commandments were written on tablets of stone that were brought down from Mount Sinai by Moses. It was also used once by Jesus in the Gospel of Luke to describe how He had cast out demons.

The phrase *"finger of God"* is mentioned four times in the Old Testament:

1. Exodus 8:16-20
2. Exodus 31:18
3. Deuteronomy 9:10
4. Daniel 5:5

The first time the phrase *"finger of God"* appears is in the Hebrew Bible, in chapter 8 of the book of Exodus, which reads:

> *Then the LORD said to Moses, "Say to Aaron, 'Stretch out your staff and strike the dust of the earth, so that it may become gnats throughout the whole land of Egypt.'" And they did so; Aaron stretched out his hand with his staff and struck the dust of the earth, and gnats came on humans and animals alike; all the dust of the earth turned into gnats throughout the whole land of Egypt. The magicians tried to produce gnats by their secret arts, but they could not. There were gnats on both humans and animals. And the magicians said to Pharaoh, "This is the finger of God!" But Pharaoh's heart was hardened, and he would not listen to them, just as the LORD had said* (Exodus 8:16-20 NIV).

The second time the phrase "finger of God" appears is in the last verse, Exodus 31:18 (NKJV): *"And when He had made an end of speaking with him on Mount Sinai, He gave Moses two tablets of the Testimony, tablets of stone, written with the finger of God."*

The third time the phrase appears is as a second reference to the tablets of the Ten Commandments, and is found in Deuteronomy 9:10

(NKJV), *"Then the LORD delivered to me two tablets of stone written with the finger of God; and on them were all the words which the LORD had spoken to you from the midst of the fire in the day of the assembly."*

It is important to understand that the prophetic and the supernatural work hand in glove when it comes to the demonstration of miracles, signs, and wonders. The power of the prophetic is the forerunner of experiencing God in the supernatural. The first healing was done by a prophet (Genesis 20:7; 17-18). The first sign was demonstrated by a prophet. The first wonder work of God was exercised by a prophet, and the first exhibition of power was done by a prophet. Finger of God meant "an act of God"; the magicians said to Pharoah it was the finger of God, meaning an act of God. It was something that the human hand cannot do.

This phenomenon is regarded and referred to in Scripture as the "finger of God." The finger of God is identified by the works of the Spirit of God, which speaks directly to the authenticity of God's power. Miraculous signs are God's endorsement and validation. It is His way of approving a matter and us recognizing it was His finger on it. The finger of God is simply God leaving His fingerprints so we can identify His work. In the same way a painter signs his or her name in the bottom right corner to provide authenticity and originality. It also allows those who see and witness the masterpiece to identify who's hand created it.

Similarly, the finger of God gives God's signature in a particular matter, which is His stamp of approval, heavenly royal seal, notoriety or authorization. God puts His stamp of approval and signature on His people to distinguish them on earth with heavenly credentials. When it is the finger of God, it is identified as the very act of God.

Jesus was approved, authorized, and accredited of God by miracles, signs, and wonders according to Acts 2:22 (NIV): *"Fellow Israelites, listen to this: Jesus of Nazareth was a man accredited by*

God to you by miracles, wonders and signs, which God did among you through him, as you yourselves know."

Jesus as a prophet was accredited of God with working the power of the miraculous. These signs, wonders, and miracles further gave Him accreditation as One anointed by God. Prophets are licensed, credentialed, and accredited practitioners of God to work miraculous healings, signs, and wonders. They are ancient and modern-day practitioners of the supernatural. God endorses the words and ministry of the prophets with accompanying signs as validation. These signs bear witness of the truth. This is an example of power prophecy. God has supernaturally accredited prophets and prophetic people working with Him to manifest His will on earth.

PROPHETIC ACCREDITATION

Samuel was an accredited and recognized prophet. He developed and emerged as a reputable voice with evidence that his words from God were fulfilled. When Samuel prophesied, his words came to pass. This is a powerful example of establishing such prominence, power, and presence with God that when he spoke, it manifested as God spoke without failure:

> *The LORD was with Samuel as he grew up, and he let none of Samuel's words fall to the ground* (1 Samuel 3:19 NIV).

One very key and interesting point is the accreditation of Samuel's prophetic ministry—God was with him and He did not let any of Samuel's words fail. The prophetic does not just carry the word of the Lord, it carries the presence of God. Prophets are ambassadors of the supernatural. Their very words carry power and presence. God is with His prophets and with all those who are carriers of His words.

Moses understood that the presence of God was critically important to him as he carried out God's will, and for the people to recognize him as being chosen as a judge and prophet of God. Moses asked for the presence of the Lord to go before and with him and the children of Israel.

Moses knew that only the presence and glory of the Lord could distinctively separate them from all other nations (Exodus 33:16). The presence of God makes the difference in ministering the prophetic. The presence of the Lord would go before the children of Israel and fight their battles. When God is before us, who can be against us (Romans 8:31; Exodus 14:14; Deuteronomy 20:4; 2 Chronicles 20:17; Isaiah 40:31 and 54:17).

According to the Scriptures, it is the finger of God that both distinguishes the divine and equally dismantles the demonic. The power of prophecy is unparallel and unmatched by the powers of darkness. We have seen examples of that with the magicians in Egypt trying to duplicate the plagues of God against Pharoah and the Egyptians to discredit the validity and authenticity of the power of God through Moses the prophet. When God performs a miracle, no one in Heaven and earth can match His unlimited creative power.

Jesus, by the same finger of God, expelled demonic forces. This same power was done by the Spirit of God. The finger of God that Jesus references in Luke 11:20 is the power of the Holy Spirit hurling demonic spirits: *"But if I drive out demons by the finger of God, then the kingdom of God has come upon you"* (Luke 11:20).

The Lord is a man of war (Exodus 15:3). God has given us authority to tread on serpents and scorpions and He fights for us (Luke 10:19; Joshua 23:10).

CREATIVE MIRACLES

Having said these things, he spit on the ground and made mud with the saliva. Then he anointed the man's eyes with the mud and said to him, "Go, wash in the pool of Siloam" (which means Sent). So he went and washed and came back seeing (John 9:6-7 ESV).

Jesus worked a miracle literally with His finger. Near Decapolis, some people brought Jesus a deaf man who could hardly talk. Jesus healed the man, of course, but in an interesting manner: *"...Jesus put his fingers into the man's ears. Then he spit and touched the man's tongue"* (Mark 7:33 NIV). Later, in the town of Bethsaida, Jesus healed a blind man. Again, the miracle was preceded by spitting: *"He...spit on the man's eyes and put his hands on him"* (Mark 8:23 NIV). To heal a man born blind, Jesus *"spit on the ground, made some mud with the saliva, and put it on the man's eyes"* (John 9:6 NIV).

Certainly, Jesus, the divine Son of God, does not need physical props to work miracles. In many cases, Jesus merely spoke and healing followed (see Matthew 15:28; Luke 17:12-14). Yet, in three cases, Jesus used His spittle in the process of healing. One possible reason for Jesus's use of His saliva has to do with the beliefs of His contemporary culture. Several Roman writers and Jewish rabbis considered saliva to be a valid treatment for blindness. Since the people of that day had a high view of saliva's healing properties, Jesus used spit to communicate His intention to heal. Those being healed would have naturally interpreted Jesus's spitting as a sign that they would soon be cured. Saliva was used by Jesus as a physical ointment to heal.

Mud was created as an ointment—creative in essence and applied on the body for healing. Jesus created new vision (new eyes) with this man who had never seen before, consequently an unheard and unseen miracles. Jesus, who is God, can certainly create new eyes as Creator by His own fingers. The greater need of each of those healed was the need for increased faith. Jesus recognized this spiritual need and offered a physical action as a means of raising their expectations and focusing their faith on Himself.

Thus, in Mark 8, the man's spiritual sight was strengthened even as physical sight was imparted to him. It is possible that Jesus's use of mud in John 9 was meant to parallel God's original creation of man: *"The LORD God formed a man from the dust of the ground"* (Genesis 2:7 NIV). In other words, Jesus showed His power as the Creator by imitating the original creation of man—He used the *"dust of the ground"* to give the man born blind new sight. The creative power of Jesus's miracle was understood by the man who was healed, saying,

> *Now that is remarkable! You don't know where he comes from, yet he opened my eyes. We know that God does not listen to sinners. He listens to the godly person who does his will. Nobody has ever heard of opening the eyes of a man born blind. If this man were not from God, he could do nothing* (John 9:32-33 NIV).

Jesus performed creative miracles. I have used my own body fluid, such as sweat, as a form of anointing oil when praying over people for healing. When I sweat due to the anointing on me as I am preaching, praying, or prophesying, I recognize that when I am under a strong prophetic anointing, I sweat heavily and oil is produced on my head and hands.

Jesus healed many people in His ministry; in fact, there was no sickness or infirmity that He could not heal (Matthew 4:23). Significantly, the details of each miracle vary. Jesus never healed the same way twice. The variety of methods used by the Lord eliminates confidence in any one technique or modus operandi. Healing is not the product of any talisman, amulet, spell, or process. Healing comes from the power of God.

When Jesus healed, with or without spit, the response was usually something like this: *"This amazed everyone and they praised God, saying, 'We have never seen anything like this!'"* (Mark 2:12 NIV). Jesus declared, *"In that day you will not [need to] ask Me about anything. I assure you and most solemnly say to you, whatever you ask the Father in My name [as My representative], He will give you"* (John 16:23 AMP). That means whatever we ask in prayer or speak.

The term *accredited* speaks of a person, organization, or course of study officially recognized or authorized, according to the Merriam-Webster Dictionary. It is to give official authorization to or approval of or to provide with credentials, especially to send (an envoy) with letters of authorization, accredit an ambassador. To recognize or vouch for someone.

Prophets are sent with words in their mouths as official ambassadors of God with full authorization. We can see an example of this with Moses being sent by God to Pharoah to speak with the full weight of Heaven with accompanying signs, plagues, and executing judgments against the Egyptians.

God called, chose, and provided Moses with credibility with a personal revelation that He had given him a ministry of signs, wonders, and miracles with two miraculous signs: the rod turning into a snake and Moses's hand being leprous and being restored (see Exodus 4:1-8). Moses's rod and hand were signs that God had not only sent Moses with a word but with powerful reinforcement. He was an authorized governmental official carrying the very words from the Kingdom of God.

THE FINGERPRINT—UNIQUE IDENTIFIER

Fingerprinting is one form of biometrics, a science that uses people's physical or biological characteristics to identify them. No two people have the same fingerprints, not even identical twins. Neither do fingerprints change, even as we get older—unless the deep or basal layer is destroyed or intentionally changed by plastic surgery. There are three main fingerprint patterns: *arches, loops,* and *whorls.* The shape, size, number, and arrangement of minor details in these patterns make each fingerprint unique. Similarly, God's miracles are unique and unusual, which proves He alone has performed it. When you are touched by God, all will know that His hand and fingerprints are over it.

Why Our Fingerprints Are Unique

As a baby moves in the womb, their fingers can rub against the side of the womb. These tiny forces push the skin as it grows, molding the direction of the growing ridges. The result is a unique fingerprint unlike anyone else's. Your fingerprints are unique—no one else in the world has the exact same set of ridges and lines that you have on your fingers. Latent fingerprints usually can't be seen by the naked eye. Most criminals or thieves wear gloves in order that their fingerprints are not left behind for investigators and detectives to track or trace their identity. The finger of God causes us to track and trace the actions of God. When someone is touched with healing or a miracle, we can identify that it was by the finger or actions of God.

Have you ever tiptoed into the kitchen to sneak a cookie out of the jar when no one was looking? Unless you wore gloves, you left behind evidence of your snack attack. A fingerprint expert could likely find fingerprints on the cookie jar and match them to the unique prints at the end of your fingers. Fortunately, most parents are neither fingerprint experts nor crime scene investigators (CSIs). However, the cookie crumbs on your chin might still give you away!

Take a close look at your palms and the tips of your fingers. Do you see the tiny ridges and lines? If you pressed a finger onto an inkpad and then onto a piece of paper, it would leave a print of the lines and ridges on your finger—a fingerprint! Your fingerprints are unique and stay the same from the time you're born until death. Their uniqueness and lasting quality make fingerprints one of the best ways to identify a person.

Did you realize that you do not have to dip your fingers in ink to leave fingerprints? Sweat and body oils are constantly pushed out through tiny pores in our skin. These substances coat the ridges and lines of your fingers. When you touch something, you transfer these substances to whatever you touch, leaving an impression of the ridges and lines on your fingers. These latent fingerprints that usually can't be seen by the naked eye, sometimes show up on certain objects, such as a glass bottle.

EVIDENCE OF PROOF

Fingerprint evidence can play a crucial role in criminal investigations as it can confirm or disprove a person's identity. Scientists have known about these invisible fingerprints since the 19th century. As early as 1892, English scientist Sir Francis Galton wrote a book about using fingerprints to solve crimes. It was not until 1896, however, that Sir Edward Richard Henry developed a way to classify fingerprints based upon their general ridge patterns: loops, whorls, and arches.

Henry's system of fingerprint identification—dactyloscopy— has been modified slightly over time. Today, it is still used by law enforcement agencies worldwide. Over the past 100 years, advances in technology have helped law enforcement make even better use of fingerprints. Today, fingerprints can be "lifted"—identified and copied for later comparison—from just about any surface using special fingerprint powder.

Moreover, scientists do not even need complete fingerprints anymore. With the help of advanced computers and software, even half a fingerprint can be identified and matched with a comparison sample. Computers can make comparisons automatically, although final verification of a fingerprint match is still done by scientists who carefully study and compare the fingerprints to ensure a proper match is found.

WHY FINGERPRINTS ARE IMPORTANT IN FORENSIC SCIENCE

Forensic science helps detectives identify persons of interest regarding their involvement in a crime. The fingerprint is uniquely designed by God and reveals person's identity. When God does a miracle by the works of His hand, it reveals His identify. A miracle done by the finger of God proves it was done by the hand of God. We can see this through a few examples in Exodus when God worked with His prophets Moses and Aaron. The Egyptian magicians identified that it was God who was behind the plagues when they saw how He stretched out His hand and struck Egypt with all His wonders.

The Egyptian magicians could not put a finger on how the power of God works—pun intended. Due to their inability to produce this kind of sign to discredit the power of God, they conceded to accept the harsh reality that it was done by the finger of God. It was understood clearly by the magicians that it was the work of God. There was no question that it was God behind the act.

GOD'S FINGER IDENTIFIED

Let's consider the following four Old Testament examples of God being identified by His finger: 1) the third plague; 2) and 3) God's signature; 4) God's sign language:

1. The Third Plague of Gnats

> *Then the LORD said to Moses, "Say to Aaron, 'Stretch out your staff and strike the dust of the earth, so that it may become gnats in all the land of Egypt.'" And they did so. Aaron stretched out his hand with his staff and struck the dust of the earth, and there were gnats on man and beast.*

All the dust of the earth became gnats in all the land of Egypt. The magicians tried by their secret arts to produce gnats, but they could not. So there were gnats on man and beast. Then the magicians said to Pharaoh, "This is the finger of God" (Exodus 8:16-19 ESV).

God said that He would work through His prophets, Moses and Aaron, and that He would harden Pharoah's heart and multiply His signs and wonders in the land of Egypt. The prophetic word to His prophets was that Pharaoh will not take heed them, which would consequently cause God to lay His hand on Egypt in full power and bring His people, His army forces or hosts, out of Egypt by great judgments (Exodus 7:1-4).

2. and 3. God's Personal Signature

The second and third examples of the phrase *"finger of God"* appears as His personal signature. Exodus 31:18 records that when Moses had concluded communing with God on Mount Sinai, God gave Moses two tablets of stone handwritten personally by God. Both represented God approving His own written word.

The Ten Commandments were written by the finger of God: *"When the LORD finished speaking to Moses on Mount Sinai, he gave him the two tablets of the covenant law, the tablets of stone inscribed by the finger of God"* (Exodus 31:18 NIV). God gave Moses the Ten Commandments on two tablets of stone handwritten with the finger of God of all His words for Moses the prophet to communicate as a spokesperson to the people.

Moses told the people of Israel, *"Then the LORD delivered to me two tables of stone written with the finger of God, and on them were all the words which the LORD had spoken to you on the mountain from the midst of the fire in the day of the assembly"* (Deuteronomy 9:10 NKJV).

It is interesting to note here that as I was studying the finger of God, something very fascinating was revealed to me—God's used His own finger as His pen. What do I mean? Let us examine closely the term "finger," which gives a better understanding of the word contextually and prophetically.

The word *finger* in Hebrew is the word *etsba,* which means something to seize with. It is used in the sense of grasping or grabbing. But as I researched the root etymology of the word *finger,* I discovered that the root word *tseba,* means to "dip" into coloring fluid or liquid substance. It also means a "dye" or something dyed. Therefore, the finger in the Hebrew sense and root etymology describes someone dipping their finger into a dye or coloring liquid.

In other words, the Hebrew text is illustrating God dipping His finger into a coloring dye, or better into ink, that we use to write. Therefore, God prophetically used His finger as a pen to write on the two tablets of stone—the Ten Commandments.

The finger of God is by revelation His divine signature or approval, which is making a statement or addressing something. Therefore, whenever there is a miracle done by the finger of God, it is God's distinctive mark, signature, or stamp.

A person is uniquely identified by two things:

- Fingerprint—an impression or mark made on a surface by a person's fingertip, especially as used for identifying individuals from the unique pattern of whorls and lines.

- Signature—a person's name written in a distinctive way as a form of identification in authorizing a check or document or concluding a letter.

The finger of God is a sign from God that simply makes a prophetic statement. It is God's way of leaving an impression on a person, place, authorizing, or notarizing a thing. This is God's kingly royal seal or signet ring, similarly where we see it in Scripture concerning earthly kings. The Lord God describes in Haggai 2:23 having a signet ring, *"On that day,' declares the LORD Almighty, 'I will take you, my servant Zerubbabel son of Shealtiel,' declares the LORD, 'and I will make you like my signet ring, for I have chosen you....'"* What did God mean when He said Zerubbabel was His signet ring?

Ancient kings used signet rings to designate authority, honor, or ownership. A signet contained an emblem unique to the king. Official documents were sealed with a dollop of soft wax impressed with the king's signet, usually kept on a ring on his finger. Such a seal certified the document as genuine, much like a notary public's stamp today.

In First Kings 21:8 (NKJV) we are told that the evil Queen Jezebel took King Ahab's signet ring and *"wrote letters in Ahab's name, sealed them with his seal."* The ring's stamp gave her letters the king's authority. In Daniel 6:17 (ESV), a signet ring was used to seal a stone covering a lions' den: *"A stone was brought and laid on the mouth of the den, and the king sealed it with his own signet and with the signet of his lords, that nothing might be changed concerning Daniel."* A royal signet ring is also featured in Genesis 41:41-43 and Esther 8:8.

Detecting invisible fingerprints is an important task in forensic science, a branch of science that helps criminal investigations by collecting and analyzing evidence from crime scenes. Each fingerprint pattern is unique to a specific person, therefore a very reliable way of identifying a suspect. Criminals linked to a crime through their fingerprints may not be happy that they were born with uniquely designed patterns of wrinkles, swirls and grooves on their fingertips.

But we can all be glad that God gave us fingerprints because they greatly improve our sense of touch.

Fingerprints are used by investigators to identify who was at the scene and what they touched. In prophetic science, when someone receives a healing, sign, wonder, or miracle, we can easily identify that the individual or individuals were touched by God. We can say like the Egyptian magicians that it was certainly the *finger of God.*

There is an excellent quote that says, "God gave you a fingerprint that no else has, so you can leave an imprint that one else can." The fingerprint is God's mark; Job said, *"He seals the hand of every man, that all men may know His work"* (Job 37:7 NKJV).

The fingerprint or finger of God touching the lives of people through miracles is emphatically God leaving His mark. Job 37:7 provides a principle—that the hand of all men may know God's work. Therefore, the hand of God will cause people to come to know His word. Those who are touched by the hand of God will see His word. This is the epitome and picture of *power prophecy*. God's mark is on each of us, on our human hands. Fingerprints are His mark. I am always in awe of how God makes Himself evident to a hurting world in so many ways—if we take a moment to realize it.

One of the most amazing proofs or evidence is our fingerprint. God uses His own hand or finger in working a miracle for us to see evidence or provide proof that it was God who did it. He leaves an indelible mark on us through miraculous signs. No one has the same fingerprint. No one has the same talent or gifts, because God gave each of us His work to do and He calls us to excellence because whatever we do, we are to do it with all our hearts as unto the Lord whom we serve—as Colossians 3:23 reminds us.

One of the most important uses for fingerprints is to help investigators link one crime scene to another involving the same person.

Fingerprint identification also helps investigators track a criminal's record, their previous arrests and convictions, to aid in sentencing, probation, parole, and pardoning decisions.

4. God's Sign Language—Interpreting God's Handwriting.

The fourth biblical mention is during Belshazzar's Feast recorded in Daniel 5, when "fingers of a man's hand" wrote on the wall: *"In the same hour the fingers of a man's hand appeared and wrote opposite the lampstand on the plaster of the wall of the king's palace; and the king saw the part of the hand that wrote"* (Daniel 5:5 NKJV).

Prophets are interpreters of divine messages and of the revelation in the Holy Scriptures. Daniel the prophet was given by God extraordinary knowledge and skill in all literature and wisdom. He also carried a special anointing in understanding all visions and dreams (Daniel 1:17). He had a prophetic capacity in all matters.

Daniel, along with Hananiah, Mishael, and Azariah (whose names were changed to Babylonian names: Shadrach, Meshach and Abed-Nego; Daniel 1:6-7), met certain qualifications suitable to royal service or ministry, according to Daniel 1:3-4:

- Young men
- No blemish (skin issues), good-looking
- Gifted in all wisdom
- Possessing knowledge
- Quick to understand
- Ability to serve in the king's palace
- Taught the language and literature of the Chaldeans

TESTING AND EXAMINATION

Daniel and the three Hebrews were strenuously tested and examined thoroughly by the king:

306

As for these four young men, God gave them knowledge and skill in all literature and wisdom; and Daniel had understanding in all visions and dreams. Now at the end of the days, when the king had said that they should be brought in, the chief of the eunuchs brought them in before Nebuchadnezzar. Then the king interviewed them, and among them all none was found like Daniel, Hananiah, Mishael, and Azariah; therefore they served before the king. And in all matters of wisdom and understanding about which the king examined them, he found them ten times better than all the magicians and astrologers who were in all his realm (Daniel 1:17-20 NKJV).

It is important to note that Daniel was a young prophet with extraordinary prophetic gifting. He also studied the books and had a wealth of wisdom and knowledge beyond his age. This is to encourage and to quiet those who say that you have to be old to be used powerfully by God. Daniel did not compromise by eating King Nebuchadnezzar's food of Babylon. He did not compromise; he consistently obeyed the dietary law of Israel. He purposed in his heart that he would not defile himself with the king's delicacies, nor with wine (Daniel 1:8). God showed him favor and goodwill among the chief eunuchs.

Daniel and the three young men were tested in these two areas: diet and all matters of wisdom and understanding.

Diet

So Daniel said to the steward whom the chief of the eunuchs had set over Daniel, Hananiah, Mishael, and Azariah, "Please test your servants for ten days, and let them give us vegetables to eat and water to drink. Then let our appearance be examined before you, and the appearance of the young men who eat the portion of the king's delicacies; and as you see fit, so deal with your servants." So he consented with them in this matter, and tested them ten days. And at the end of ten days their features appeared better and fatter in flesh than all the young men who ate the portion of the king's delicacies. Thus the steward took away their portion of delicacies and the wine that they were to drink, and gave them vegetables (Daniel 1:11-16 NKJV).

In all matters of wisdom and understanding

As for these four young men, God gave them knowledge and skill in all literature and wisdom; and Daniel had understanding in all visions and dreams. Now at the end of the days, when the king had said that they should be brought in, the chief of the eunuchs brought them in before Nebuchadnezzar. Then the king interviewed them, and among them all none was found like Daniel, Hananiah, Mishael, and Azariah; therefore they served before the king (Daniel 1:17-19 NKJV).

After examination, the king found these four young men much better than the others: *"And in all matters of wisdom and understanding about which the king examined them, he found them ten times better than all the magicians and astrologers who were in all his realm"* (Daniel 1:20 NKJV).

Prophets are ten times better than all the magicians, astrologers, psychics, clairvoyants, diviners, soothsayers, mediums, witches, warlocks, prognosticators, false prophets, priests, satanists, and practitioners of darkness. Prophets are in a class and league all by themselves. The kings of the earth will recognize the emerging power prophets with extraordinary ability by God so that the world will take notice and they will be summoned to bring solution and resolutions to all matters. The spirit of Daniel will rest upon this powerful prophetic company, and rulers will seek their divine wisdom, knowledge, understanding, strategy, and revelation.

The kings of earth will approve the wisdom of God upon these Daniel-type prophets who will meet certain qualifications to have access into the various nations, kingdoms, and rooms. The position of prophetic advisors will be restored in the prophetic mantle and office. Prophets will be equipped in the church and sent into all the world. The kings of earth will find these prophets as Nebuchadnezzar saw—as being *"ten times better."*

The word *better* in the Hebrew is *yad,* which means "hand or power." The word *better* means "hand" in Hebrew indicating power. In other words, it means spiritual power. In the context of the verse when the king found Daniel and the Hebrew boys ten times better, it simply meant that he found them to be ten times more powerful than all the magicians and astrologers.

Better also describes the hand used as a pointer, sign, or indicator. Therefore, the king recognized a spiritual or powerful hand on them. In other words, he saw the hand of the Lord on them that distinguished them from all the other powers in his realm. He had to sense a special hand impression on Daniel. There was a special touch of God on the four young men. We can see that even before the writing on the wall manifested, God's hand was already resting on Daniel prophetically. Prophets have the hand of the Lord on them.

The following Scriptures tell us of prophets encountering the *"hand"* of the Lord upon them to minister:

- Moses—Exodus 3:19-20
- Ezekiel—Ezekiel 1:3; 3:14; 33:22

309

- Jeremiah—Jeremiah 32:21
- Samuel—1 Samuel 6:3
- David—Psalm 60:5
- Ezra—Ezra 7:6
- Stephen—Acts 7:55
- Barnabas the prophet and Saul—Acts 11:21

THE KING'S POWER IS UPON YOU!

Jesus said He cast out devils by the finger of God. Here Jesus borrows a phrase used by the Egyptian magicians in Exodus 8:19, recognizing the power of God executing judgment against Egypt. In Egypt the magicians were trying to duplicate the miraculous signs, and wonders demonstrated by God through the prophetic ministry of Moses. They were trying to discredit and diminish the power of God by copying the same plague so that Pharoah could believe that the signs and wonders done in Egypt were not of God, but produced by men. The phrase is a figure of speech for the power of God (see Exodus 8:19; 31:18 and Psalm 8:3).

Jesus was making a clear distinction of the power being demonstrated in deliverance. This is a revelation of deliverance, that when demons are cast out in the unseen realm, the king is exercising His power over spirits and expelling them. Jesus casting out demons is the execution of His kingly anointing to overthrow the kingdom or powers of darkness. This is simply acknowledging the Kingdom of God sovereignty over the kingdom of satan. Jesus proves total dominion; when He overthrows demons He is establishing that now the King's domain has come upon you—*God's Kingdom!*

When you consider the following two Scripture verses in Luke and Matthew, you will get a sense of what Jesus was referring to regarding the finger of God:

But if I drive out demons by the finger of God, then the kingdom of God has come upon you (Luke 11:20 NIV).

But if I cast out devils by the Spirit of God, then the kingdom of God is come unto you (Matthew 12:28 KJV).

The phrase is also used by Jesus in the New Testament when proving that He did not cast out demons by the power of beelzebub (lord of flies or dung or prince of demons).

The following are just a few New Testament examples of the *"finger of God"* being exercised to deconstruct demonic powers through dismantling the demonic by a finger:

- Mark 5:1-15—Jesus exercising power over the demoniac
- Acts 8:9-13—Peter the apostle rebuking Simon the sorcerer
- Acts 13:6-12—Elymas the sorcerer
- Acts 16:16-21—Paul casting out the spirit of divination from the fortune-teller
- Acts 19:24-27—Paul confronting the goddess Diana

REVISION IN THE NEW TESTAMENT LAW

They said this to test him, so that they might have some charge to bring against him. Jesus bent down and wrote with his finger on the ground (John 8:6 ESV).

The word *revision* means to make changes to something that has been written or decided. Revision provides improvements. The word *addendum* is an additional material, statement, or an appendix to the law. The purpose of an addendum is used to clarify the original agreement. Jesus draws up and revels a new line in the Law that the Pharisees misunderstood in the Old Testament Law. He did not come to abolish the Law but to fulfill it (Matthew 5:17). Jesus was revealing the spirit of the Law with regard to the penalty of death and the woman who had been caught in the act of adultery (John 8:1-11). They did not have the right argument to stone this woman.

In the New Testament story of Jesus and the woman taken in adultery, Jesus writes in the dust of the earth with His finger. This prophetic act can be seen as a reenactment of Christ or making a revision or addendum as the Divine Legislator in His New Testament. Jesus's actions in writing in the dust with His finger are reminiscent of the finger of God writing the Law on tablets of stone in the Old Testament.

Jesus demonstrates healing with the finger of God when He put His *fingers* into the man's ears. Then He spit and touched the man's tongue: *"After he took him aside, away from the crowd, Jesus put his fingers into the man's ears. Then he spit and touched the man's tongue"* (Mark 7:33 NIV).

‖ 13 ‖

AGENTS OF THE IMPOSSIBLE

*But without faith it is impossible to please Him, for he
who comes to God must believe that He is* [exists], *and
that He is a rewarder of those who diligently seek Him.*
—Hebrews 11:6 NKJV

*"Faith, mighty faith, the promise sees, and looks to that
alone; laughs at impossibilities, and cries it shall be done."*
—Charles Wesley

Faith Activates the Impossible

Praying and asking from God is our activation of faith that unlocks
supernatural provision in our life and welcomes God into our affairs
to engage with Him on His plane. Those who pray to God are men
and women of faith. Those without faith do not pray. Faith is the
only dynamic that pleases God and opens up doors of impossibility.
We are a people of faith, believers who were born for the impossible.

True Christians operate and function from the realm of impossibility. The realm of impossibility is the realm of faith. Faith activates
God to release. People of faith seek God. Believers live by faith (see
Galatians 3:11; Romans 1:17; Hebrews 10:38). In other words, we as
the just live by faith, we live in that realm. It's time to walk in *"Now*

faith" that is the substance of things hoped for and being the proof of things unseen before (Hebrews 11:1).

Faith helps us to depend on God alone and see His promises. Faith gives us the strength to do the impossible. With faith we can walk in confidence that what we hope for will come to pass. Faith sets the impossible in motion.

What is faith? One definition is that faith is believing in the unseen. *Faith* according to Strong's Concordance is translated from the Greek *pi'stis,* and was primarily used in the New Testament to mean: believe, be persuaded, to obey, trust or confidence. Faith is simply a strong and powerful conviction of truth in God.

We live for the impossible. The supernatural is our spiritual hub. Agents of the impossible will be a people of the impossible who through their faith and unmovable belief in the existence of God know that He will perform for those who are tenacious and laborious. They are diligent seekers of God. Faith unlocks the *impossible realm: "But without faith it is impossible to please Him, for he who comes to God must believe that He is* [exists], *and that He is a rewarder of those who diligently seek Him"* (Hebrews 11:6 NKJV).

Knowing the very existence of God as a people will produce supernatural strength to do great exploitations of God according to the prophet Daniel: *"...the people who know their God shall be strong, and carry out great exploits"* (Daniel 11:32 NKJV).

THE REALMS OF FAITH AND IMPOSSIBILITY

The gift of faith is simply extraordinary faith to see and function in the realm of the supernatural. In other words, this is the manifestation of the Spirit that empowers the believer to believe, see and do the impossible. This is that impossible faith type of gift. It gives believers the ability to move into the realm of impossibility, where believers can believe the unexplainable The gift of faith is defined by Paul the apostle as *"all faith"* where he could move mountains. This is mountain-moving faith. Mountains are described metaphorically or spiritually to represent something *impossible* or something *impossible to move.*

Paul was essentially saying that he had all faith to be able to move in the impossible. He could move in the impossible by faith. The gift of faith gives us the ability to do, move, and believe the impossible. It gives believers the capacity of faith that is beyond and outside of human comprehension.

MOVING MOUNTAINS

The gift of faith is mountain-moving faith to believe the impossible: *"And though I have the gift of prophecy, and understand all mysteries and all knowledge, and though I have all faith, so that I could remove mountains, but have not love, I am nothing"* (1 Corinthians 13:2 NKJV).

All faith without love renders the believer powerless and useless to the church. Love makes the impossible possible by faith. Faith unlocks the impossible in our lives. Agents of the impossible display the type of faith that do the impossible and remove mountainous issues in other people's lives. Jesus Christ taught His disciples a lesson on a certain *"kind"* of faith and its hidden supernatural potential and properties and what it can do in healing and deliverance:

> *Then the disciples came to Jesus privately and said, "Why could we not cast it out?" So Jesus said to them, "Because of your unbelief; for assuredly, I say to you, if you have faith as a mustard seed, you will say to this mountain, 'Move from here to there,' and it will move; and nothing will be impossible for you. However, this kind does not go out except by prayer and fasting"* (Matthew 17:19-21 NKJV).

Jesus reveals a powerful key that essentially unlocks the kind of faith that produces the impossible for you. This is a realm of the supernatural that comes through exceptional prayer and fasting. Truthfully, Jesus is teaching His students the kind of prayer and faith needed to deal and drive out certain kinds of demonic entities. When His disciples came to Him and questioned why they could not cast out the spirits, He told them it was because of their unbelief that hindered their power and authority over demonic spirits. Their lack of or underdeveloped faith was the primary reason.

However, He went on to further explain that not only was it their unbelief, it was the kind of demonic spirits they were dealing with that needed specialized tactical prayer and fasting to remove. He was teaching them a lifestyle of cultivating faith and prayer and fasting. Agents of the impossible will be a people of faith in prayer and fasting that deal with certain kinds of spirits, situations, problems, dilemmas, crises, and circumstances.

God will move mountains for you in partnership with your mouth to speak words of faith in prayer and prophecy. Faith without action will not work (see James 2:17-21). Faith is about taking risks. Those who are daring and even controversial live and walk by faith and demonstrate faith in believing in miracles, signs, and wonders. If you believe in healing, you will pray for the sick. Agents of the impossible declare to those "show me your faith without your works, and I will show you my faith by my works." Faith can be seen; it is active, alive, and animated.

MUSTARD-SEED POWER

Jesus said this kind of spirit does not go out except by prayer and fasting. Exceptional deliverance requires exceptional faith, prayer, and fasting to cast out this kind of spirit. This is a principle not only in deliverance but a key to accessing the impossible. Certain kinds of miracles require a certain kind of faith and lifestyle in prayer and fasting. Faith has the capacity to move mountainous things that seem or appear impossible. Mustard-seed faith must be cultivated and developed through practice and prayer and fasting.

A small mustard seed can grow into one of the largest trees. Therefore, there is so much potency and potential in the mustard seed; but essentially Jesus is saying that it must be watered over time to be able to deal with bigger demonic problems. We must develop our faith. The mustard seed is our faith capacity.

MUSTARD-SEED FAITH CAPACITY

Faith as small as a mustard seed has the capacity to do the impossible. Faith is like a mustard seed planted in the spirit of a believer where it can grow massively to produce great faith to do the impossible. The gift of faith is a seed of faith that I believe is imparted into every believer. Faith has size, and there are Scriptures that teach us how we can water our seed of faith to do the supernatural. Every believer carries a capacity of faith that needs to be developed. Jesus provides us with a key and the type of faith that unlocks the unexplainable. Faith is a seed that must be watered and will eventually take root.

Jesus reveals in Matthew 17:20 that our faith has size. The gift of faith is like a seed planted with incredible power to exercise a realm of authority to speak to things and they will obey you. Faith also gives the believer a measure of assurance and authority with which to operate. Jesus clearly teaches His disciples that even mustard-seed size faith in God has the power to do the unfathomable.

Here is another example of the apostles asking Jesus to increase their faith capacity. See what He tells them in Luke 17:5-6 (NASB):

The apostles said to the Lord, "Increase our faith!" And the Lord said, "If you had faith the size of a mustard seed, you could say to this mulberry tree, 'Be uprooted and be planted in the sea'; and it would obey you."

We can see that they were asking Jesus to increase their faith and Jesus answered them with the condition of faith. They were seeking increase outwardly and Jesus was saying faith is like a seed planted inwardly by the Spirit. It was up to them to grow and cultivate the seed of faith. The interesting part of Jesus's statement was predicated on the condition of *"if they had faith the size of a mustard seed."* He had already planted the seed of faith, therefore it was not that they needed per se to increase in faith—it was to walk in the authority of it and do it. Faith is like a major sports corporation's slogan, "Just Do It."

Faith has the supernatural and extraordinary potential to grow exponentially in believers:

And He said, "How shall we picture the kingdom of God, or what parable shall we use to illustrate and explain it? It is like a mustard seed, which, when it is sown on the ground, even though it is smaller than all the [other] seeds that are [sown] on the soil, yet when it is sown, it grows up and becomes larger than all the garden herbs; and it puts out large branches, so that the birds of the sky are able to make nests and live under its shade" (Mark 4:30-32 AMP).

The gift of faith has massive growing properties that causes others to see it and will cause you to stand out and others will benefit from you and operate under that realm of faith. The word of God helps to increase our faith, and faith comes to the believer by hearing the word: *"So faith comes from hearing, and hearing through the word of Christ"* (Romans 10:17 ESV).

The key to growing, increasing, and moving in the realm of faith is to keep hearing and getting around those who teach and preach faith, those who operate in that realm. Men and women of great faith continue to hear the words of Christ through studying His words in the Bible. They eat, sleep, and live by faith. Get around those who continue to teach faith about the prophetic, miracles, signs, and wonders. The more you hear it, the more you will have faith to move in it. Watch videos, listen to audio tapes, attend teaching and preaching on the subject of faith and the supernatural. Read about it and recite it. The more you hear and hear and hear the word of God, the more faith will grow in you to see and do the impossible. It will increase the authority to function at that higher degree of faith.

The kind of faith Jesus was revealing to His disciples releases a measure of authority to speak to impossible situations in the natural and causes it to adhere. Prophets and those with the gift of faith will have the ability to speak things that may seem insane, unbelievable, and even unreal—to see and speak to things that seem insurmountable. Those who function in this realm of gifting, will believe that nothing will be impossible for them. The disciples could not cure the man who was an epileptic and was suffering severely with a demon that was trying to kill him by causing him to fall into the fire and often into the water. Jesus cured the man—He had "that" kind of faith.

The following are other variables of faith revealed in the New Testament:

- All things are possible—Mark 9:23-24 and Mark 11:22-24
- Only believe and you will see the glory of God in Lazarus being raised from the dead with the prayer and command of Jesus—John 11:1-44
- The cursing of the fig tree by Jesus as a lesson to His apprentices—Matthew 21:18-21

- God-given faith is doubt-free—Mark 9:24

There is immeasurable power of God unleashed in the lives of believers with true faith. The gift of faith unlocks the unexplainable where you can speak to fig trees, move mountains, and ask in prayer for whatever believing you *will* (not might or perhaps) receive.

- Matthew 21:22—And whatever things you ask in prayer, believing, you will receive.
- Luke 1:37—For with God nothing will be impossible.
- Paul says "all faith," which implies that there are various types, degrees, levels, measures, and realms of faith.

The *gift of faith* is God's own faith active in a believer to see the impossible happen in the unseen realm first, then manifested in the seen realm. They can literally see things happen through the lens of faith before it manifests in the natural. God gives believers the ability to see into a reality apart from what it looks like in the natural. They are given a set of spiritual lenses to not see things as they are in the natural realm but through the lens of faith to see as God sees them. In other words, a person may be lying on their deathbed with a terminal, incurable disease that is impossible for humans to heal or remedy. But the person with the gift of faith will not see the situation in the natural; rather, the person sees through the eyes of faith as being cured. The person's mind's eye doesn't see the sickness, only healing.

James 5:15 (ESV) reveals that the prayer of faith unlocks the anointing for healing to be released and forgiven of sins: *"And the prayer of faith will save the one who is sick, and the Lord will raise him up. And if he has committed sins, he will be forgiven."*

HALL OF FAITH

In the "hall of fame of faith," the Bible records those who lived, walked, and demonstrated faith. Hebrews 11:2-30 describes the faith of the *agents of the impossible*. By faith:

- The elders obtained a testimony
- We understand Enoch was taken away and translated having pleased God
- Noah became an heir
- Abraham obeyed and dwelled in a land of the promise
- Sarah received strength to conceive a child in her old age and judged God as faithful
- Abraham received God's promises
- Isaac blessed his son
- Joseph gave prophecy of what would happen following his death
- Moses's parents preserved him, seeing he was special
- Moses refused to be aligned with the whole Egyptian system and chose instead to be rejected by people
- Joshua obeyed and the walls of Jericho fell
- Rahab and her family did not perish
- The hall of famers subdued kingdoms, worked righteousness, obtained promises, shut the mouths of lions, quenched the violence of fire, escaped the edge of sword, and were made strong and valiant in battle as they turned to fight their enemies.

PROPHETIC GRACE AND FAITH

Having then gifts differing according to the grace that is given to us, let us use them: if prophecy, let us prophesy in proportion to our faith; or ministry, let us use it in our ministering; he who teaches, in teaching; he who exhorts, in exhortation; he who gives, with liberality; he who leads, with diligence; he who shows mercy, with cheerfulness (Romans 12:6-8 NKJV).

We prophesy according to our faith. It is understood clearly that a person can prophesy with a measure of faith and grace distributed by God and through impartation. Each person ministers out of their own portion, percentage, ratio, and measurement. When a person is ministered to through prophetic utterance by a prophesier and/or a prophet, that person should experience God through: edification, exhortation, and comfort. Prophets who have matriculated through the school of the prophetic understand this to be a fundamental level of prophecy and that it is the purpose of prophecy and the launching pad and true basis to prophesy.

When someone leaves the presence of a prophet, someone with the gift of prophecy or a prophesier, they should feel edified, exhorted, and comforted, if it is a true prophecy from the Lord. Only the prophet in the office has the spiritual authority and latitude to function beyond the realm of edification, exhortation, and comfort that brings levels of correction, alignment, rebuke, order, affirmation, direction, strategy, confirmation, impartation, revelation, activation, and ordination.

This is for higher degrees of prophetic authority. The gift of prophecy has a higher level of strength, power, and more capacity to edify, exhort, and comfort for building than testifying of Jesus Christ by the spirit of prophecy. Each level and dimension in the realm of the prophetic adds a greater level of strength, power, and purpose in its function.

The grace of God on our lives makes our gifts in the church different. For instance, there may be three prophets in a church all possessing the gift of prophecy and other prophetic abilities, but what differentiates their gift as a prophet is according to their individual graces. God's grace makes them different even though all three are prophets. Yet when they operate and manifest the Spirit, there will be a distinction in each of their prophetic ministries that is uniquely and clearly identified.

One may have the grace to prophesy to ten people with forensic and laser details and specifics, while another may have the grace to prophesy to a hundred people with prophetic endurance and acuity, and the third may have the grace and ministry to prophesy corporately over thousands in a meeting regarding the detailed intelligence from God regarding the state of the people of a city, community and/or nation. Each can visibly display a grace that differs, and as they prophesy they minister according to the ratio of their faith. Each one has a different gift, grace, and measure of faith.

MEASURE OF FAITH

For I say, through the grace given to me, to everyone who is among you, not to think of himself more highly than he ought to think, but to think soberly, as God has dealt to each one a measure of faith. For as we have many members in one body, but all the members do not have the same function, so we, being many, are one body in Christ, and individually members of one another (Romans 12:3-5 NKJV).

The word *measure* in the Greek is *metron*, which means "a limited portion, degree, or measurement." A *metron* is an instrument or vessel for receiving and determining the quantity of things whether liquid or dry. A measure is simply a measuring rod and can be similar to a ruler, measuring tape, or container that determines extension, portion, or limit. Proverbially, it is the rule or standard of judgment. What does it mean in terms of the measure of faith? It means that God has given each believer a limit, portion, and degree of faith to exercise their grace.

There is a measure or limit of faith that we can flow in the gift and grace. God initially determined the level, degree, or limitation for each one of us to operate. He draws the line of how much and what portion of faith only we can use. For instance, He fills our vessels with various gifts; but in our spiritual vessels, there is a limit and measure of faith for each gift. This limit is our capacity of faith.

God determines how much faith we have and its limitation. That is why those who have the gift of prophecy may have a greater levels of faith to speak words of knowledge or to prophesy to more than ten people. Each person is dealt a different level or limit of faith per spiritual gift. The same is for someone who has been given the gifts of healings; one person may manifest a level of faith to believe and heal a few from back issues, while someone else with same gift of healing may believe and heal those who are blind or deaf. Respectfully, not one gift is better or unimportant to the body.

Prophets in particular must be careful not to become haughty, arrogant, prideful or puffed up in comparing themselves to others. Some prophets may have the ability to prophesy very detailed, forensic, and specific words of knowledge in the realm of disclosing names, addresses and happenings in a person's life. Other may not get those kinds of details but may have the measure of faith to see and unfold what is about to happen in someone's life, through the word of wisdom, providing strategy and the mind of God on matters. They counsel kings and leaders of nations with the purposes of God.

My point is that the gifts of God are not given to us to think either highly or lowly of ourselves; what we were given was already predetermined according to the purpose of God to the specific function in the Body. Because we have different functions and roles, there are different gifts, grace, and proportion of faith in which we minister (see Romans 12:6).

God conceals matters and counsels the kings to search them out. Prophets were instrumental in directing kings as they searched their hearts. Rulers would see God through the prophets as they disclosed the heart of a matter. We can see this example in Proverbs 25:2 (NIV) *"It is the glory of God to conceal a matter; to search out a matter is the glory of kings."* The New Living Translation says it this way: *"It is God's privilege to conceal things and the king's privilege to discover them."*

Each member in the church has been given gifts, grace, and purpose with which to serve God. It is crucial to understand that just as our human body is made up of many parts, each with a specific function to keep the body functioning properly and healthy, so have we been given spiritual gifts to keep the church healthy and functioning properly. Every part of our bodies whether big, small, cellular or microscopic, seen or unseen, conspicuous, inconspicuous or significant or insignificant in our own eyes, has a vital job in the human body. They all work interchangeably together. Any breakdown or malfunction or shutdown of any one of the parts in the human or spiritual body could irreversibly hurt the body as a whole. Similarly, the body of Christ is made up of many believers and each plays a role and function in His body.

Therefore, we should not think that we are overly significant or think more highly of ourselves than we ought, as Paul states in Romans 12:3-5. Nor should we think or allow others to make us think that we are insignificant and unimportant to the church. We all have a work to accomplish God's will and purpose. Our gifts serve the body and every joint supplies in the body of Christ, though we are many members (believers in Christ); we are all one body and not separate or cut off from the body. Ephesians 4:16 (NKJV) says, *"from whom the whole body, joined and knit together by what every joint supplies, according to the effective working by which each part does its share, causes growth of the body for the edifying of itself in love."*

We as believers serve God with our spiritual gifts. Therefore, it is understood that each one in the body of Christ is different and grace is given to each to function. God has given each one of us as believers a measure of faith. Grace is God's limited space in us to operate. God measures out in each of us a space in which He will work and display His ability. There is a grace for the space. In other words, you are limited by the amount of grace you received from God. The space becomes God's room or the realm in us to occupy and work from. It is like God is working "from home" in us. Grace is His ability, but our boundary or limitation.

The grace of God is the realm of space from which we can function. The realm of the prophetic is the limited space that God gives to us. Every believer should operate in the realm or space of the prophetic in one or more levels of prophecy. We should seek more into a greater measure of the prophetic realm. The spirit of prophecy should not be enough.

Each room in a house is made up of multiple dimensions, some rooms are smaller or larger than others. Therefore, each room in the spirit represents a realm. We are given a realm of grace to function in. Some prophets function in smaller or greater dimensions and realms of prophetic grace differ according to what God has measured out for each one. Each room speaks of capacity. Your grace is your capacity.

Prophetic grace is measuring the level of your prophetic capacity. Your capacity can be developed and this happens as we grow more into the knowledge of the Lord Jesus Christ. As we mature in Christ our spiritual space, capacities and grace enlarges. There is always room to grow in the grace of God. We can grow in the prophetic grace, anointing, and power. The more we increase in the knowledge of Christ, the more we grow in His grace.

With every room you can upgrade your room and even expand it. Scriptures tell us that we can grow in our capacity: *"But grow in the grace and knowledge of our Lord and Savior Jesus Christ..."* (2 Peter 3:18 NKJV).

When the spirit of prophecy is strong in the local church, it opens a portal of prophecy for more believers to have access to different realms in the prophetic. The more believers who function in the diversity of the prophetic, the more others learn and discover this multidimensional realm and they can be edified while seeing how others are built up by other prophetic expressions.

ACTIVATING PROPHETIC GRACE

The word *activate* means "to stir up, wake up, arouse, and rekindle." It also means "to wake up and make active out of dormancy." Many of our prophetic gifts are dormant, dead, idle, inert, inoperative, vacant, or asleep. To activate the prophetic in our lives is to simply activate faith to operate in the gift of prophecy. The Holy Spirit has given us grace in the prophetic for all believers to prophesy according to the proportion of his or her faith according to what Paul wrote in Romans 12:6-8.

The same faith we activated to receive the gift of salvation from the Lord Jesus Christ to save and redeem us, is the very same faith we can activate to believe and operate in the gift of prophecy. Again, it takes faith to prophesy. The Holy Spirit is a gentleman; therefore, He will not force us to prophesy. The Holy Spirit does not forcefully open our mouths to prophesy. He does not grab our tongues and force us to speak. He will simply move upon our heart, mind, and spirit giving us the words and inclinations to interpret what we by faith believe He desires to say.

The Holy Spirit inspires and gives us the utterance. However, there will be times when those with the gift of prophecy will not have to wait for an inspired utterance because the gift of edification, exhortation, and comfort resides already in you, and therefore you can prophesy at will and anytime to build up, encourage, strengthen, comfort, console, and instruct others and the whole church. This gift is fluent in the mouths of those who are encouragers and builders of the body of Christ. Therefore, the gift of prophecy can be stirred up, activated. We already have the Holy Spirit in us who equipped us with this precious gift to use whenever needed, not always whenever influenced.

I have heard those without a strong biblical foundation of teaching say, "I only prophesy when the Holy Spirit is upon me," or, "I prophesy only when the Holy Spirit is speaking." Though I understand their sensitivity to respect and to ensure they are not speaking when the Holy Spirit is not speaking, the reality is that if we only wait for the Holy Spirit to come upon us to speak, then we are essentially functioning in an Old Testament understanding of prophecy when the prophets of God spoke as the Spirit moved upon them in anointing. They were carried away to prophesy as they were inspired by the Holy Spirit coming *"upon them."*

During that time the prophetic was under a different set of laws; and if a prophet spoke without the Spirit coming upon them and their words did not come to pass or fell to the ground, they would have been put to death, stoned, and regarded as a false prophet. They were under the Law during that era; however, it is extremely important to comprehend that we are under grace and are ministers of grace in Christ Jesus.

Therefore, there is a prophetic grace we can minister out of and we do not have to wait for the Holy Spirit to come *upon us* in power in order to prophesy. In fact, the prophets of Old have the gift and spirit of the prophet. At times they would ask for a minstrel in order to stir up and activate the prophetic anointing. There was a strong reliance upon an external assistance or agent to activate the prophetic.

Today we are under grace and we do not have to wait for the Spirit of God to come "upon us" to prophesy, where many ignorantly or respectfully do not want to operate outside of the leading or grace of the Spirit, which I totally understand. Truthfully, we must examine this in light of what the Bible teaches. There is a grace of prophecy, which is the gift of prophecy. Any believer with this gift can minister in this realm because the gift is your grace to prophesy.

You have permission by right of the gift being resident in you; therefore you do not have to wait on the Holy Spirit—in truth, the Holy Spirit is waiting on you. You have to activate it. Yes there are those who function in the spirit of prophecy who are induced to prophesy as a result of external means of contact such as: atmosphere, worship, music, and being around prophets and prophetic people. In contrast, those with the gift of prophecy do not need that level of influence because the Helper is within them.

Though I respect many people's position who want to ensure they do not grieve the Holy Spirit by speaking or prophesying, so to speak, out of turn or grace, I would be remiss not to encourage them to adjust their way of thinking. The Holy Spirit is not outside the believer; He is not a visitor—rather, He in grace and truth lives, abodes, dwells and resides PERMANENTLY in them. We grieve the Holy Spirit when we do not exercise the gift of prophecy that He has given us.

Some say that they believe wholeheartedly it is a sign of spiritual maturity to wait on the Lord in the context of only prophesying when the Holy Spirit comes on them or is only speaking directly to them. Unfortunately, this is not a measure of spiritual maturity but in fact reveals an obscured understanding of Scripture, lack of faith, and even pride to limit God's ability at the idea of being wrong, making a mistake, or facing criticism if they miss or are off prophetically.

The gift of prophecy is to be used regularly in the church. Most Christians who tend to wait for the Spirit to come upon them do not fully understand that the Spirit is inside them spiritually to prophesy; they usually do not have a high quality of prophetic words and when they finally release the prophetic, it is laced with ten thousand tongues (meaning speaking in tongues) and what is usually spoken prophetically is weak and carries little insight, specifications, and strength. They tend to have low frequency, and they may only prophesy once or twice a month or even once a year. I have seen this often and they are typically deep in appearance but very shallow in prophetic.

I prefer to be around someone who activates and prophesies often, than someone waiting on the Holy Spirit to move them in an Old Testament context. Who do you believe will be more accurate and have practiced it enough to get better, stronger, and more detailed at it? If you said the one who prophesies and practices it often, you are absolutely correct. Give me the person who practices their gift of prophecy versus someone who is waiting on prophecy. If I have to wait on someone who is waiting on the Lord to speak to them to prophesy, they usually do not have the *gift of prophecy* but have the lowest level of prophecy is which is the *spirit of prophecy*. These types of prophesiers or utterers will give words like, "Jesus loves you," or, "The best is yet come." They are limited in testifying of the Lord Jesus over anyone's life.

Prophecy is generally out of the gift of prophecy. It is a resident gift. The gift of prophecy inhabits the believers and is not a visitor. The Holy Spirit is always speaking and the word of the Lord should continually be in our mouths to witness to the unbelievers, unchurched, unlearned, and unorthodox.

Jesus Christ died on the Cross for us to be representatives, ambassadors, and spokespeople about Him to others. He gave us the gift of the Holy Spirit; and by His Spirit was given what I call His "love gifts." The love of God gave us gifts. Therefore, by His unconditional love, goodness, and kindness, He gave us grace. The gifts of the Holy Spirit were given to us not because of any religious works or merit of our own to earn it. There is grace in the prophetic that is accessible and readily available for us as believers to operate in the gift of prophecy NOW, not later. Prophetic grace has been extended to His church and to all of His sons and daughter to express His heart, mind, love, will, and purpose to humankind. His grace gives us the permission and ability to minister in a measure of the gift of prophecy, even if not quite our regular flow.

This gift of prophecy is activated only by the proportion of our faith. No faith, no prophecy. No faith, no miracles. No faith, no healing. No faith, no salvation. Hebrews 11:6 (NLT) says, *"And it is impossible to please God without faith. Anyone who wants to come to him must believe that God exists and that he rewards those who sincerely seek him."* We cannot prophesy without faith. Faith activates the gift of prophecy by believing that He has given us this precious gift and by believing that God, in the gift of the Holy Spirit, exists and is in you.

The gift of Holy Spirit through the gift of prophecy is the inworking of God in us to speak prophetically to others to build them up. If we cannot build and encourage others in the church, then the love of God is not in us, or we are not walking in the Spirit, or the works of the flesh have outweighed the fruit of the Spirit (see Galatians 5:16-26). Those who are genuinely led by the Sprit are not under the law but by the grace of God (Galatians 5:18).

RATIO OF PROPHECY

As mentioned previously, we prophecy according to the proportion of our faith. The word *proportion* refers to a ratio or measurement. This proportion or ration of faith gives an individual believer the faith to prophesy to one person, while to another person the faith to prophesy to ten or more people, and to another the faith to prophesy to prophesy to more than one hundred people.

My twin brother, Dr. Hakeem Collins, best-selling author of the book *Heaven Declares,* and I are known widely as the "Twin Prophets." We travel as a team ministering prophetically, and people are amazed primarily at the uniqueness and rarity of twin prophets—and importantly the grace and faith in which my brother and I are able to prophesy accurately and specifically with detail to more than hundreds of people.

In a number of conferences and meetings we have prophesied to hundreds of people one by one and have given personal and specific prophecies. This takes a higher ratio and measure of faith and grace to do so without burning out. We even have prophesied to many in a congregation all night and into the morning. There are examples of those in the Bible who prophesied all night under the auspices of the prophetic and in the company of the office prophet (see 1 Samuel 19:24). We both have what some call *prophetic rivers,* where the prophetic gift and anointing continually flow out of us.

Prophets can operate in a very high frequency, endurance, and continuum of prophecy. This is best described as our *prophetic grace* where there is a continual reservoir of grace from which we flow. We have a greater space and room to prophesy out of than those who may not have the same ratio of faith. Prophetic streams are in us prophetically—the gift of prophecy is the reservoir of prophecy in believers to minister out of. This flowing river in us refreshes and gives life to those to whom we minister. My brother and I have learned to tap into the rivers given to us by the Holy Spirit. We believe in the gifts of the Spirit and the gift of prophecy; therefore, we unlock that dimension of prophetic power by faith.

There are untapped gifts of the prophetic and the supernatural because of fear, doubt, and unbelief. If you can just believe and by faith unlock the gift of prophecy that is in you, you will flow in the realm of the prophetic that you have never known. The primary reason my brother and I can minister all night in the prophetic and can effortlessly prophesy to hundreds personally, is because we do not limit or stop up or quench or deactivate the flow of the Spirit that is in us. There are rivers of life in us that God desires us to pour out upon His people who need to drink for refreshing.

The key to unlocking your prophetic flow out of the streams, reservoirs, and rivers in you is found in John 7:38 (NIV) where Jesus says, *"Whoever believes in Me, as Scripture has said, rivers of living water will flow from within them."* The Holman Christian Standard Bible says that verse this way: *"The one who believes in Me, as the Scripture has said, will have streams of living water flow from deep within him."*

The key to walking and operating in the gift of prophecy is to believe in Jesus Christ and the teaching of Scripture—then God's rivers of living water will spring up out of you to cause others to drink from your prophetic utterance and release. Many people struggle in the Spirit and the supernatural because they do not believe in Jesus or the Bible. I teach the prophetic and study Scriptures on matters that impart faith in me to do the same works of Christ and greater because He resides in me by the Spirit.

We need to take the limits off and the muzzles off our mouths and believe that there are wells, fountains, and rivers of the Spirit that we can tap into, plunge into, be immersed into, and drawn into. Many of our prophetic rivers are stopped up by thoughts of doubt, fear of the supernatural, unbelief, lack of solid and thorough teaching of Scripture, doctrines of men and devils, and lack of exposure to the prophetic, prophets, and the gifted. The apostle Paul challenged Timothy to arouse from dormancy the gift that was given to him (2 Timothy 1:6). This is a time to unlock the prophetic realm to pour out the living words of Jesus Christ.

QUICKENED TO PROPHESY

The gift of prophecy will be quickened by the Spirit to speak life to you: *"It is the spirit that quickeneth; the flesh profiteth nothing: the words that I speak unto you, they are spirit, and they are life. But there are some of you that believe not..."* (John 6:63-64 KJV).

The New International Version says it this way: *"The Spirit gives life; the flesh counts for nothing. The words I have spoken to you— they are full of the Spirit and life. Yet there are some of you who do not believe...."*

The word *quicken* in the Greek is *zoopoieo*, which means "to vitalize, produce alive, cause to live and give life" according to Strong's Concordance. It is the spiritual power to arouse and invigorate or to restore life. This power aspect of the prophetic must be seriously considered when operating and functioning in any realm of the prophet. There is life-giving power of words spoken out of prophetic utterance that restores life or causes life to come into someone's life. There is a quicken mechanism to prophecy that makes it very powerful in the realm of the spirit that is key and an essential part of the ministry of the prophetic. Not only does the prophet have this power, but the believer has the same prophetic grace and capabilities to speak life to people who are spiritually dead, dormant, and deactivated.

I will go on to say that although the church, all believers, may not have the ministry office of prophet, I believe we all have the ministry of the prophetic where we all can actively function in prophetic activities of prophesying, building and encouraging, and speaking life to one another in Christ. Those with the gift of prophecy can quicken to prophesy.

This is the same as activating or stirring up the gift to prophesy. The Holy Spirit is our example who quickened Jesus to speak spiritual words of life. Because the Holy Spirit is a living and lively Spirit in all believers, there is therefore no reason why the gifts of the Spirit are inactive, deactivated, inert, and dead without life. The Spirit continually quickens our gifts to be alive in us to operate whenever needed. In other words, the Holy Spirit gifts are already charged up and waiting for the saints to activate and use their gifts.

The word *quicken* spiritually gives us the picture or idea of seeds quickened to life—germinating, springing up, growing. What does this mean? The words we speak in prophecy causes the words imparted to grow, germinate, or spring up. Jesus was saying that His words have the power spiritually to cause you to come forth, grow up, and be awakened. His words carry life and the very breath of God.

Inspired and quickened words spoken by the Spirit out of the mouth of a prophet or one with the gift of prophecy cause the seeds sown in your life to manifest. The word of prophecy can revitalize those who may feel wasted, desolate, and spiritually deprived. There is revival in the mouths of the prophets to quicken your mortal bodies and cause a great awakening. Prophecy tends to release new grace, strength, and greater power of life into others.

Through my prophetic ministry as a prophet, I have spoken life to organs, tissues, and ligaments in people's bodies that were malfunctioning and inactive to the point they needed organ transplants. Miraculous healings were released in their physical bodies as I prophesied over them. They could feel the Spirit healing them as the prophetic was being released. Their organ responded to the life-quickening words in my mouth.

The secret to the prophetic realm is to simply speak life. Prophets are at times intercessors between life and death. They can be someone's lifeline.

The prophetic can extend and expand life expectancy with the word of the Lord that is in us spiritually. Jesus is releasing a mystery key to us to understand that we as believers have the spiritual power to arouse, invigorate, restore and increase life spiritually and physically and cause others to grow exponentially from what is stored in our mouth. The power of life and death is in the tongue, and today I challenge you by the quickening of the Spirit to release life. You are the power cord that someone may need to live. Elijah prayed through his intercession and called life back (restoration) into the dead child. Prophets stand in the space with grace to impart life by the power of prophecy.

AGENTS OF THE IMPOSSIBLE'S TWELVE TENANTS

The following are the twelve tenants of faith Scriptures for all believers who I believe are called to be agents of the impossible:

1. *Jesus looked at them and said, "With man this is impossible, but with God all things are possible"* (Matthew 19:26 NIV).

2. *For nothing will be impossible with God* (Luke 1:37 ESV).

3. *Ah, Lord God! It is you who have made the heavens and the earth by your great power and by your outstretched arm! Nothing is too hard for you* (Jeremiah 32:17 ESV).

4. *Is anything too hard for the LORD? At the appointed time I will return to you, about this time next year, and Sarah shall have a son* (Genesis 18:14 ESV).

5. *I can do all things through him who strengthens me* (Philippians 4:13 ESV).

6. *And Jesus said to him, "If you can'! All things are possible for one who believes"* (Mark 9:23 ESV).

7. *He said to them, "Because of your little faith. For truly, I say to you, if you have faith like a grain of mustard seed, you will say to this mountain, 'Move from here to there,' and it will move, and nothing will be impossible for you"* (Matthew 17:20 ESV).

8. *And without faith it is impossible to please him, for whoever would draw near to God must believe that he exists and that he rewards those who seek him* (Hebrews 11:6 ESV).

9. *Jesus looked at them and said, "With man it is impossible, but not with God. For all things are possible with God"* (Mark 10:27 ESV).

10. *But he said, "What is impossible with man is possible with God"* (Luke 18:27 ESV).

11. *Behold, I am the LORD, the God of all flesh. Is anything too hard for me?* (Jeremiah 32:27 ESV)

12. *I know that you can do all things, and that no purpose of yours can be thwarted* (Job 42:2 ESV).

ABOUT THE AUTHOR

Dr. Naim Collins is an emerging leader and catalyst with an apostolic heart and prophetic voice. He carries a peculiar anointing in the prophetic, healings, and the supernatural. He has been featured on various multimedia outlets including *Sid Roth's It's Supernatural!* and The Word Network. He is the visionary leader of Naim Collins Ministries and Fan the Flames Global Ministries based in Wilmington, Delaware.